☆ ☆

The World Turned Upside Down

☆ ☆

The World Turned Upside Down

Prose and Poetry of the American Revolution

Edited and with an Introduction by James H. Pickering

National University Publications
KENNIKAT PRESS • 1975
Port Washington, N.Y. • London

Manufactured in the United States of America

Published by
Kennikat Press Corp.
Port Washington, N.Y. / London

Library of Congress Cataloging in Publication Data

Main entry under title:

The World turned upside down.

(National university publications)
Includes bibliographical references.
1. American literature—Revolutionary period,
1775-1783. I. Pickering, James H
PS533.W6   810'.8'002   75-15551
ISBN 0-8046-9082-0

For David and Susan

CONTENTS

PART TWO
THE LITERATURE OF REVOLUTION, 1775–83
THE PATRIOTS

CONTENTS

PART THREE
THE LITERATURE OF REVOLUTION, 1775-83
THE LOYALISTS

☆ ☆

The World Turned Upside Down

☆ ☆

INTRODUCTION

*In establishing American independence, the pen and
the press had a merit equal to that of the sword.*

David Ramsay The History of the
American Revolution (1789)

In 1763, at the close of the struggle with France for control of North America, England turned to the task of reorganizing an overseas empire badly strained by seven long years of war. The colonial and commercial policies governing this empire had been established in the seventeenth century, at a time when England had but few colonies; now she had thirty, of which the thirteen in North America had all but arrived at a state of political and economic maturity and semi-independence. When applied to such powerful dependencies as these, changes in the policies regulating taxation, trade, credit, and territorial expansion were bound to create uneasiness and friction. In the years of controversy that followed, it was through the written word—through "literature" conceived of in its broadest terms—that America's growing sense of her own political and cultural identity found its richest and most effective expression.

The literature of the American Revolution, with which the present volume is concerned, deals directly with the motives, desires, and emotions of a people engaged not only in a revolution against the world's greatest military and naval power but in the creative act of establishing for themselves a new society and government. Far from being dry and uninteresting, as readers will discover, the body of revolutionary literature is a large and impressive one. It consists of songs, ballads, essays, plays, allegories, satires, poems, narratives, and various kinds of public oratory (to cite the most obvious examples), written and published over a period of twenty years by men who found themselves caught up in a conflict that hung precariously in the balance until almost the very end. That the quality of such productions should be uneven, given the conditions under which most of them were rushed to

3

print, goes almost without saying. Yet there is about them a robustness and vitality that the passage of two hundred years has scarcely diminished. Of most importance, however, is the insight and understanding that such literature affords us of the American Revolution itself: perhaps in no other way can the modern American come to appreciate that bitter struggle for the "minds and hearts of the people" which John Adams insisted was "the real American Revolution."

The selections included in this volume, with a few exceptions, reached their original audiences through one of three principal media: broadsides, pamphlets, and newspapers. Though all three often shared audiences and often carried the same kind of subject matter, each medium had its distinctive uses; and in the hands of writers gifted in the art of public persuasion each became a weapon of considerable importance in advancing the revolutionary cause. The dominant contemporary form of instant communication was, of course, the broadside—single sheets of paper hawked through city streets or posted, often in the dead of night, in conspicuous public places— carrying news of important events, notices of meetings and calls to political action, resolutions and proclamations, speeches, and personal attacks on public officials, as well as songs, ballads, poetry, and cartoons on topics of the hour. As instruments of propaganda* aimed at the "people" themselves, broadsides possessed a number of distinct advantages, among them the speed and cheapness with which they could be struck off and rushed into circulation, and the anonymity they promised their authors and printers. By design they were ephemeral—of the tens of thousands of broadsides called forth by the Revolution, but few remain today. Those that survive are noteworthy primarily, for our purposes at least, because of the songs and ballads they contain, a kind of literature as close to the actual pulsebeat of the times as we are likely to get.

Of far greater impact on shaping and promoting the ideological basis of the Revolution was the pamphlet, the form of journalism to which the revolutionary author invariably turned when serious and sustained writing was to be done. In addition to being inexpensive and easy to produce the pamphlet had the advantages of greater size and flexibility, the very two factors which most limited the effectiveness of the broadside. Adaptable as it was to a wide variety of uses, the paperbound pamphlet offered the revolutionary writer a nearly ideal format through which to develop the full complexity of a constitutional argument or to place in print the latest sermon, drama,

---

* The term "propaganda," for all the negative connotations it so often carries for the contemporary reader, is used here in its most basic dictionary sense: "the spreading of ideas, information, or rumor for the purposes of helping or injuring an institution, a cause, or a person" (Webster's New Collegiate Dictionary).

INTRODUCTION

lengthy poem, public oration, or sustained prose satire. The dissemination of ideas in pamphlet form, moreover, came naturally to the colonial writer. Not only did he live in an age in which the pamphlet was the accepted medium of public debate (the so-called golden age of pamphleteering), but as an Englishman he partook of a long and honorable tradition of pamphlet literature which included Swift, Defoe, Locke, Dryden, and Milton. Though few American writers could hope to rival a Dean Swift or a John Milton, the number of surviving revolutionary pamphlets suggests at least a willingness to try.

As a vehicle for public persuasion, the pamphlet reached the height of its success with the publication of Thomas Paine's *Common Sense* early in 1776. Within a matter of months Paine's two-shilling pamphlet had sold over 100,000 copies and been reprinted at New York, Norwich, Providence, Newport, Salem, Newburyport, Charleston, and Boston, as well as at Philadelphia —this in a country whose total population was scarcely more than 2½ million and where adult literacy was far from universal. Few pamphlets, of course, could claim the wide readership or popularity of a *Common Sense*. By the very weightiness of their subject matter, those pamphlets which contributed most significantly to the developing intellectual history of the Revolution addressed themselves to a far more select and well-educated audience, including the intellectual leadership of the patriot party itself, without whose unified thinking and concurrence no ideological movement could finally hope to succeed.

Of all the available media at the revolutionary writer's disposal, however, it was the newspaper, rather than the pamphlet or broadside, that finally proved to be most crucial in crystallizing, propagandizing, and sustaining the public mind in the cause of revolution. The newspaper, of course, could be expected to reach a much more diverse audience than either the pamphlet or broadside, and patriot leaders like Boston's wily Sam Adams were quick to discover its value in shaping public sentiment and moving men to action. Thanks in good measure to the Stamp Act of 1765, which required newspapers to carry the hated blue revenue stamp and thus united colonial editors in opposition to the Parliament that imposed it, the press from the very outset of the revolutionary controversy was largely in the hands of the Whigs.[*] Thereafter, patriot editors used their newspapers as a convenient means of publicizing—and, by stirring up anger and resentment, implementing—the activities and programs of local patriot groups.

---

[*] The terms "Whig" and "Tory" did not actually enter the lexicon of the American Revolution until about 1774. To use them as I do to describe the two emerging points of view of colonial Americans seems permissible as long as one remembers that they were not hard and fast political labels denoting organized political parties in the modern sense.

Though newspapers carried official proclamations, the proceedings of Congress and local revolutionary committees, letters to the editor, poems, and short satirical pieces, as well as news (which then, as now, could be slanted), their principal stock in trade was the political essay, a powerful weapon in the colonies' ideological and constitutional quarrel with Britain. To be sure, many of these essays were not unlike pamphlets in miniature, particularly when they were written sequentially by a single author. Such was the case, in fact, with John Dickinson's celebrated *Letters from a Farmer in Pennsylvania* which first appeared serially in the *Pennsylvania Chronicle* (December, 1767, to February, 1768) before being circulated anew in pamphlet form several weeks later.

The colonial newspaper, as it existed throughout the period of the American Revolution, was, at best, a precarious enterprise. To begin with, its general overall appearance was scarcely designed to please the eye. Typically, the colonial newspaper consisted of four three-column pages, ten by fifteen inches in size, printed in correspondingly small typeface, not infrequently of poor quality. Add to this its relatively small weekly circulation (500–600 copies seems to have been about average, though circulation naturally rose and fell with the tide of events), its small advertising revenues, and its inadequate system of distribution, and it is a wonder that any newspapers were able to survive. Those that did survive often managed to do so because the printer—who also performed the modern functions of editor and publisher —was either fortunate or conniving enough to attach himself as "publick printer" to the local government. But survive they did. By 1764, the year in which Parliament passed the Sugar Act, there were twenty-three colonial papers; and by 1775 that number had grown to something like thirty-eight, seven of which were found in Philadelphia, five in Boston, and three in the city of New York.

The dislocation of war naturally brought about a basic realignment of the press. Before the end of 1775 nine papers had disappeared completely, two had sought the security of areas controlled by American arms, and two new ones had been founded. Though both sides were quick to recognize and seize upon the newspaper as a psychological weapon of war, and to use it with considerable skill in mounting propaganda campaigns, the Americans never surrendered their initial advantage. For them, indeed, the newspaper was at times the only means at their disposal to counter British victories and sustain morale, especially through the dark days preceding Burgoyne's unexpected defeat at Saratoga. Only in New York City, where the notorious Tory printer James Rivington and his *Royal Gazette* held sway, and where most of the leading Loyalist writers took refuge for the duration of the war, were the British able to use the press consistently to their advantage. There their success was significant, as is amply illustrated by the sustained fury of the attack which Whig writers unleashed against Jamie Rivington and his "lying Gazette."

The road to American independence was a long one, filled with twists and turns. Before there could be independence, basic attitudes had to be changed, long-standing opinions altered, and a whole traditional way of thinking discredited and destroyed. In the final analysis, it was the writer's ability to accomplish precisely these ends that made American independence possible. As is so often the case where revolutionary causes are concerned, the Whig writers exercised an influence far in excess of their actual numbers. Their success can be credited to their determination, their aggressiveness, their ingenuity, and, finally, of course, to the persuasiveness of their argument.

With perhaps the single exception of Benjamin Franklin, the leading Whig writers of the American Revolution were not professional authors—though it is true that the cause of America made some of them so. They were, for the most part, successful, well-educated, fairly prosperous men—lawyers, planters, ministers, and merchants—many of whom by 1763 had reached positions of influence and leadership within their respective colonies, not infrequently as a direct result of their political astuteness. Not surprisingly, many of the most prominent and articulate of the Whig writers were lawyers, schooled in the British legal tradition, for whom constitutional debate posed few terrors. A number—James Otis, John Dickinson, and Thomas Jefferson, to cite but three—possessed not only considerable literary talent but were endowed with original, highly creative minds capable of constructing from their knowledge of English law and the revolutionary principles associated with eighteenth-century natural-rights philosophy closely reasoned arguments limiting (and then denying altogether) the sovereignty of Parliament and crown. In response to Parliament's attempt to raise revenue through taxation, these writers initiated a broad and sweeping inquiry into the rights of Englishmen and into the very nature and source of political power itself. What emerged, at length, was not only a revolutionary ideology justifying colonial resistance to British imperial policy but the beginnings of a national self-consciousness, a uniquely "American" formulation of the world, whose dynamic implications are very much with us yet.

Original thinking, of and by itself, however, was by no means a necessary prerequisite for a successful revolutionary writer. In a day when the average American had but little real grasp of the subtleties of constitutional polemics, the most widely influential Whig writers were those who were able to convince their readers—through appeals that went as much to the heart as to the head—of the truth and legitimacy of ideas and feelings already perceived but till then only half-believed and half-understood. Such men—Thomas

Paine, the author of *Common Sense,* is the perfect example—were, in the best sense of the word, popularizers, who, having read perfectly the public mind, distilled from ideas already in the air self-evident, "common sense" arguments, delivered in a language and with a force and a conviction that could be readily appreciated by men and women of all ranks. At each successive crisis of the revolutionary period—The Stamp Act (1765), the Townshend Acts (1767), the Boston Massacre (1770), the Boston Tea Party (1773), and Lexington and Concord (1775)—patriot writers emerged to set forth with increasing urgency and eloquence the colonial case against Great Britain. So effective was their appeal that they succeeded at length in persuading an ever-increasing number of Americans that their cherished liberties were being deliberately and systematically undermined by evil ministers and an unsympathetic king, and that nothing short of independence and a recourse to arms would possibly suffice to preserve them.

This momentous decision, made by the delegates to the Second Continental Congress and announced to an incredulous world by the Declaration of Independence, irrevocably ended the long period of colonial debate. Jefferson's ringing words made clear and final what had been a fact since the preceding April: the American colonies were in a state of rebellion against Great Britain, and any hope for reconciliation had given way before the pressure of events themselves.

Americans soon learned, however, that winning a war was something more than a military problem—that the times, as Washington himself noted, called for literary efforts capable of impressing "upon the mind of every man, from the first to the lowest, the importance of the cause, and what it is that they are contending for." Though Washington's injunction went all but unheeded during the first months of independence—a letdown attributable, in part at least, to the fact that many of the major literary figures of the prerevolutionary period, their immediate goals attained, were now otherwise engaged—Whig writers soon began to rise to the occasion.

The continuing need for propaganda was particularly acute in a war like the American Revolution. Though the immediate threat posed by Sir William Howe and the British army understandably dominated the day-to-day concerns of Congress and its generals, the Revolution remained, in its larger dimensions, a civil struggle. On the one hand, there were those patriotic Whigs who accepted the leadership of Congress and embraced, with greater or less unanimity, the cause of independence. Directly opposing them were those Americans variously labeled "Tories" or "Loyalists" who just as unequivocally maintained the authority of Great Britain. Between the two was still another group, the uncertain and the uncommitted, who chose, by conviction or design, neutrality. This third group, whose membership fluctuated with the fortunes of war, posed the greatest challenge to revolutionary writers. Once military operations shifted from Boston to New York and the middle colonies in the late summer and fall of 1776—an area where neutralist sentiment was strong—it became a principal goal of the writers of both sides to attempt, through threat or entreaty, to convert or at least neutralize this wavering group of middle Americans. (Witness, for example, the first of Paine's *Crisis* papers, Burgoyne's "Proclamation," and William Livingston's satiric response.)

Not surprisingly, the literature produced by Whig writers during the war years differed noticeably in theme and purpose from the literature of the prewar period. The time for long, elaborate legal and constitutional arguments was over and done with, save for an occasional reminder that the cause for which Americans were contending was both honorable and just. The literature of the Revolution was, by and large, a literature of passion and emotional appeal, which sought, even in the face of adversity—and at times precisely because of adversity—to sustain the high ideological level of American patriotism. The writer's job became one of buoying up morale, of winning new converts by holding forth the advantages and glorious prospect of final victory, of neutralizing the counterarguments of enemy writers, and of attempting to sow seeds of dissension and despair among the ranks of the British army and their supporters and sympathizers. Bitter, unrelenting, and blatantly propagandistic, the literature of the Revolution is a literature filled with satire, ridicule, and invective, aimed at creating a sense of indignation and moral outrage. In its most extreme form it becomes a literature of hatred, dramatizing in lurid detail the atrocities committed by British troops and their Hessian and Indian allies against defenseless men, women, and children.

The Whig literary effort did not, of course, go either unchallenged or unanswered. From the beginning of the revolutionary controversy there were many good and honorable Americans who opposed on principle any attempt to limit or proscribe British authority. These "Tories" (or "Loyalists" as they themselves preferred to be known), while drawn from the whole spectrum of colonial society, tended to be identified, particularly in the North, with a number of special groups: with government officials, great and small, who held office at the pleasure of the crown; with the Anglican clergy, who in taking orders from the Bishop of London had sworn allegiance to George III and in many cases received part of their yearly stipend directly from the Church of England; and with wealthy merchants and large landowners, especially those dependent on the favors of local British officialdom. Generalizations in this respect, however, are dangerous, for historians have shown that American Toryism was inspired as much by temperament and deep-rooted patriotism as it was by narrow economic, religious, or political self-interest. As the quarrel with Great Britain mounted in intensity, as violence and mob action replaced peaceful remonstrance, and as expressions of loyalty gave way to treasonable whispers of independence, these conservatives moved steadily away from their more "patriotic" countrymen to support, however reluctantly, the political status quo.

Though Loyalist writers were no less dedicated and able than their Whig counterparts, they nonetheless found themselves during the prewar years at a decided disadvantage. To begin with, theirs was a delayed response. Initially, in fact, there was scarcely any response at all. Faced with the unhappy choice of speaking out as apologists for the ill-conceived, inconsistent, and poorly executed economic program of the British ministry, or of remaining silent, hoping that the whole problem of imperial relations would resolve itself or simply disappear, most Loyalist spokesmen understandably chose the latter course. In so doing, of course, they followed the fatal lead of George III's ministers in underestimating the strength of colonial opposition and the lengths to which patriot leaders were prepared to go in securing redress for their grievances.

It was not, in fact, until the tempo of events quickened in late 1773 and 1774 and the final polarization of colonial society was well under way, that Loyalist writers grasped the seriousness of the political situation and attempted to counter the constitutional arguments of Whig writers with arguments of their own. Even then, instead of coming forward as advocates of a positive program that might have solved the constitutional crisis and preserved British authority, their public posture remained essentially negative and defensive. In place of evolution and change they offered an elitist appeal to order, social stability, and respect for traditional authority. Inhibited by a sense of the weakness of their own position, and lacking organized, effective leadership, many simply succumbed to the temptation to seek refuge behind the protection of British arms. By then, too, the initiative had already passed into the hands of the Whigs, who used the First Continental Congress, their control of the lower houses of the provincial assemblies, and their interconnected and well-organized network of associations, committees, and political action groups to intimidate and silence those who might be tempted to raise their voices in opposition.

Though a number of conservative writers eventually did speak out—Samuel Seabury, Daniel Leonard, Charles Inglis, and Joseph Galloway among them—on the whole, the Loyalists' prewar appeal to their countrymen was relatively ineffectual, at least in comparison to that of their better-organized and more aggressive opponents. At a time when the "Intolerable Acts" had turned the city of Boston into an armed camp and patriots everywhere had been roused to new levels of resistance and determination, it was next to useless to engage in constitutional polemics or sing the praises of a paternal ministry and king. To appreciate fully the dilemma that confronted Loyalist writers, one must also remember that during the final, climactic year before independence the colonies were already in a state of undeclared war. Blood had been shed on the village green at Lexington, Congress had placed an American army in the field, Bunker Hill had been stormed, and the British, after a lengthy siege, had been forced to evacuate Boston by sea. As Thomas Paine put it so pointedly in *Common Sense:* "All plans, proposals, etc. prior to the nineteenth of April, i.e. to the commencement of hostilities, are like the almanacs of the last year; which though proper then, are superseded and useless now."

The role of the American Loyalists in the long war that followed was a significant one. In sheer numbers alone—estimates run to as high as one-third of the colonial population—they were a force to be reckoned with, especially in New York, New Jersey, Pennsylvania, Delaware, and Maryland, where Loyalism was particularly widespread. Before the war was over, some 50,000 American Loyalists had taken up arms either with regular units of the British army or in special Loyalist corps of their own and had participated—not infrequently with distinction—in virtually every major military engagement.

Loyalist writers, taking their cue from the series of British successes that marked the summer and fall of 1776, began the war on a note of lighthearted optimism, an attitude which became increasingly more sober as hostilities dragged on. Though limited in number and restricted geographically to those areas protected by British troops (two factors which, in turn, reduced the potential size of their audience), Loyalist propagandists functioned briskly throughout the war. After mid-1776 most of the leading Loyalist writers were drawn from the ranks of the Anglican clergy, a fact which becomes doubly interesting when one surveys the literature that such men produced. Where one might expect to find a literature of argumentative discussion or high moral tone, one finds, on the contrary, as Moses Coit Tyler, America's first literary historian, characterized it so well, "a literature of emotional appeal, exultant, hortatory, derisive, denunciatory—a literature chiefly lyrical and satirical." Satire, mainly poetic satire, was their forte.

The reiterated themes of Loyalist writers were predictable: the appeal to enlightened self-interest; the illegality of the Revolution; the rascality of Congress (a Congress composed of "obscure pettifogging attorneys, bankrupt shopkeepers, outlawed smugglers, wretched banditti, the refuse and dregs of mankind"); the depreciated state of Continental currency; the demoralization of the Continental army and its self-serving leaders; the invincibility of British arms; and the ironies and snares of an alliance with Catholic France. Loyalist writers, of course, seized upon every opportunity to deflate rebel victories, to cast disdain upon opposing military leaders, to spread tales about the cruelty and rapacity of American soldiers, and to per-

11

suade their readers that the war was indeed a lost and desperate cause. Their task, however, was not always an easy one, particularly after Burgoyne's humiliating surrender at Saratoga in October, 1777. At such moments of frustration Loyalist writers were not above criticizing the British army for failing to come to the aid of their fellow Loyalists or for refusing (as in the case of the methodical, overly cautious Sir William Howe) to pursue a more active and aggressive military policy.

The American Loyalists, in the end, paid a high price for their allegiance to the crown. Before the war was over, many of those who had looked so confidently to the British to vindicate their loyalty saw their estates and property confiscated and their lives proscribed by new state governments composed, in many instances, of former friends and neighbors. At its conclusion upwards of 100,000 American Loyalists were forced to flee into exile, many to the maritime provinces of Canada where, after great trials and hardships, they managed to build new lives on the shattered remains of the old. Some eventually chose to return to make whatever peace they could in the land of their nativity; for most, however, the road to exile had but one direction.

The individual selections which comprise this collection were chosen primarily because of (1) their recognized importance to the developing intellectual history of the American Revolution; (2) the degree to which they serve to illustrate the various literary types, genres, and techniques employed most frequently by revolutionary writers; and (3) the intrinsic literary merit of the selections themselves. Each has a brief introduction which attempts to place the selection in its proper historical context and to provide the essential details about the author and his role in the American Revolution. Revolutionary texts provide many problems for the present-day editor, particularly in regard to their punctuation and typography, which often follow no other standard, convention, or consistency than the author's or printer's own. With the needs of the modern American reader in mind, I have made a number of silent emendations and corrections in the typography, punctuation, capitalization, and spelling. The aim in each case has been to improve the readability of the text without fundamentally altering the author's desired meaning or emphasis. The historical footnotes, unless otherwise indicated, are my own.

Part One

The Literature of
Colonial Debate, 1763-76

JAMES OTIS

1

from *The Rights of the British Colonies Asserted and Proved* (1764)

James Otis (1725–83), one of Massachusetts's earliest revolutionary leaders, was born at West Barnstable into a family which could trace its New England roots back a full five generations. Following his graduation from Harvard College in 1743, Otis took up the study of law and began his practice at Plymouth in 1748. Two years later he moved to Boston and began to rise rapidly in legal circles. Otis served as advocate general (chief prosecutor) of the Massachusetts vice-admiralty court from 1756 to 1761, but resigned the lucrative position in order to represent a group of Boston merchants in their unsuccessful attempt to prevent the renewal of the Writs of Assistance, which gave customs officials the right to enter private homes and warehouses in search of dutiable goods. His dogged opposition to royal governors Bernard and Hutchinson and to the policies of the British ministry made him the leader of the popular party in Boston, which elected him to the provincial legislature in 1761. Otis's active, at times tempestuous, political career climaxed in September, 1769, when he was involved in the famous British Coffee House brawl with customs official John Robinson. The sword blow on the head that Otis suffered soon healed; but increasing mental instability, culminating in madness, led to his withdrawal from all political life. Seldom seen in public thereafter, Otis died in 1783 when he was struck down by lightning.

James Otis's reputation as the "first writer of the Revolution" rests primarily on his 120-page pamphlet The Rights of the British Colonies Asserted and Proved, *published at Boston on July 23, 1764. It was the first pamphlet to appear after the arrival of the news of the proposed Stamp Act. For Otis, as for those who came after him, the issue on taxation was clear: taxation*

without representation violated the British constitution and was hence illegal.
Furthermore, the colonists have an "equitable right . . . to be represented in
Parliament, or to have some new subordinate legislature among themselves.
It would be best if they had both. Deprived however of their common rights
as subjects they cannot lawfully be while they remain such." Though Otis's
tract established what was in fact a legal, constitutional basis for colonial
resistance, his aim throughout was conciliatory, his tone mild and restrained.
And though some of his assertions—most notably his acknowledgment of
the supremacy of Parliament—were soon to become outmoded, the essentials
of his argument were to be echoed and reechoed in the years ahead.

☆ ☆

Of the Political and Civil Rights of the British Colonists

Here indeed opens to view a large field; but I must study brevity. Few
people have extended their enquiries after the foundation of any of their
rights, beyond a charter from the crown. There are others who think when
they have got back to old *Magna Charta* that they are at the beginning of all
things. They imagine themselves on the borders of Chaos (and so indeed in
some respects they are) and see creation rising out of the unformed mass, or
from nothing. Hence, say they, spring all the rights of men and of citizens.
. . . But liberty was better understood and more fully enjoyed by our ancestors before the coming in of the first Norman tyrants than ever after, 'till it
was found necessary, for the salvation of the kingdom, to combat the arbitrary and wicked proceedings of the Stuarts.

The present happy and most righteous establishment is justly built on the
ruins which those princes brought on their family; and two of them on their
own heads. The last of the name sacrificed three of the finest kingdoms in
Europe to the councils of bigoted old women, priests and more weak and
wicked ministers of state. He afterward went a grazing in the fields of St.
Germain, and there died in disgrace and poverty, a terrible example of God's
vengeance on arbitrary princes!

The deliverance under God wrought by the prince of Orange, afterwards
deservedly made King Wm. 3rd., was as joyful an event to the colonies as to
Great Britain. In some of them steps were taken in his favor as soon as in
England.

They all immediately acknowledged King William and Queen Mary as
their lawful sovereign. And such has been the zeal and loyalty of the colonies ever since for that establishment, and for the protestant succession in

his Majesty's illustrious family, that I believe there is not one man in a hundred (except in Canada) who does not think himself under the best national civil constitution in the world.

Their loyalty has been abundantly proved, especially in the late war.[1] Their affection and reverence for their mother country is unquestionable. They yield the most cheerful and ready obedience to her laws, particularly to the power of that august body the Parliament of Great Britain, the supreme legislative of the kingdom and in dominions. These I declare are my own sentiments of duty and loyalty. I also hold it clear that the act of Queen Anne, which makes it high treason to deny "that the King, with and by the authority of Parliament, is able to make laws and statutes of sufficient force and validity to *limit and bind* the crown, and the descent, limitation, inheritance and *government* thereof," is founded on the principles of liberty and the British constitution. And he that would palm the doctrine of unlimited passive obedience and non-resistance upon mankind, and thereby or by any other means serve the cause of the Pretender, is not only a fool and a knave, but a rebel against common sense, as well as the laws of God, of nature, and his country.

I also lay it down as one of the first principles from whence I intend to deduce the civil rights of the British colonies, that all of them are subject to and dependent on Great Britain; and that therefore as over subordinate governments, the Parliament of Great Britain has an undoubted power and lawful authority to make acts for the general good, that by naming them, shall and ought to be equally binding as upon the subjects of Great Britain within the realm. This principle, I presume, will be readily granted on the other side of the Atlantic. It has been practiced upon for twenty years to my knowledge in the province of the *Massachusetts Bay*; and I have ever received it that it has been so from the beginning in this and the sister provinces through the continent.

I am aware some will think it is time for me to retreat, after having expressed the power of the British Parliament in quite so strong terms. But 'tis from and under this very power and its acts, and from the common law, that the political and civil rights of the colonists are derived. And upon those grand pillars of liberty shall my defense be rested. At present, therefore, the reader may suppose that there is not one provincial charter on the continent; he may, if he pleases, imagine all taken away, without fault, without forfeiture, without trial or notice. All this really happened to some of them in the last century. I would have the reader carry his imagination still further, and suppose a time may come when instead of a process at common law the Parliament shall give a decisive blow to every charter in America, and declare them all void. Nay it shall also be granted that 'tis barely possible the time may come when the real interest of the whole may require an act of Parliament to annihilate all those charters. What could follow from all this that would shake one of the essential, natural, civil or religious rights of the colonists? Nothing. They would be men, citizens and British subjects after all. No act of Parliament can deprive them of the liberties of such, unless any will contend that an act of Parliament can make slaves not only of one, but of two millions of the commonwealth. And if so, why not of the whole? I freely own that I can find nothing in the laws of my country that would justify the Parliament in making one slave, nor did they ever professedly undertake to make one. . . .

Every British subject born on the continent of America, or in any other of the British dominions, is by the law of God and nature, by the common law, and by act of Parliament (exclusive of all charters from the crown) entitled to all the natural, essential, inherent and inseparable rights of our fellow subjects in Great Britain. Among those rights are the following, which it is humbly conceived no man or body of men, not excepting the Parliament, justly, equitably and consistently with their own rights and the constitution, can take away.

1st. *That the supreme and subordinate powers of the legislation should be free and sacred in the hands where the community have once rightfully placed them.*

2dly. *The supreme national legislative cannot be altered justly 'till the commonwealth is dissolved, nor a subordinate legislative taken away without forfeiture or other good cause.* Nor then can the subjects in the subordinate government be reduced to a state of slavery, and subject to the despotic rule of others. A state has no right to make slaves of the conquered. Even when the subordinate right of legislature is forfeited, and so declared, this cannot affect the natural persons either of those who were invested with it, or the inhabitants, so far as to deprive them of the rights of subjects and of men. The colonists will have an equitable right, notwithstanding any such forfeiture of charter, to be represented in Parliament, or to have some new subordinate legislature among themselves. It would be best if they had both. Deprived however of their common rights as subjects they cannot lawfully be while they remain such. A representation in Parliament from the several colonies, since they are become so large and numerous as to be called on not to maintain provincial government, civil and military among themselves, for this they have cheerfully done, but to contribute towards the support of a national standing army, by reason of the heavy national debt, when they themselves owe a large one contracted in the common cause, can't be thought an unreasonable thing, nor if asked, could it be called an immodest request. *Qui sentit commodum sentire debet et onus* has been thought a maxim of equity. But that a man should bear a burden for other people as well as himself, without a return, never long found a place in any lawbook or decrees but those of the most despotic princes. Besides the equity of an American representation in Parliament, a thousand advantages would result from it. It would be the most effectual means of giving those of both countries a thorough knowledge of each others' interests, as well as that of the whole, which are inseparable.

Were this representation allowed, instead of the scandalous memorials and depositions that have been sometimes, in days of old, privately cooked up in an inquisitorial manner, by persons of bad minds and wicked views, and sent from America to the several boards, persons of the first reputation among their countrymen might be on the spot, from the several colonies, truly to represent them. Future ministers need not, like some of their predecessors, have recourse for information in American affairs to every vagabond stroller that has run or rid post through America from his creditors, or to the people of no kind of reputation from the colonies, some of whom, at the time of administering their sage advice, have been as ignorant of the state of the country as of the regions in Jupiter and Saturn.

No representation of the colonies in Parliament alone would, however, be equivalent to a subordinate legislative among themselves, nor so well answer the ends of increasing their prosperity and the commerce of Great Britain. It would be impossible for the Parliament to judge so well of their abilities to bear taxes, impositions on trade, and other duties and burdens, or of the local laws that might be really needful, as a legislative here.

3dly. *No legislative, supreme or subordinate, has a right to make itself arbitrary.*

It would be a most manifest contradiction for a free legislative, like that of Great Britain, to make itself arbitrary.

4thly. *The supreme legislative cannot justly assume a power of ruling by extempore arbitrary decrees, but is bound to dispense justice by known settled rules, and by duly authorized independent judges.*

5thly. *The supreme power cannot take from any man any part of his property,* without his consent in *person, or by representation.*

6thly. *The legislature cannot transfer the power of making laws to any other hands.*

These are their bounds, which by God and nature are fixed; hitherto have they a right to come, and no further.

1. *To govern by stated laws.*

2. *Those laws should have no other end ultimately but the good of the people.*

3. *Taxes are not to be laid on the people but by their consent in person, or by deputation.*

4. *Their whole power is not transferable.*

These are the first principles of law and justice, and the great barriers of a free state, and of the British constitution in particular. I ask, I want no more.—Now let it be shown how 'tis reconcilable with these principles, or to many other fundamental maxims of the British constitution, as well as the natural and civil rights which by the laws of their country all British subjects are entitled to as their best inheritance and birthright, that all the northern colonies, who are without one representative in the House of Commons, should be taxed by the British Parliament.

That the colonists, black and white, born here are free-born British subjects, and entitled to all the essential civil rights of such, is a truth not only manifest from the provincial charters, from the principles of the common law, and acts of Parliament, but from the British constitution, which was re-established at the revolution with a professed design to lecture the liberties of all the subjects to all generations.

In the 12 and 13 of Wm. cited above, the liberties of the subjects are spoken of as their best birthrights. No one ever dreamt, surely, that these liberties were confined to the realm. At that rate, no British subjects in the dominions could, without a manifest contradiction, be declared entitled to all the privileges of subjects born within the realm, to all intents and purposes which are rightly given foreigners by Parliament after residing seven years. These expressions of Parliament, as well as of the charters, must be vain and empty sounds unless we are allowed the essential rights of our fellow-subjects in Great Britain.

Now can there be any liberty where property is taken away without consent? Can it with any color of truth, justice or equity be affirmed that the northern colonies are represented in Parliament? Has this whole continent of near three thousand miles in length, and in which and his other American dominions his Majesty has, or very soon will have, some millions of as good, loyal and useful subjects, white and black, as any in the three kingdoms, the election of one member of the House of Commons?

Is there the least difference, as to the consent of the colonists, whether taxes and impositions are laid on their trade, and other property, by the crown alone, or by the Parliament? As it is agreed on all hands, the crown alone cannot impost them, we should be justifiable in refusing to pay them, but must and ought to yield obedience to an act of Parliament, though erroneous, 'till repealed.

I can see no reason to doubt but that the imposition of taxes, whether on trade, or on land, or houses, or ships, on real or personal, fixed or floating property, in the colonies, is absolutely irreconcilable with the rights of the colonists as British subjects and as men. I say men, for in a state of nature no man can take my property from me without my consent. If he does, he deprives me of my liberty, and makes me a slave. If such a proceeding is a breach of the law of nature, no law of society can make it just. The very act of taxing, exercised over those who are not represented, appears to me to be depriving them of one of their most essential rights as freemen; and if continued, seems to be in effect an entire disfranchisement of every civil right. For what one civil right is worth a rush after a man's property is subject to be taken from him at pleasure, without his consent. If a man is not his *own assessor* in person, or by deputy, his liberty is gone, or lies entirely at the mercy of others. . . .

With regard to the Parliament, as infallibility belongs not to mortals, 'tis possible *they* may have been misinformed and deceived. The power of Parliament is uncontrollable, but by themselves, and we must obey. They only can repeal their own acts. There would be an end of all government if one or a number of subjects or subordinate provinces should take upon them so far to judge of the justice of an act of Parliament as to refuse obedience to it. If there was nothing else to restrain such a step, prudence ought to do it, for forcibly resisting the Parliament and the king's laws is high treason. Therefore let the Parliament lay what burdens they please on us, we must, it is our duty to, submit and patiently bear them till they will be pleased to relieve us. And 'tis to be presumed the wisdom and justice of that august assembly always will afford us relief by repealing such acts, as through mistake or other human infirmities, have been suffered to pass, if they can be convinced that their proceedings are not constitutional, or not for the common good. . . .

To say the Parliament is absolute and arbitrary is a contradiction. The Parliament cannot make 2 and 2, 5; Omnipotency cannot do it. The supreme power in a state is *jus dicere* only; *jus dare,* strictly speaking, belongs alone to God. Parliaments are in all cases to *declare* what is for the good of the whole; but it is not the *declaration* of Parliament that makes it so. There must be in every instance a higher authority, viz. *God.* Should an act of Parliament be against any of *his* natural laws, which are *immutably* true, their declaration would be contrary to eternal truth, equity and justice, and consequently void: and so it would be adjudged by the Parliament itself, when convinced of their mistake. Upon this great principle, parliaments repeal such acts as soon as they find they have been mistaken in having declared them to be for the public good, when in fact they were not so. When such mistake is evident and palpable, as in the instances in the appendix, the judges of the executive courts have declared the act "of a whole Parliament void." See here the grandeur of the British constitution! See the wisdom of our ancestors! The supreme *legislative* and the supreme *executive* are a perpetual check and balance to each other. If the supreme executive errs, it is informed by the supreme legislative in Parliament. If the supreme legislative errs, it is informed by the supreme executive in the king's courts of law. Here, the king appears, as represented by his judges, in the highest luster and majesty, as supreme executor of the commonwealth; and he never shines brighter but on his throne, at the head of the supreme legislative. This is government! This, is a constitution! to preserve which, either from foreign or domestic foes, has cost oceans of blood and treasure in every age; and the blood and the treasure have upon the whole been well spent. . . .

The colonies have been so remarkable for loyalty that there never has been any instance of rebellion or treason in them. This loyalty is in very handsome terms acknowledged by the author of the administration of the colonies. "It has been often suggested that care should be taken in the administration of the plantations lest, in some future time, these colonies should become independent of the mother country. But perhaps it may be proper on this occasion, and it is justice to say it, that if by becoming independent is meant a revolt, nothing is further from their nature, their interest, their thoughts. If a defection from the *alliance* of the mother country be suggested, it ought to be and can be truly said that their spirit abhors the sense of such; their attachment to the protestant succession in the house of Hanover will ever stand unshaken; and nothing can eradicate from their hearts their natural and almost mechanical affection to Great Britain, which they conceive under no other sense nor call by any other name than that of *home.* Any such suggestion, therefore, is a false and unjust aspersion on their principles and affections; and can arise from nothing but an entire ignorance of their circumstances." . . .

We all think ourselves happy under Great Britain. We love, esteem and reverence our mother country, and adore our king. And could the choice of independency be offered the colonies, or subjection to Great Britain upon any terms above absolute slavery, I am convinced they would accept the latter. The ministry in all future generations may rely on it that British America will never prove undutiful till driven to it, as the last fatal resort against ministerial oppression, which will make the wisest mad, and the weakest strong. . . .

JOHN DICKINSON

2

from *Letters from a Farmer in Pennsylvania* (1767–68)

On June 26, 1767, Parliament passed the Townshend Revenue Act, named after its chief architect Charles Townshend, chancellor of the exchequer, which sought through a series of import duties on glass, paper, paint, lead, and tea to raise revenues to pay the salaries of British customs officers. Three days later Parliament suspended the New York Assembly for its failure to obey the Quartering Act of 1765. Americans were at once alarmed. By attempting to raise revenue under the guise of regulating trade, Parliament had in effect declared null and void the distinction between "internal" and "external" taxation which it had itself acknowledged, however tacitly, in the repeal of the Stamp Act the year before. When coupled with the unprecedented suspension of a colonial legislature, an institution whose prerogatives Americans jealously guarded, this action created overnight a new crisis in imperial relations.

Into this crisis stepped John Dickinson (1732–1808), perhaps the best legal mind in the colonies, who, masquerading as a plain-speaking Pennsylvania farmer, published twelve letters to the press (1767–68) setting forth the historical origin of colonial rights and arguing that while Parliament might regulate trade it had no legal or constitutional right to tax the colonies. Dickinson brushed aside the distinction between "external" and "internal" taxation: as long as the colonies remained unrepresented in Parliament, any form of taxation was illegal. Such a limitation on the powers of Parliament served, of course, to open up a whole new phase in the debate over colonial rights. Dickinson's Letters from a Farmer in Pennsylvania *gained immediate notoriety and approval. Published and republished in virtually every colonial newspaper and then in pamphlet form, their influence was unprecedented, and once their authorship was revealed Dickinson's reputation as a defender of American freedom became second only to Benjamin Franklin's.*

John Dickinson was born in Maryland but raised on his parents' estate near Dover, Delaware. Tutored at home until 1750, he studied law in Philadelphia for three years before going abroad to complete his legal education at the Middle Temple in London (1753–57). Returning to Philadelphia, where he was admitted to the bar and opened his own practice, Dickinson quickly became known in legal circles as a young lawyer of unusual abilities, and prospered accordingly. His political career began in 1760 with his election to the Delaware assembly, followed two years later by his election to the Pennsylvania assembly, where he served from 1762 to 1765, and again from 1770 to 1776. As a delegate to the Stamp Act Congress of 1765, Dickinson was called upon by his colleagues to write its major resolutions; two years later came the Townshend Acts and his celebrated response. Conservative by nature, a moderate who hoped to the last for reconciliation, Dickinson gradually moved into the background as the movement towards independence reached its climax, and temporarily fell into disfavor for his refusal to sign the Declaration of Independence. Interestingly enough, however, though no one hated violence more than he, Dickinson was one of the few congressmen to take up arms against the British. Dickinson's interest in public affairs lasted long after the war was over (he served as president of Delaware from 1781 to 1782 and as president of Pennsylvania from 1782 to 1785) and well into the turbulent decade of the 1790s, after which he retired to the quietude of the Delaware countryside.

☆ ☆

LETTER I

My dear Countrymen,

I am a Farmer, settled, after a variety of fortunes, near the banks of the river Delaware in the province of Pennsylvania. I received a liberal education, and have been engaged in the busy scenes of life; but am now convinced that a man may be as happy without bustle as with it. My farm is small; my servants are few, and good; I have a little money at interest; I wish for no more; my employment in my own affairs is easy; and with a contented grateful mind, undisturbed by wordly hopes or fears relating to myself, I am completing the number of days allotted to me by divine goodness.

Being generally master of my time, I spend a good deal of it in a library, which I think the most valuable part of my small estate; and being acquainted with two or three gentlemen of abilities and learning, who honor me with their friendship, I have acquired, I believe, a greater knowledge in history and the laws and constitution of my country than is generally attained by men of my class, many of them not being so fortunate as I have been in the opportunities of getting information.

From my infancy I was taught to love *humanity* and *liberty*. Enquiry and experience have since confirmed my reverence for the lessons then given me by convincing me more fully of their truth and excellence. Benevolence towards mankind excites wishes for their welfare, and such wishes endear the means of fulfilling them. *These* can be found in liberty only, and therefore her sacred cause ought to be espoused by every man, on every occasion, to the utmost of his power. As a charitable but poor person does not withhold his *mite* because he cannot relieve *all* the distresses of the miserable, so should not any honest man suppress his sentiments concerning freedom, however small their influence is likely to be. Perhaps he "may touch some wheel," that will have an effect greater than he could reasonably expect.

These being my sentiments, I am encouraged to offer to you, my countrymen, my thoughts on some late transactions that appear to me to be of the utmost importance to you. Conscious of my own defects, I have waited some time in expectation of seeing the subject treated by persons much better qualified for the task; but being therein disappointed, and apprehensive that longer delays will be injurious, I venture at length to request the attention of the public, praying that these lines may be *read* with the same zeal for the happiness of British America with which they were *wrote*. . . .

LETTER II

My dear Countrymen,

There is another late act of Parliament which appears to me to be unconstitutional, and as destructive to the liberty of these colonies as that mentioned in my last letter; that is the act for granting the duties on paper, glass, etc.[2]

The Parliament unquestionably possesses a legal authority to *regulate* the trade of Great Britain and all her colonies. Such an authority is essential to the relation between a mother country and her colonies; and necessary for the common good of all. He who considers these provinces as states distinct from the British Empire has very slender notions of *justice*, or of their *interests*. We are but parts of a *whole*; and therefore there must exist a power somewhere to preside and preserve the connection in due order. This power is lodged in the Parliament; and we are as much dependent on Great Britain as a perfectly free people can be on another.

I have looked over *every statute* relating to these colonies from their first settlement to this time; and I find every one of them founded on this principle till the Stamp Act administration. *All before* are calculated to regulate trade and preserve or promote a mutually beneficial intercourse between the several constituent parts of the empire; and though many of them imposed duties on trade, yet those duties were always imposed *with design* to restrain the commerce of one part that was injurious to another, and thus to promote the general welfare. The raising a revenue thereby was never intended. Thus the king, by his judges in his courts of justice, imposes fines which all together amount to a very considerable sum, and contribute to the support of government. But this is merely a consequence arising from restrictions that only meant to keep peace and prevent confusion; and surely a man would argue very loosely who should conclude from hence that the king has a right to levy money in general upon his subjects. Never did the British Parliament, till the period above-mentioned, think of imposing duties in America for the purpose of raising a revenue. Mr. Grenville first introduced this language in the preamble to the 4th of *Geo.* III., Chap. 15, which has these words: "And whereas it is just and necessary that a revenue be raised in your Majesty's said dominions in America *for defraying the expenses of defending, protecting, and securing the same,* We your Majesty's most dutiful and loyal subjects, the Commons of Great Britain, in Parliament assembled, being desirous to make some provision in this present session of Parliament towards raising the said revenue in America, have resolved to give and grant unto your Majesty the several rates and duties herein after mentioned," etc.

A few months after came the Stamp Act, which reciting this, proceeds in the same strange mode of expression, thus—"And whereas it is just and necessary that provision be made for raising a further revenue within your Majesty's dominions in America *towards defraying the said expenses,* we your Majesty's most dutiful and loyal subjects, the Commons of Great Britain, etc., give and grant," etc., as before.

The last act, granting duties upon paper, etc., carefully pursues these modern precedents. The preamble is, "Whereas it is expedient that a revenue should be raised in your Majesty's dominions in America *for making a more certain and adequate provision for defraying the charge of the administration of justice, and the support of civil government in such provinces where it shall be found necessary, and towards the further defraying the expenses of defending, protecting and securing the said dominions,* we your Majesty's most dutiful and loyal subjects, the Commons of Great Britain, etc., give and grant," etc., as before.

Here we may observe an authority *expressly* claimed and exerted to impose duties on these colonies; not for the regulation of trade; not for the preservation or promotion of a mutually beneficial intercourse between the several constituent parts of the empire, heretofore the *sole objects* of parliamentary institutions; *but for the single purpose of levying money upon us.*

This I call an innovation; and a most dangerouse innovation. It may perhaps be objected that Great Britain has a right to lay what duties she pleases upon her exports, and it makes no difference to us whether they are paid here or there.

To this I answer. These colonies require many things for their use which the laws of Great Britain prohibit them from getting anywhere but from her. Such are paper and glass.

That we may legally be bound to pay any *general* duties on these commodities relative to the regulation of trade is granted; but we being *obliged by the laws* to take from Great Britain, any *special* duties imposed on their exportation *to us only, with intention to raise a revenue from us only,* are as much *taxes* upon us as those imposed by the Stamp Act.

What is the difference in *substance* and *right* whether the same sum is raised upon us by the rates mentioned in the Stamp Act on the *use* of paper, or by these duties on the *importation* of it. It is only the edition of a former book, shifting a sentence from the *end* to the *beginning.*

Suppose the duties were made payable in Great Britain.

It signifies nothing to us whether they are to be paid here or there. Had the Stamp Act directed that all the paper should be landed at Florida, and the duties paid there before it was brought to the British colonies, would the act have raised less money upon us, or have been less destructive of our rights? By no means: for as we were under a necessity of using the paper, we should have been under the necessity of paying the duties. Thus, in the present case, a like *necessity* will subject us, if this act continues in force, to the payment of the duties now imposed.

Why was the Stamp Act then so pernicious to freedom? It did not enact that every man in the colonies *should* buy a certain quantity of paper—No: it only directed that no instrument of writing should be valid in law, if not made on stamped paper, etc.

The makers of that act knew full well that the confusions that would arise from the disuse of writings would compel the colonies to use the stamped paper and therefore to pay the taxes imposed. For this reason the Stamp Act was said to be a law that would execute itself. For the very same reason, the last act of Parliament, if it is granted to have any force here, will execute itself, and will be attended with the very same consequences to American liberty. . . .

Great Britain has prohibited the manufacturing *iron* and *steel* in these colonies without any objection being made to her *right* of doing it. The *like* right she must have to prohibit any other manufacture among us. Thus she is possessed of an undisputed *precedent* on that point. This authority, she will say, is founded on the *original intention* of settling these colonies; that is, that we should manufacture for them, and that they should supply her with materials. The *equity* of this policy, she will also say, has been universally acknowledged by the colonies, who never have made the least objections to statutes for that purpose; and will further appear by the *mutual benefits* flowing from this usage ever since the settlement of these colonies.

Our great advocate, Mr. Pitt,[3] in his speeches on the debate concerning the repeal of the Stamp Act, acknowledged that Great Britain could restrain our manufactures. His words are these: "This kingdom, as the supreme governing and legislative power, has always bound the colonies by her regulations and restrictions in trade, in navigation, in manufactures—in everything *except that of taking their money out of their pockets* without their consent." Again he says, "We may bind their trade, confine their manufactures, and exercise every power whatever, *except that of taking their money out of their pockets* without their consent."

Here then, my dear countrymen, rouse yourselves, and behold the ruin hanging over your heads. If you ONCE admit that Great Britain may lay duties upon her exportation to us *for the purpose of levying money on us only,* she then will have nothing to do but to lay those duties on the articles which she prohibits us to manufacture—and the tragedy of American liberty is finished. We have been prohibited from procuring manufactures in all cases anywhere but from Great Britain (excepting linens which we are permitted to import directly from Ireland). We have been prohibited, in some cases, from manufacturing for ourselves; and may be prohibited in others. We are therefore exactly in the situation of a city besieged, which is surrounded by the works of the besiegers in every part *but one.* If *that* is closed up, no step can be taken *but to surrender at discretion.* If Great Britain can order us to come to her for necessaries we want, and can order us to pay what taxes she pleases before we take them away, or when we land them here, we are as abject slaves as France and Poland can show in wooden shoes, and with uncombed hair. . . .

From what has been said, I think this uncontrovertible conclusion may be deduced, that when a ruling state obliges a dependent state to take certain commodities from her alone, it is implied in the nature of that obligation; is essentially requisite to give it the least degree of justice; and is inseparably united with it, in order to preserve any share of freedom to the dependent state; *that those commodities should never be loaded with duties* for the sole purpose of levying money on the dependent state.

Upon the whole, the single question is whether the Parliament can legally impose duties to be paid *by the people of these colonies only,* for the sole purpose of raising a revenue, *on commodities which she obliges us to take from her alone,* or, in other words, whether the Parliament can legally take money out of our pockets without our consent. If they can, our boasted liberty is but

> *Vox et praeterea nihil.*
> A sound and nothing else.
>
> A Farmer

LETTER IV

My dear Countrymen,

An objection, I hear, has been made against my second letter which I would willingly clear up before I proceed. "There is," say these objectors, "a material difference between the Stamp Act and the late Act for laying a duty on paper, etc., that justifies the conduct of those who opposed the former, and yet are willing to submit to the latter. The duties imposed by the Stamp Act were *internal* taxes; but the present are *external,* and therefore the Parliament may have a right to impose them."

To this I answer with a total denial of the power of Parliament to lay upon these colonies any "tax" whatever.

This point, being so important to this and to succeeding generations, I wish to be clearly understood.

To the word "tax" I annex that meaning which the constitution and history of England require to be annexed to it; that is, that it is *an imposition on the subject for the sole purpose of levying money.*

In the early ages of our monarchy, certain services were rendered to the crown *for the general good.* These were personal. But in process of time, such institutions being found inconvenient, *gifts* and *grants* of their own property were made by the people under the several names of aids, tallages, tasks, taxes and subsidies, etc. These were made, as may be collected even from the names, *for public service* upon "need and necessity." All these sums were levied upon the people by virtue of their voluntary gift. Their design was to support the *national honor and interest.* Some of those grants comprehended duties arising from trade, being imposts on merchandises. These Lord Chief Justice *Coke* classes under "subsidies" and "parliamentary aids." They are also called "customs." But whatever the *name* was, they were always considered as *gifts of the people to the crown to be employed for public uses.*

Commerce was at a low ebb, and surprising instances might be produced how little it was attended to for a succession of ages. The terms that have been mentioned, and among the rest that of "tax," had obtained a national, parliamentary meaning, drawn from the principles of the constitution, long before any Englishman thought of *imposition of duties for the regulation of trade.*

Whenever we speak of "taxes" among Englishmen, let us therefore speak of them with reference to the *principles* on which and the *intentions* with which they have been established. This will give certainty to our expression and safety to our conduct. But if, when we have in view the liberty of these colonies, we proceed in any other course, we pursue a *Juno* indeed, but shall only catch a cloud.

In the national, parliamentary sense insisted on, the word "tax" was certainly understood by the congress at New York, whose resolves may be said to form the American "bill of rights." . . .

Here is no distinction made between *internal* and *external* taxes. It is evident from the short reasoning thrown into these resolves that every imposition "to grant to his Majesty *the property of the colonies*" was thought a "tax;" and that every such imposition, if laid any other way than "with their consent, given personally, or by their representatives," was not only "unreasonable, and inconsistent with the principles and spirit of the British constitution," but destructive "to the freedom of a people."

This language is clear and important. A "tax" means an imposition to raise money. Such persons therefore as speak of *internal* and *external* "taxes," I pray may pardon me, if I object to that expression as applied to the privileges and interests of these colonies. There may be *internal* and *external* impositions, founded on *different principles* and having *different tendencies,* every "tax" being an imposition, though every imposition is not a "tax." But *all taxes* are founded on the *same principles,* and have the *same tendency.*

External impositions for the regulation of our trade do not "grant to his Majesty *the property of the colonies.*" They only *prevent the colonies acquiring property,* in things not necessary, in a manner judged to be injurious to the welfare of the whole empire. But the last statute respecting us, "grants to his Majesty *the property of the colonies*" by laying duties on the manufactures of Great Britain which they must take, and which she settled on them on purpose that they should take.

What *tax* can be more *internal* than this? Here is money drawn, *without their consent,* from a society who have constantly enjoyed a constitutional mode of raising all money among themselves. The payment of their *tax* they have no possible method of avoiding, as they cannot do without the commodities on which it is laid, and they cannot manufacture these commodities themselves. Besides, if this unhappy country should be so lucky as to elude this act by getting parchment enough in the place of paper, or by reviving the ancient method of writing on wax and bark, and by inventing something to serve instead of glass, her ingenuity would stand her in little stead; for then the Parliament would have nothing to do but to prohibit such manufactures, or to lay a tax on *hats* and *woolen cloths,* which they have already prohibited the colonies *from supplying each other with,* or on instruments and tools of *steel* and *iron*, which they have prohibited the provincials *from manufacturing at all.* And then what little gold and silver they have must be torn from their hands, or they will not be able in a short time to get an ax for cutting their firewood, nor a plow for raising their food. In what respect, therefore, I beg leave to ask, is the late act preferable to the Stamp Act, or more consistent with the liberties of the colonies? For my own part, I regard them both with equal apprehensions; and think they ought to be in the same manner opposed.

Habemus quidem senatus consultum, tanquam gladium in vagina repositum.
We have a statute, laid up for future use, like a sword in the scabbard.

A Farmer

3

"An Edict by the King of Prussia"
(1773)

A man of amazing versatility, who combined shrewd practicality with wit, humor, and homespun wisdom, Benjamin Franklin (1706–90) rose from humble beginnings to become the most widely known and respected colonial American of his time. By turns a printer, bookseller, inventor, scientist, civic organizer, author, colonial agent, and, in his final years, elder statesman of the republic, Franklin had a long career which is the embodiment of the American success story, a story so successful that at the age of forty-two he was able to retire from active business to devote his attention to public service. Interestingly enough, Franklin spent most of the revolutionary years abroad, first in England (1764–75) where he was sent as agent for the colony of Pennsylvania, and then in France (1776–83), where he delighted the French as commissioner to the French court.

An accomplished writer, with a gift for satire and burlesque, Franklin was always ready to turn his pen to the service of his country. In so doing, he wrote a number of satiric essays which are not only classics of their kind but excellent examples of how newspapers and magazines could be effectively used to further the cause of political advocacy. "An Edict by the King of Prussia" was written in 1773, while Franklin was in England, and published anonymously in the Gentleman's Magazine *in October of that year. It was quickly picked up and reprinted by the newspapers. Franklin subsequently reported its effect on British readers in a letter to his son William:*

> *I was down at Lord Despencer's when the post brought that day's papers. Mr. Whitehead was there, too . . . who runs early through all the papers, and tells the company what he finds remarkable. He had*

them in another room, and we were chatting in the breakfast parlor, when he came running in to us, out of breath, with the paper in hand. Here! says he, here's news for ye! Here's the King of Prussia, claiming a right to this kingdom! *All stared. . . . When he had read two or three paragraphs, a gentleman present said,* Damn his impudence, I dare say, we shall hear by next post that he is upon his march with one hundred thousand men to back this. *Whitehead, who is very shrewd, soon after began to smoke it, and looking in my face said,* I'll be hanged if this is not some of your American jokes upon us. *The reading went on, and ended with abundance of laughing, and a general verdict that it was a fair hit. . . .*

Franklin's "Edict" is a "fair hit" indeed. It is political satire at its very best. What better way to bring America's case home to the British than by having the king of Prussia make the very same demands on England that England had been making on America?

☆ ☆

Danzig, 5 September, 1773.

We have long wondered here at the supineness of the English nation under the Prussian impositions upon its trade entering our port. We did not till lately know the claims, ancient and modern, that hang over that nation; and therefore could not suspect that it might submit to those impositions from a sense of duty or from principles of equity. The following Edict, just made public, may, if serious, throw some light upon this matter.

"Frederic, by the grace of God, King of Prussia, etc., etc., etc.,[4] to all present and to come (*à tous présens et à venir*), health. The peace now enjoyed throughout our dominions, having afforded us leisure to apply ourselves to the regulation of commerce, the improvement of our finances, and at the same time the easing our *domestic* subjects in their taxes; for these causes, and other good considerations us thereunto moving, we hereby make known that, after having deliberated these affairs in our council, present our dear brothers, and other great officers of the state, members of the same; we, of our certain knowledge, full power, and authority royal have made and issued this present Edict, viz.

Whereas it is well known to all the world that the first German settlements made in the island of Britain were by colonies of people subject to our renowned ducal ancestors, and drawn from their dominions, under the conduct of Hengist, Horsa, Hella, Uffa, Cerdicus, Ida, and others; and that the said colonies have flourished under the protection of our august house for ages past; have never been emancipated therefrom; and yet have hitherto yielded little profit to the same; and whereas we ourself have in the last war fought for and defended the said colonies against the power of France, and thereby enabled them to make conquests for the said power in America, for which we have not yet received adequate compensation; and whereas it is just and expedient that a revenue should be raised from the said colonies in Britain towards our indemnification; and that those who are descendants of our ancient subjects, and thence still owe us due obedience, should contribute to the replenishing of our royal coffers (as they must have done, had their ancestors remained in the territories now to us appertaining); we do therefore hereby ordain and command that from and after the date of these presents there shall be levied and paid to our officers of the *customs* on all goods, wares, and merchandises, and on all grain and other produce of the earth, exported from the said island of Britain, and on all goods of whatever kind imported into the same, a duty of four and a half per cent. *ad valorem*, for the use of us and our successors. And that the said duty may more effectually be collected, we do hereby ordain that all ships or vessels bound from Great Britain to any other part of the world, or from any other part of the world to Great Britain, shall in their respective voyages touch at our port of Koningsberg, there to be unladen, searched, and charged with the said duties.

And whereas there hath been from time to time discovered in the said island of Great Britain, by our colonists there, many mines or beds of ironstone; and sundry subjects of our ancient dominion, skilful in converting the said stone into metal, have in time past transported themselves thither, carrying with them and communicating that art; and the inhabitants of the said island, presuming that they had a natural right to make the best use they could of the natural productions of their country for their own benefit, have not only built furnaces for smelting the said stone into iron, but have erected plating-forges, slitting-mills, and steel-furnaces for the more convenient manufacturing of the same; thereby endangering a diminution of the said manufacture in our ancient dominion; we do therefore hereby further ordain that from and after the date hereof no mill or other engine for slitting or rolling of iron, or any plating-forge to work with a tilt-hammer, or any furnace for making steel, shall be erected or continued in the said island of Great Britain. And the lord lieutenant of every county in the said island is hereby commanded, on information of any such erection within his county, to order, and by force to cause, the same to be abated and destroyed; as he shall answer the neglect thereof to us at his peril. But we are nevertheless graciously pleased to permit the inhabitants of the said island to transport their iron into Prussia, there to be manufactured, and to them returned; they paying our Prussian subjects for the workmanship with all the costs of commission, freight, and risk, coming and returning; anything herein contained to the contrary notwithstanding.

We do not, however, think fit to extend this our indulgence to the article of *wool*; but, meaning to encourage not only the manufacturing of woolen cloth, but also the raising of wool, in our ancient dominions, and to prevent both, as much as may be, in our said island, we do hereby absolutely forbid the transportation of wool from thence, even to the mother country, Prussia; and that those islanders may be further and more effectually restrained in making any advantage of their own wool in the way of manufacture, we command that none shall be carried out of one county into another; nor shall any worsted, bay, or woolen yarn, cloth, says, bays, kerseys, serges, frizes, druggets, cloth-serges, shalloons, or any other drapery stuffs or woolen manufactures whatsoever made up or mixed with wool in any of the said counties, be carried into any other county, or be water-borne even across the smallest river or creek, on penalty of forfeiture of the same, together with the boats, carriages, horses, etc., that shall be employed in removing them. Nevertheless, our loving subjects there are hereby permitted (if they think proper) to use all their wool as manure for the improvement of their lands.

And whereas the art and mystery of making *hats* hath arrived at great perfection in Prussia, and the making of hats by our remoter subjects ought to be as much as possible restrained; and forasmuch as the islanders before-mentioned, being in possession of wool, beaver, and other furs, have presumptuously conceived they had a right to make some advantage thereof by manufacturing the same into hats, to the prejudice of our domestic manufacture; we do therefore hereby strictly command and ordain that no hats or felts whatsoever, dyed or undyed, finished or unfinished, shall be loaded or put into or upon any vessel, cart, carriage, or horse, to be transported or conveyed out of one county in the said island into another county, or to any other place whatsoever, by any person or persons whatsoever; on pain of forfeiting the same, with a penalty of five hundred pounds sterling for every offense. Nor shall any hatmaker, in any of the said counties, employ more than two apprentices, on penalty of five pounds sterling per month; we intending hereby that such hatmakers, being so restrained, both in the production and sale of their commodity, may find no advantage in continuing their business. But, lest the said islanders should suffer inconveniency by the want of hats, we are further graciously pleased to permit them to send their beaver furs to Prussia; and we also permit hats made thereof to be exported from Prussia to Britain; the people thus favored to pay all costs and charges of manufacturing, interest, commission to our merchants, insurance and freight going and returning, as in the case of iron.

And, lastly, being willing further to favor our said colonies in Britain, we do hereby also ordain and command that all the *thieves,* highway and street robbers, housebreakers, forgerers, murderers, s—d—tes, and villains of every denomination, who have forfeited their lives to the law of Prussia, but whom we in our great clemency do not think fit here to hang, shall be emptied out of our gaols into the said island of Great Britain for the better peopling of that country.

We flatter ourselves that these our royal regulations and commands will be thought *just and reasonable* by our much favored colonists in England; the said regulations being copied from their statutes of 10th and 11th William III. c. 10, 5th George II. c. 22, 23d George II. c. 26, 4th George I. c. 11, and from other equitable laws made by their Parliaments; or from instructions given by their princes; or from resolutions of both houses, entered into for the good government of their *own colonies in Ireland and America.*

And all persons in the said island are hereby cautioned not to oppose in any wise the execution of this our Edict, or any part thereof, such opposition being high treason; of which all who are suspected shall be transported in fetters from Britain to Prussia, there to be tried and executed according to the Prussian law.

Such is our pleasure.

Given at Potsdam, this twenty-fifth day of the month of August, one thousand seven hundred and seventy-three, and in the thirty-third year of our reign.

By the King in his Council.

Rechtmaessig, *Sec.*"

Some take this edict to be merely one of the king's *jeux d'esprit;* others suppose it serious, and that he means a quarrel with England; but all here think the assertion it concludes with, "that these regulations are copied from acts of the English Parliament respecting their colonies," a very injurious one; it being impossible to believe that a people distinguished for their love of liberty, a nation so wise, so liberal in its sentiments, so just and equitable towards its neighbors, should, from mean and injudicious views of petty immediate profit, treat its own children in a manner so arbitrary and tyrannical!

THOMAS JEFFERSON

4

from *A Summary View of the Rights of British America* (1774)

Following the repeal of the Townshend duties on all items but tea in April, 1770, and the removal of British troops from Boston, the colonies entered upon a two-year period of comparative calm in their relationship with the mother country. Tensions were revived, however, in the fall and winter of 1773, following Britain's attempt to rescue from bankruptcy the fortunes of the East India Company by giving it a monopoly to sell its huge surplus of tea directly to select agents in the colonies (the Tea Act, May, 1773). American resistance culminated in the famous Boston Tea Party (December 16, 1773). British response was almost immediate: it came in a series of measures known as the "Intolerable Acts" aimed at punishing Boston for the Tea Party and its long history of intransigent behavior.

When news of the first of these measures, the Boston Port Bill, reached Williamsburg, Virginia, Thomas Jefferson and Charles Lee drafted a series of resolutions, adopted by the House of Burgesses, calling for a general day of fasting and prayer to coincide with the closing of Boston harbor on June 1. Royal Governor Dunmore promptly dissolved the assembly, whereupon its members withdrew to a room in the Raleigh Tavern and issued a call for an intercolonial congress. It fell to Jefferson, who as John Adams later said had "a happy talent for composition," to prepare a series of resolutions for presentation to the Virginia convention in August, 1774, as the official set of instructions for Virginia's representatives to the First Continental Congress at Philadelphia. Jefferson himself was too ill to attend the convention, where his resolutions were circulated but not adopted, apparently because they were considered too revolutionary; subsequently, and without Jefferson's knowledge, they were carried to a printer in Williamsburg and published in pamphlet form as A Summary View of the Rights of British America *(August, 1774).*

Setting forth in clear and precise prose Jefferson's understanding of the history of British-American relations, A Summary View *firmly denies the sovereignty of Parliament and rests the case of colonial allegiance on loyalty to the king alone. Though Jefferson lays the responsibility for events jointly on Parliament and crown, his enumeration of the charges against George III clearly anticipates the ringing indictment of the Declaration of Independence. Unfortunately, Jefferson's warning to the king—"Let not the name of George the Third be a blot in the page of history"—was to go unheeded.*

Thomas Jefferson (1743–1826) was born at Shadwell, one of his father's tobacco plantations, in Albemarle County, Virginia. He graduated from William and Mary College at Williamsburg in 1762, after which he studied law and was admitted to the bar. In 1764 Jefferson was elected Albermarle County's representative to the House of Burgesses, and entered his long and distinguished career of service to colony, state, and nation. As a member of the Second Continental Congress (1775–76), Jefferson drafted the Declaration of Independence, after which he returned to Virginia where he set to work reforming the new state's legal system before being elected governor in 1779. From 1784 to 1789 Jefferson served as minister plenipotentiary to France, succeeding Franklin, and then returned home to become Washington's secretary of state. Throughout the decade that followed, Jefferson with his states' rights, agrarian philosophy, was the leader of the anti-Federalists. He served as vice president under John Adams (1797–1801) before beginning the first of his two terms in the presidency (1801–09). Thereafter Jefferson retired to Monticello, his home in Albermarle County, where he kept very much alive his philosophical, agricultural, and scientific interests, as well as the acquaintanceship with his wide circle of friends.

☆ ☆

Resolved, That it be an instruction to the said deputies, when assembled in general congress with the deputies from the other states of British America, to propose to the said congress that a humble and dutiful address be presented to his Majesty, begging leave to lay before him as Chief Magistrate of the British empire the united complaints of his Majesty's subjects in America; complaints which are excited by many unwarrantable encroachments and usurpations, attempted to be made by the legislature of one part of the empire upon those rights which God and the laws have given equally and independently to all. To represent to his Majesty that these his states have often individually made humble application to his imperial throne to obtain, through its intervention, some redress of their injured rights, to none of which was ever even an answer condescended; humbly to hope that this their joint address, penned in the language of truth, and divested of those expressions of servility which would persuade his Majesty that we were asking favors and not rights, shall obtain from his Majesty a more respectful acceptance. And this his Majesty will think we have reason to expect when he reflects that he is no more than the chief officer of the people, appointed by the laws, and circumscribed with definite powers, to assist in working the great machine of government, erected for their use, and consequently subject to their superintendence. And in order that these our rights as well as the invasions of them may be laid more fully before his Majesty, to take a view of them from the origin and first settlement of these countries. . . .[5]

That thus we have hastened through the reigns which preceded his Majesty's, during which the violations of our rights were less alarming, because repeated at more distant intervals, than that rapid and bold succession of injuries which is likely to distinguish the present from all other periods of American history. Scarcely have our minds been able to emerge from the astonishment into which one stroke of Parliamentary thunder had involved us, before another more heavy and more alarming is fallen on us. Single acts of tyranny may be ascribed to the accidental opinion of a day; but a series of oppressions begun at a distinguished period, and pursued unalterably through every change of ministers, too plainly prove a deliberate and systematical plan of reducing us to slavery.

That the act, passed in the 4th year of his Majesty's reign, entitled "An act for granting certain duties in the British colonies and plantations in America, etc.";

One other act, passed in the 5th year of his reign, entitled "An act for granting and applying certain stamp duties and other duties in the British colonies and plantations in America, etc.";

One other act, passed in the 6th year of his reign, entitled "An act for the better securing the dependency of his Majesty's dominions in America upon the Crown and Parliament of Great Britain;" and one other act, passed in the 7th year of his reign, entitled "An act for granting duties on paper, tea, etc.," form that connected chain of parliamentary usurpation which has already been the subject of frequent applications to his Majesty, and the Houses of Lords and Commons of Great Britain; and no answers having yet been condescended to any of these, we shall not trouble his Majesty with a repetition of the matters they contained.

But that one other act, passed in the same 7th year of the reign, having been a peculiar attempt, must ever require peculiar mention; it is entitled "An act for suspending the legislature of New York." One free and inde-

pendent legislature hereby takes upon itself to suspend the powers of another, free and independent as itself; this exhibiting a phenomenon unknown in nature, the creator and creature of his own power. Not only the
principles of common sense but the common feelings of human nature must
be surrendered up before his Majesty's subjects here can be persuaded to believe that they hold their political existence at the will of a British Parliament. Shall these governments be dissolved, their property annihilated, and
their people reduced to a state of nature at the imperious breath of a body
of men whom they never saw, in whom they never confided, and over whom
they have no powers of punishment or removal, let their crimes against the
American public be ever so great? Can any one reason be assigned why
160,000 electors in the island of Great Britain should give law to four millions in the states of America, every individual of whom is equal to every individual of them in virtue, in understanding, and in bodily strength? Were
this to be admitted, instead of being a free people as we have hitherto supposed, and mean to continue ourselves, we should suddenly be found the
slaves not of one but of 160,000 tyrants, distinguished too from all others
by this singular circumstance, that they are removed from the reach of fear,
the only restraining motive which may hold the hand of a tyrant.

That by "an act to discontinue in such manner and for such time as they are
therein mentioned the landing and discharging, lading or shipping, of goods,
wares, and merchandise at the town and within the harbor of Boston, in the
province of Massachusetts Bay, in North America" which was passed at the
last session of British Parliament; a large and populous town, whose trade
was their sole subsistence, was deprived of that trade and involved in utter
ruin. Let us for a while suppose the question of right suspended in order to
examine this act on principles of justice. An act of Parliament had been
passed imposing duties on teas to be paid in America, against which act the
Americans had protested as inauthoritative. The East India Company, who
till that time had never sent a pound of tea to America on their own account,
step forth on that occasion the asserters of parliamentary right, and send
hither many shiploads of that obnoxious commodity. The masters of their
several vessels, however, on their arrival to America wisely attended to ad-
monition and returned with their cargoes. In the province of New England
alone the remonstrances of the people were disregarded, and a compliance,
after being many days waited for, was flatly refused. Whether in this the
master of the vessel was governed by his obstinacy, or his instructions, let
those who know say. There are extraordinary situations which require extraordinary interposition. An exasperated people who feel that they possess
power are not easily restrained within limits strictly regular. A number of
them assembled in the town of Boston, threw the tea into the ocean, and
dispersed without doing any other act of violence. If in this they did wrong,

they were known and were amenable to the laws of the land, against which it could not be objected that they had ever in any instance been obstructed or diverted from their regular course in favor of popular offenders. They should therefore not have been distrusted on this occasion.

But that ill-fated colony had formerly been bold in their enmities against the house of Stuart, and were now devoted to ruin by that unseen hand which governs the momentous affairs of this great empire. On the partial representations of a few worthless ministerial dependents, whose constant office it has been to keep that government embroiled, and who by their treacheries hope to obtain the dignity of the British knighthood, without calling for the party accused, without asking a proof, without attempting a distinction between the guilty and the innocent, the whole of that ancient and wealthy town is in a moment reduced from opulence to beggary. Men who had spent their lives in extending the British commerce, who had invested in that place the wealth their honest endeavors had merited, found themselves and their families thrown at once on the world for subsistence by its charities. Not the hundredth part of the inhabitants of that town had been concerned in the act complained of, many of them were in Great Britain and in other parts beyond sea, yet all were involved in one indiscriminate ruin by a new executive power unheard of till then, that of a British Parliament. A property of the value of many millions of money was sacrificed to revenge, not repay, the loss of a few thousands. This is administering justice with a heavy hand indeed! And when is this tempest to be arrested in its course? Two wharves are to be opened again when his Majesty shall think proper. The residue which lined the extensive shores of the bay of Boston are forever interdicted the exercise of commerce. This little exception seems to have been thrown in for no other purpose than that of setting a precedent for investing his Majesty with legislative powers. If the pulse of his people shall beat calmly under this experiment, another and another shall be tried till the measure of despotism be filled up. It would be an insult on common sense to pretend that this exception was made in order to restore its commerce to that great town. The trade which cannot be received at two wharves alone must of necessity be transferred to some other place; to which it will soon be followed by that of the two wharves. Considered in this light, it would be insolent and cruel mockery at the annihilation of the town of Boston. . . .

That these are acts of power, assumed by a body of men, foreign to our constitutions, and unacknowledged by our laws, against which we do on behalf of the inhabitants of British America enter this our solemn and determined protest; and we do earnestly entreat his Majesty, as yet the only mediatory power between the several states of the British empire, to recommend to his Parliament of Great Britain the total revocation of these acts which, however nugatory they be, may yet prove the cause of further discontents and jealousies among us.

That we next proceed to consider the conduct of his Majesty, as holding the executive powers of the laws of these states, and mark out his deviations from the line of duty. By the constitution of Great Britain, as well of the several American states, his Majesty professes the power of refusing to pass into a law any bill which has already passed the other two branches of legislature. His Majesty, however, and his ancestors, conscious of the impropriety of opposing their single opinion to the united wisdom of two houses of Parliament, while their proceedings were unbiassed by interested principles, for several ages past have modestly declined the exercise of this power in that part of his empire called Great Britain. But by change of circumstances other principles than those of justice simply obtained an influence on their determinations; the addition of new states to the British empire has produced an addition of new and sometimes opposite interests. It is now, therefore, the great office of his Majesty to resume exercise of his negative power, and to prevent the passage of laws by any one legislature of the empire which might bear injuriously on the rights and interests of another. Yet this will not excuse the wanton exercise of this power which we have seen his Majesty practice on the laws of the American legislatures. . . .

With equal inattention to the necessities of his people here has his Majesty permitted our laws to lie neglected in England for years, neither confirming them by his assent nor annulling them by his negative: so that such of them as have no suspending clause we hold on the most precarious of all tenures, his Majesty's will; and such of them as suspend themselves till his Majesty's assent be obtained we have feared might be called into existence at some future and distant period when the time and change of circumstances shall have rendered them destructive to his people here. And to render this aggrievance still more oppressive, his Majesty by his instructions has laid his governors under such restrictions that they can pass no law of any moment unless it have such suspending clause: so that, however immediate may be the call for legislative interposition, the law cannot be executed till it has twice crossed the Atlantic, by which time the evil may have spent its whole force. . . .

That in order to force the arbitrary measures before complained of, his Majesty has from time to time sent among us large bodies of armed forces not made up of the people here nor raised by the authority of our laws. Did his Majesty possess such a right as this, it might swallow up all our other rights whenever he should think proper. But his Majesty has no right to land a single armed man on our shores, and those whom he sends here are liable to our laws made for the suppression and punishment of riots, routs, and unlawful assemblies, or are hostile bodies invading us in defiance of the law.

When in the course of the late war it became expedient that a body of Hanoverian troops should be brought over for the defense of Great Britain, his Majesty's grandfather, our late sovereign, did not pretend to introduce them under any authority he possessed. Such a measure would have given just alarm to his subjects in Great Britain, whose liberties would not be safe if armed men of another country and of another spirit might be brought into the realm at any time without the consent of their legislature. He therefore applied to Parliament, who passed an act for that purpose, limiting the number to be brought in and the time they were to continue. In like manner is his Majesty restrained in every part of the empire. He possesses, indeed, the executive power of the laws in every state, but they are the laws of the particular state which he is to administer within that state, and not those of any one within the limits of another. Every state must judge for itself the number of armed men which they may safely trust among them, of whom they are to consist, and under what restrictions they shall be laid.

To render these proceedings still more criminal against our laws, instead of subjecting the military to the civil powers his Majesty has expressly made the civil subordinate to the military. But can his Majesty thus put down all law under his feet? Can he erect a power superior to that which erected himself? He has done it indeed by force, but let him remember that force cannot give right.

That these are our grievances which we have thus laid before his Majesty, with that freedom of language and sentiment which becomes a free people claiming their rights, as derived from the laws of nature, and not as the gift of their chief magistrate. Let those flatter who fear; it is not an American art. To give praise which is not due might be well from the venal, but would ill beseem those who are asserting the rights of human nature. They know, and will therefore say, that kings are the servants not the proprietors of the people. Open your breast, sire, to liberal and expanded thought. Let not the name of George the Third be a blot in the page of history. You are surrounded by English counsellors, but remember that they are parties. You have no minister for American affairs, because you have none taken up from among us, nor amenable to the laws on which they are to give you advice. It behooves you, therefore, to think and to act for yourself and your people. The great principles of right and wrong are legible to every reader; to pursue them requires not the aid of many counsellors. The whole art of government consists in the art of being honest. Only aim to do your duty, and mankind will give you credit where you fail. No longer persevere in sacrificing the rights of one part of the empire to the inordinate desires of another, but deal out to all equal and impartial right. Let no act be passed by any one legislature which may infringe on the rights and liberties of another. This is the important post in which fortune has placed you, holding the balance of a great if a well-poised empire. This, sire, is the advice of your great American council, on the observance of which may perhaps depend your felicity and future fame, and the preservation of that harmony which alone can continue both in Great Britain and America the reciprocal advantages of their connection. It is neither our wish nor our interest to separate from her. We are willing, on our part, to sacrifice everything which reason can ask to the restoration of that tranquillity for which all must wish. On their part, let them be ready to establish union and a generous plan. Let them name their terms, but let them be just. Accept of every commercial preference it is in our power to give for such things as we can raise for their use, or they make for ours. But let them not think to exclude us from going to other markets to dispose of those commodities which they cannot use, or to supply those wants which they cannot supply. Still less let it be proposed that our properties within our own territories shall be taxed or regulated by any power on earth but our own. The God who gave us life gave us liberty at the same time; the hand of force may destroy, but cannot disjoin them. This, sire, is our last, our determined resolution; and that you will be pleased to interpose with that efficacy which your earnest endeavors may ensure to procure redress of these our great grievances, to quiet the minds of your subjects in British America against any apprehensions of future encroachment, to establish fraternal love and harmony through the whole empire, and that these may continue to the latest ages of time, is the fervent prayer of all British America.

FRANCIS HOPKINSON

5

from *A Pretty Story* (1774)

Francis Hopkinson (1737-91), a lawyer by vocation but also an accomplished musician, composer, mathematician, chemist, and man of letters, was born in Philadelphia and became the first graduate of the College of Philadelphia (now the University of Pennsylvania). Following a two-year visit to relatives in England, Hopkinson took up residence in Bordentown, New Jersey, where he married and settled down to the practice of law. Hopkinson represented New Jersey at the Second Continental Congress, became a signatory of the Declaration of Independence, and during the war served as chairman of the Navy Board and then judge of the admiralty for Pennsylvania (1779-89). Perhaps his greatest wartime service, however, was the skillful use to which he put his pen as author of numerous satires and ballads, a role in which he had few peers. His ballad "The Battle of the Kegs," first published in the Pennsylvania Packet *in March, 1778, and later set to music, became one of the most popular songs of the war.*

A Pretty Story, published in Philadelphia in September of 1774, apparently to coincide with the opening sessions of the First Continental Congress, is an historical allegory which from a decidedly American point of view holds up to satire the political events which had culminated in the then-current impasse with Great Britain. In Hopkinson's allegory the old farm is England, the new farm America; the nobleman is the king of England, his wife Parliament, his steward the prime minister, and his children and grandchildren his faithful, if abused, subjects.

☆ ☆

FRANCIS HOPKINSON

Chapter I

Once upon a time, a great while ago, there lived a certain nobleman who had long possessed a very valuable farm, and had a great number of children and grandchildren.

Besides the annual profits of his land, which were very considerable, he kept a large shop of goods; and being very successful in trade, he became, in process of time, exceedingly rich and powerful; insomuch that all his neighbors feared and respected him. . . .

Chapter II

Now it came to pass that this nobleman had by some means or other obtained a right to an immense tract of wild, uncultivated country at a vast distance from his mansion house. But he set little store by this acquisition, as it yielded him no profit; nor was it likely to do so, being not only difficult of access on account of distance, but was also overrun with innumerable wild beasts very fierce and savage; so that it would be extremely dangerous to attempt taking possession of it.

In process of time, however, some of his children, more stout and enterprising than the rest, requested leave of their father to go and settle on this distant tract of land. Leave was readily obtained; but before they set out certain agreements were stipulated between them. The principal were [that] the old gentleman, on his part, engaged to protect and defend the adventurers in their new settlements, to assist them in chasing away the wild beasts, and to extend to them all the benefits of the government under which they were born, assuring them that although they should be removed so far from his presence they should nevertheless be considered as the children of his family, and treated accordingly. At the same time he gave each of them a bond for the faithful performance of their promises; in which, among other things, it was covenanted that they should, each of them in their several families, have a liberty of making such rules and regulations for their own good government as they should find convenient, provided these rules and regulations should not contradict or be inconsistent with the general standing orders established in his farm. . . .[6]

Chapter III

Now the new settlers had adopted a mode of government in their several families similar to that their father had established in the old farm, in taking

46

a new wife at the end of certain periods of time; which wife was chosen for them by their children, and without whose consent they could do nothing material in the conduct of their affairs. Under these circumstances they thrived exceedingly, and became very numerous; living in great harmony amongst themselves, and in constitutional obedience to their father and his wife. . . .

Thus did matters go on for a considerable time to their mutual happiness and benefit. But now the nobleman's wife began to cast an avaricious eye upon the new settlements; saying to herself, if by the natural consequence of their intercourse with us my wealth and power are so much increased, how much more would they accumulate if I can persuade them that all they have belonged to us, and therefore I may at any time demand from them such part of their earnings as I please. At the same time she was fully sensible of the promises and agreements her husband had made when they left the old farm, and of the tenor and purpose of the great paper.[7] She therefore thought it necessary to proceed with great caution and art, and endeavored to gain her point by imperceptible steps. . . .

Chapter IV

As the old gentleman advanced in years he began to neglect the affairs of his family, leaving them chiefly to the management of his steward. Now the steward had debauched his wife, and by that means gained an entire ascendancy over her. She no longer deliberated what would most benefit either the old farm or the new, but said and did whatever the steward pleased. Nay, so much was she influenced by him that she could neither utter ay or no but as he directed. For he had cunningly persuaded her that it was very fashionable for women to wear padlocks on their lips, and that he was sure they would become her exceedingly. He therefore fastened a padlock to each corner of her mouth; when the one was open, she could only say ay, and when the other was loosed, could only cry no. He took care to keep the keys of these locks himself, so that her will became entirely subject to his power.

Now the old lady and the steward had set themselves against the people of the new farm, and began to devise ways and means to impoverish and distress them.

They prevailed on the nobleman to sign an edict against the new settlers, in which it was declared that it was their duty as children to pay something towards supplying their father's table with provisions, and to the supporting the dignity of his family; for that purpose it was ordained that all their spoons, knives, and forks, plates and porringers, should be marked with a certain mark by officers appointed to that end; for which marking they were to pay a certain stipend; and that they should not, under severe penalties, presume to make use of any spoon, knife or fork, plate or porringer, before it had been so marked, and the said stipend paid to the officer.[8]

The inhabitants of the new farm began to see that their father's affections were alienated from them, and that their mother was but a base mother-in-law debauched by their enemy the steward. They were thrown into great confusion and distress. They wrote the most supplicating letters to the old gentleman, in which they acknowledged him to be their father in terms of the greatest respect and affection—they recounted to him the hardships and difficulties they had suffered in settling his new farm; and pointed out the great addition of wealth and power his family had acquired by the improvement of that wilderness; and showed him that all the fruits of their labors must in the natural course of things unite, in the long run, in his money box. They also, in humble terms, reminded him of his promises and engagements on their leaving home, and of the bonds he had given them; of the solemnity and importance of the great paper with the curse annexed.[9] They acknowledged that he ought to be reimbursed the expenses he was at on their account, and that it was their duty to assist in supporting the dignity of his family. All this they declared they were ready and willing to do; but requested that they might do it agreeable to the purport of the great paper, by applying to their several wives for the keys of their money boxes and furnishing him from thence; and not be subject to the tyranny and caprice of an avaricious mother-in-law, whom they had never chosen, and of a steward who was their declared enemy. . . .

The new settlers, observing how matters were conducted in their father's family, became exceedingly distressed and mortified. They met together and agreed one and all that they would no longer submit to the arbitrary impositions of their mother-in-law and their enemy the steward. They determined to pay no manner of regard to the new decree, considering it as a violation of the great paper. But to go on and eat their broth and pudding as usual. The cooks also and butlers served up their spoons, knives and forks, plates and porringers, without having them marked by the new officers.[10]

The nobleman at length thought fit to reverse the order which had been made respecting the spoons, knives and forks, plates and porringers of the new settlers.[11] But he did this with very ill grace: for he, at the same time, avowed and declared that he and his wife had a right to mark all their furniture, if they pleased, from the silver tankard down to the very chamber pieces; that as he was their father he had an absolute control over them, and that their liberties, lives and properties were at the entire disposal of him and his wife;[12] that it was not fit that he who was allowed to be omnipresent, immortal, and incapable of error should be confined by the shackles of the great paper or obliged to fulfill the bonds he had given them, which he averred he had a right to cancel whenever he pleased. . . .

The people of the new farm however took little notice of these pompous declarations. They were glad the marking decree was reversed, and were in hopes that things would gradually settle into their former channel.

Chapter V

In the meantime the new settlers increased exceedingly, and as they increased their dealings at their father's shop were proportionably enlarged. . . .

Now the steward continued to hate the new settlers with exceeding great hatred, and determined to renew his attack upon their peace and happiness. . . .

For this purpose another decree was prepared and published, ordering that the new settlers should pay a certain stipend upon particular goods, which they were not allowed to purchase anywhere but at their father's shop; and that this stipend should not be deemed an advance upon the original price of the goods, but be paid on their arrival at the new farm, for the express purpose of supporting the dignity of the old gentleman's family, and of defraying the expenses he affected to afford them.[13]

This new decree gave our adventurers the utmost uneasiness. They saw that the steward and their mother-in-law were determined to oppress and enslave them. They again met together and wrote to their father, as before, the most humble and persuasive letters; but to little purpose: a deaf ear was turned to all their remonstrances, and their dutiful requests treated with contempt.

Finding this moderate and decent conduct brought them no relief, they had recourse to another expedient. They bound themselves in solemn agreement not to deal any more at their father's shop until this unconstitutional decree should be reversed; which they declared to be a violation of the great paper.[14]

This agreement was so strictly adhered to that in a few months the clerks and apprentices in the old gentleman's shop began to make a sad outcry. They declared that their master's trade was declining exceedingly, and that his wife and steward would, by their mischievous machinations, ruin the whole farm. They forthwith sharpened their pens and attacked the steward, and even the old lady herself, with great severity. Insomuch that it was thought proper to withdraw this attempt likewise upon the rights and liberties of the new settlers. One part only of the new decree remained unreversed—viz. the tax upon water gruel.[15]

Now there were certain men on the old farm who had obtained from the nobleman an exclusive right of selling water gruel. . . . [The steward, finding

his "designs once more frustrated,"] formed another scheme so artfully contrived that he thought himself sure of success. He sent for the persons who
had the sole right of vending water gruel, and after reminding them of the
obligations they were under to the nobleman and his wife for their exclusive
privilege, he desired that they would send sundry wagonloads of gruel to the
new farm, promising that the accustomed duty which they paid for their exclusive right should be taken off from all the gruel they should send amongst
the settlers; and that in case their cargoes should come to any damage, he
would take care that the loss should be repaired out of the old gentleman's
coffers. . . .[16]

Chapter VI

On the arrival of the water gruel, the people of the new farm were again
thrown into great alarms and confusions. Some of them would not suffer
the wagons to be unloaded at all, but sent them immediately back to the
gruel merchants. Others permitted the wagons to unload, but would not
touch the hateful commodity; so that it lay neglected about their roads and
highways until it grew sour and spoiled.[17] But one of the new settlers, whose
name was Jack,[18] either from a keener sense of the injuries attempted against
him, or from the necessity of his situation, which was such that he could not
send back the gruel because of a number of mercenaries whom his father had
stationed before his house to watch and be a check upon his conduct: he, I
say, being almost driven to despair, fell to work, and with great zeal stove to
pieces the casks of gruel which had been sent him and utterly demolished the
whole cargo.[19]

These proceedings were soon known at the old farm. Great and terrible
was the uproar there. The old gentleman fell into great wrath, declaring that
his absent children meant to throw off all dependence upon him and to become altogether disobedient. His wife also tore the padlocks from her lips,
and raved and stormed like a billingsgate. The steward lost all patience and
moderation, swearing most profanely that he would leave no stone unturned
'till he had humbled the settlers of the new farm at his feet, and caused their
father to trample on their necks. . . .

A very large padlock was, accordingly, prepared to be fastened upon
Jack's great gate; the key of which was to be given to the old gentleman,
who was not to open it again until he had paid for the gruel he had spilt,
and resigned all claim to the privileges of the great paper: nor then neither
unless he thought fit.[20] Secondly, a decree was made to new model the regulations and economy of Jack's family in such manner that they might for
the future be more subject to the will of the steward.[21] And, thirdly, a large

gallows was erected before the mansion house in the old farm, and an order made that if any of Jack's children or servants should be suspected of misbehavior, they should not be convicted or acquitted by the consent of their brethren, agreeable to the purport of the great paper, but be tied neck and heels and dragged to the gallows at the mansion house, and there be hanged without mercy. . . .[22]

Poor Jack found himself in a most deplorable condition. The great inlet to his farm was entirely blocked up, so that he could neither carry out the produce of his land for sale, nor receive from abroad the necessaries for his family.

But this was not all—his father, along with the padlock aforesaid, had sent an overseer to hector and domineer over him and his family; and to endeavor to break his spirit by exercising every possible severity: for which purpose he was attended by a great number of mercenaries, and armed with more than common authorities. . . .[23]

Chapter VII

Now Jack and his family finding themselves oppressed, insulted and tyrannized over in the most cruel and arbitrary manner, advised with their brethren what measures should be adopted to relieve them from their intolerable grievances. Their brethren, one and all, united in sympathizing with their afflictions; they advised them to bear their sufferings with fortitude for a time, assuring them that they looked on the punishments and insults laid upon them with the same indignation as if they had been inflicted on themselves, and that they would stand by and support them to the last. But, above all, earnestly recommended it to them to be firm and steady in the cause of liberty and justice, and never acknowledge the omnipotence of their mother-in-law, nor yield to the machinations of their enemy the steward.

In the meantime, lest Jack's family should suffer for want of necessaries, their great gate being fast locked, liberal and very generous contributions were raised among the several families of the new settlements for their present relief. This seasonable bounty was handed to Jack over the garden wall —all access to the front of his house being shut up.

Now the overseer observed that the children and domestics of Jack's family had frequent meetings and consultations together: sometimes in the garret, and sometimes in the stable. Understanding, likewise, that an agreement not to deal in their father's shop, until their grievances should be redressed, was much talked of amongst them, he wrote a thundering prohibition, much like a pope's bull, which he caused to be pasted up in every room in the house, in which he declared and protested that these meetings were treasonable, traitorous and rebellious, contrary to the dignity of their father, and inconsistent with the omnipotence of their father, and inconsistent with the omnipotence of their mother-in-law; denouncing also terrible punishments against any two of the family who should from thenceforth be seen whispering together, and strictly forbidding the domestics to hold any more meetings in the garret or stable.

These harsh and unconstitutional proceedings irritated Jack and the other inhabitants of the new farm to such a degree that . . .

Caetera desunt.[24]

SAMUEL SEABURY

6

from *A View of the Controversy between Great Britain and Her Colonies* (1774)

Before adjourning on October 26, 1774, the Continental Congress in answer to the Intolerable Acts passed a series of nonimportation, nonconsumption, and nonexportation agreements to go into effect on December 1, 1774, March 1, 1775, and September 1, 1775, respectively. When the news reached New York, the Reverend Samuel Seabury (1729-96), rector of St. Peter's Church in the quiet village of New Rochelle, not far from the city, set to work on the first of four pamphlets challenging these agreements on the grounds of economic self-interest and constitutional legality. Known collectively as the "Letters from a Westchester Farmer," Seabury's pamphlets provide the modern reader with an illuminating glimpse into the mind of the American Loyalist on the eve of the Revolution.

Samuel Seabury was born in North Groton, Connecticut, the son of a Congregationalist minister turned Anglican priest. He graduated from Yale College in 1748, and then entered church work under the tutelage of his father at Huntington, Long Island. At the age of twenty-four (in 1753) Seabury took orders from the Bishop of London and was assigned to New Brunswick, New Jersey. He married in 1756, and a year later moved to a parish at Jamaica, Long Island, where he remained until called to St. Peter's in March of 1767. During the years that immediately followed, Seabury became increasingly active in the debate between England and America, principally at first through his prominent role in the controversial movement by New York Anglicans to secure an American bishop for the colonies—a movement which in the eyes of many colonists (particularly New Englanders) appeared as nothing less than an attempt to establish a state church and to put an end to religious freedom.

Of the four pamphlets which bore the signature "A. W. Farmer," only the first, Free Thoughts on the Proceedings of the Continental Congress, *published in New York by James Rivington on November 24, 1774, was addressed explicitly to an agrarian audience. In the two that followed,* The Congress Canvassed; or, An Examination into the Conduct of the Delegates at Their Grand Convention *(December 22, 1774) and* A View of the Controversy between Great Britain and Her Colonies *(January 5, 1775), Seabury continued to pose as a blunt-speaking, clear-thinking farmer, but widened the scope of his inquiries to include the whole of the constitutional question between England and the colonies. Though he continued to deny the legality of the Continental Congress and to uphold the legislative authority of Parliament, Seabury, like many Americans of Loyalist persuasion, was deeply troubled by the current state of Anglo-American relations. And indeed, had the hour not been so late, the corrective solution he urged—"the settlement of an American constitution"—might well have headed off a final collision.*

Seabury's activities as an organizer of Loyalist opposition made him an obvious target of patriot reprisal, and in late November, 1775, he was taken prisoner and carried off to Connecticut where he was briefly confined. Seabury was allowed to return to Westchester in January of 1776, but in September was forced to seek refuge behind British lines on Long Island. From there he made his way to New York City, where he remained for the balance of the war. Following the cessation of hostilities in 1783, Seabury once again took up his clerical duties and in his later years served as Bishop for Connecticut and Rhode Island.

The selection reprinted below from the third of Seabury's Westchester Farmer letters, A View of the Controversy between Great Britain and Her Colonies, *was written in direct response to Alexander Hamilton, who challenged Seabury in perhaps the most celebrated pamphlet exchange of the prewar period. For Hamilton's reply, see the following selection.*

☆ ☆

Sir,

You have done me the honor "to bestow some notice upon" a little pamphlet which I lately published, entitled *Free Thoughts on the Proceedings of the Continental Congress,* in a piece which you call *A Full Vindication of the Measures of the Congress, from the Calumnies of Their Enemies.* My present business shall be to examine your Vindication, and see whether it *fully* exculpates *the measures of the Congress* from the charges brought against them by the friends of order and good government. This task I shall endeavor to perform with all that freedom of thought and expression which, as an *Englishman*, I have a right to; and which never shall be wrested from me either by *yourself* or the *Congress.*

I freely own that I wrote and published the *Free Thoughts* with a design to "diminish the influence, and prevent the effects" of the "decisions" of the Congress. You speak of the *impotence* of such attempts; of the general *indignation* with which they are treated; you say "that no material ill consequences (i. e., to your party) can be dreaded from them." Why then did you take the pains to write so long, so elaborate a pamphlet, to justify decisions against whose influence none but impotent attempts had been made?— to prevent ill consequences which were not to be dreaded? You felt, sir, the force of the stubborn facts exhibited to the view of the public in the *Free Thoughts.* You perceived the ground on which the decrees of the Congress were founded to be hollow and ready to fall in; you were willing to prop it up at any rate. You knew that at the bar of *impartial* reason and *common* sense the conduct of the Congress must be condemned. You were too much interested, too deeply engaged in party views and party heats, to bear this with patience. You had no remedy but *artifice, sophistry, misrepresentation* and *abuse.* These are your weapons, and these you wield like an old experienced practitioner. . . .

I, who am a plain Farmer, though of some education, have no manner of inclination to dispute the prize of *Wit* and *Ridicule* with the panegyrist of the late *all-accomplished* Congress. You, sir, shall bear off the palm unrivalled, unenvied by me. . . .

The Congress, sir, was founded in sedition; its decisions are supported by tyranny; and is it *presumption* to controvert its *authority*? In your opinion they "are *restless spirits*"—"enemies to the natural rights of mankind" who shall dare to speak against the *Congress,* or attempt to "diminish the influence of *their* decisions;" while *they* are friends to America, and to the natural rights of mankind, who shall traduce and slander the sovereign authority of the nation, contravene and trample under foot the laws of their country.

I have no inclination to scrutinize the characters of men who composed the Congress. It is not the dignity of their private characters but their public conduct as *Delegates* that comes under my examination. The manner in which they were chosen was subversive of all law and of the very constitution of the province. After they had met they were only a popular assembly, without check or control, and therefore unqualified to make laws, or to pass ordinances. Upon supposition that they had been chosen by all the people with once voice, they could be only the servants of the people; and every individual must have had a right to animadvert on their conduct, and to have censured it where he thought it wrong. *We* think, sir, that we have a double right to do so, seeing they were chosen by a party only, and have endeavored to tyrannize over the whole people. . . .

I wish you had explicitly declared to the public your ideas of the *natural rights of mankind.* Man in a *state of nature* may be considered as perfectly free from all restraints of law and government. And then the *weak* must submit to the *strong.* From such a state, I confess, I have a violent aversion. I think the form of government we lately enjoyed a much more eligible state to live in. And cannot help regretting our having *lost* it by the *equity, wisdom,* and *authority* of the Congress, who have introduced in the room of it confusion and violence; where all must submit to the power of a mob.

You have taken some pains to prove what would readily have been granted you—that *liberty* is a very *good* thing, and *slavery* a very *bad* thing. But then I must think that liberty under a *king, Lords* and *Commons* is as good as liberty under a republican Congress. And that slavery under a republican Congress is as bad, at least, as slavery under a *king, Lords* and *Commons.* And upon the whole, that *liberty* under the supreme authority and protection of Great Britain is infinitely preferable to *slavery* under an American Congress. I will also agree with you "that Americans are entitled to freedom." I will go further: I will own and acknowledge that not only *Americans,* but *Africans, Europeans, Asiatics,* all men, of all countries and degrees, of all sizes and complexions, have a right to as much freedom as is consistent with the security of civil society. And I hope you will not think me an "enemy to the *natural* rights of mankind" because I cannot wish them more. We must however remember that more liberty may, without inconvenience, be allowed to individuals in a small government than can be admitted of in a large empire.

But when you assert that "since Americans have not by any act of theirs impowered the British Parliament to make laws for them, it follows they can have no just authority to do it," you advance a position subversive of that dependence which all colonies must, from their very nature, have on the mother country. By the British Parliament, I suppose you mean the supreme legislative authority, the king, Lords and Commons, because no other authority in England has a right to make laws to bind the kingdom, and consequently no authority to make laws to bind the colonies. In this sense I shall understand and use the phrase *British Parliament.*

Now the dependence of the colonies on the mother country has ever been acknowledged. It is an impropriety of speech to talk of an independent colony. The words *independency* and *colony* convey contradictory ideas: much like *killing* and *sparing.* As soon as a colony becomes independent of its parent state, it ceases to be any longer a colony; just as when you *kill* a sheep, you cease to *spare* him. The British colonies make a part of the British Empire. As parts of the body they must be subject to the general laws of the body. To talk of a colony independent of the mother country is no better sense than to talk of a limb independent of the body to which it belongs.

In every government there must be a supreme, absolute authority lodged somewhere. In arbitrary governments this power is in the monarch; in aristocratical governments, in the nobles; in democratical, in the people, or the deputies of their electing. Our own government being a mixture of all these kinds, the supreme authority is vested in the king, nobles, and people, i. e., the king, House of Lords, and House of Commons elected by the people. This supreme authority extends as far as the British dominions extend. To suppose a part of the British dominions which is not subject to the power of the British legislature, is no better sense than to suppose a country, at one and the same time, to be and not to be a part of the British dominions. If therefore the colony of New York be a part of the British dominions, the colony of New York is subject and dependent on the supreme legislative authority of Great Britain.

Legislation is not an inherent right in the colonies. Many colonies have been established and subsisted long without it. The Roman colonies had no legislative authority. It was not till the later period of their republic that the privileges of Roman citizens, among which that of voting in the assemblies of the people at Rome was a principal one, were extended to the inhabitants of Italy. All the laws of the empire were enacted at Rome. Neither their colonies nor conquered countries had anything to do with legislation.

The position that we are bound by no laws to which we have not consented, either by ourselves, or our representatives, is a novel position, unsupported by any authoratative record of the British constitution, ancient or modern. It is republican in its very nature, and tends to the utter subversion of the English monarchy.

This position has arisen from an artful change of terms. To say that an Englishman is not bound by any laws but those to which the representatives of the nation have given their consent, is to say what is true. But to say that an Englishman is bound by no laws but those to which *he* hath consented in person, or by *his* representative, is saying what never was true, and never can be true. A great part of the people in England have no vote in the choice of representatives, and therefore are governed by laws to which they never consented either by *themselves* or by *their* representatives.

The right of colonists to exercise a legislative power is no natural right. They derive it not from nature, but from the indulgence or grant of the parent state, whose subjects they were when the colony was settled, and by whose permission and assistance they made the settlement.

Upon supposition that every English colony enjoyed a legislative power independent of the Parliament, and that the Parliament has no just authority to make laws to bind them, this absurdity will follow—that there is no power in the British empire, which has authority to make laws for the whole empire; i. e., we have an empire, without government; or which amounts to the same thing, we have a government which has no supreme power. All our colonies are independent of each other. Suppose them independent of the British Parliament—what power do you leave to govern the whole? None at all. You split and divide the empire into a number of petty insignificant states. This is the direct, the necessary tendency of refusing submission to acts of Parliament. Every man who can see one inch beyond his nose must see this consequence. And every man who endeavors to accelerate the independency of the colonies on the British Parliament endeavors to accelerate the ruin of the British empire.

To talk of being liege subjects to King George while we disavow the authority of Parliament is another piece of Whiggish nonsense. I love my king as well as any Whig in America or England either, and am as ready to yield him all lawful submission. But while I submit to the king, I submit to the authority of the laws of the state whose guardian the king is. The difference between a good and a bad subject is only this, that the one obeys, the other transgresses the law. The difference between a loyal subject and a rebel is that the one yields obedience to and faithfully supports the supreme authority of the state, and the other endeavors to overthrow it. If we obey the laws of the king, we obey the laws of the Parliament. If we disown the authority of the Parliament, we disown the authority of the king. There is no medium without ascribing powers to the king which the constitution knows nothing of—without making him superior to the laws, and setting him above all restraint. These are some of the ridiculous absurdities of American Whiggism. . . .

The other objection to what has been said upon the legislative authority of the British Parliament is this: that if the Parliament have authority to make laws to bind the whole empire, to regulate the trade of the whole empire, and to raise a revenue upon the whole empire, then we have nothing that we can call our own. By the same authority that they can take a penny, they can take a pound, or all we have got.

Let it be considered that no scheme of human policy can be so contrived and guarded but that something must be left to the integrity, prudence, and wisdom of those who govern. We are apt to think, and I believe justly, that the British constitution is the best scheme of government now subsisting. The rights and liberties of the people are better secured by it than by any other system now subsisting. And yet we find that the rights and liberties of Englishmen may be infringed by wicked and ambitious men. This will ever be the case, even after human sagacity has exerted its utmost ability. This is, however, not an argument that we should not secure ourselves as well as we can. It is rather an argument that we should use our utmost endeavor to guard against the attempts of ambition or avarice.

A great part of the people in England, a considerable number of people in this province, are bound by laws, and taxed without their consent, or the consent of their representatives: for representatives they have none, unless the absurd position of a *virtual* representation be admitted. These people may object to the present mode of government. They may say that they have nothing that they can call their own. That if they may be taxed a penny without their consent, they may be taxed a pound; and so on. You will think it a sufficient security to these people that the representatives of the nation or province cannot hurt *them* without hurting themselves; because they cannot tax *them* without taxing themselves. This security however may not be so effectual as at first may be imagined. The rich are never taxed so much in proportion to their estates as the poor. And even an equal proportion of that tax which a rich man can easily pay may be a heavy burden to a poor man. But the same security that these people have against being ruined by the representatives of the nation or province where they live; the same security have we against being ruined by the British Parliament. They cannot hurt us without hurting themselves. The principal profits of our trade center in England. If they lay unnecessary or oppressive burdens on it; or any ways restrain it, so as to injure us, they will soon feel the effect, and very readily remove the cause. If this security is thought insufficient, let us endeavor to obtain a more effectual one. Let it however be remembered that this security has been thought and found sufficient till within a short period; and very probably a prudent management and a temperate conduct on our part would have made it permanently effectual.

But the colonies have become so considerable by the increase of their inhabitants and commerce, and by the improvement of their lands, that they seem incapable of being governed in the same lax and precarious manner as formerly. They are arrived to that mature state of manhood which requires a different and more exact policy of ruling than was necessary in their infancy and childhood. They want and are entitled to a fixed determinate constitution of their own. A constitution which shall unite them firmly with Great Britain, and with one another; which shall mark out the line of British supremacy and colonial dependence, giving on the one hand full force to the supreme authority of the nation over all its dominions, and on the other securing effectually the rights, liberty, and property of the colonists. This is an event devoutly to be wished by all good men; and which all ought to labor to obtain by all prudent, and probable means. Without obtaining this, it is idle to talk of obtaining a redress of the grievances complained of. They naturally, they necessarily, result from the relation which we at present stand in to Great Britain.

You, Sir, argue through your whole pamphlet upon an assumed point, viz: That the British government—the *king, Lords* and *Commons*—have laid a regular plan to enslave America; and that they are now deliberately putting it in execution. This point has never been proved, though it has been asserted over, and over, and over again. If you say that they have declared their right of making laws, to *bind us in all cases whatsoever,* I answer that the declarative act here referred to means no more than to assert the supreme authority of Great Britain over all her dominions. If you say that they have exercised this power in a wanton, oppressive manner, it is a point that I am not enough acquainted with the *minutiae* of government to determine. It may be true. The colonies are undoubtedly alarmed on account of their liberties. Artful men have availed themselves of the opportunity, and have excited such scenes of contention between the parent state and the colonies as afford none but dreadful prospects. Republicans smile at the confusion that they themselves have in a great measure made, and are exerting all their influence by sedition and rebellion to shake the British empire to its very basis that they may have an opportunity of erecting their beloved commonwealth on its ruins. If greater security to our rights and liberties be necessary than the present form and administration of the government can give us, let us endeavor to obtain it; but let our endeavors be regulated by prudence and probability of success. In this attempt all good men will join, both in England and America. All who love their country and wish the prosperity of the British empire, will be glad to see it accomplished.

Before we set out to obtain this security we should have had prudence enough to settle one point among ourselves. We should have considered what security it was we wanted; what concessions on the part of Great Britain would have been sufficient to have fixed our rights and liberties on a firm and permanent foundation. This was the proper business of our assemblies, and to them we ought to have applied; and why we did not apply to them, no one tolerable reason can be assigned. A business which *our* assembly, at least, is equal to, whether we consider their abilities as men, or their authority as representatives of the province; and a business which, I doubt not, they would have executed with prudence, firmness and success. I say nothing of the other assemblies on the continent, for I know little of them; only that they were the proper persons to have managed this affair.

But we ran headlong to work without ever considering the point we aimed at, or determining what the concessions were with which we would be satisfied. Nor is this, indeed, so much to be wondered at. The present commotions were first excited not by patriotism, but [by] the selfishness of those merchants who had engrossed the tea-trade with Holland. All was quiet till *they* were alarmed by the design of sending the tea belonging to the East India Company to be sold in the colonies. Then began the cry of liberty which hath since been so loudly echoed and reechoed through the continent.

Nor have the steps we have since taken been a whit more prudent than the manner in which we set out.

Every man who wishes well either to America or Great Britain must wish to see a hearty and firm union subsisting between them, and between every part of the British empire. The first object of his desire will be to heal the unnatural breach that now subsists, and to accomplish a speedy reconciliation. All parties declare the utmost willingness to live in union with Great Britain. They profess the utmost loyalty to the king, the warmest affection to their fellow-subjects in England, Ireland, and the West Indies, and their readiness to do everything to promote their welfare that can reasonably be expected from them. Even those republicans, who with the destruction of every species and appearance of monarchy in the world, find it necessary to put on a fair face and make the same declaration.

What steps, Sir, I beseech you, has the Congress taken to accomplish these good purposes? Have they fixed any determined point for us to aim at? They have, and the point marked out by them is *absolute* independence on Great Britain—a perfect discharge from all subordination to the supreme authority of the British empire. Have they proposed any method of cementing our union with the mother country? Yes, but a queer one, viz: to break off all dealings and intercourse with her. Have they done anything to show their love and affection to their fellow-subjects in England, Ireland, and the West Indies? Undoubtedly they have—they have endeavored to starve them all to death. Is this "Equity?" Is this "Wisdom?"—Then murder is equity, and folly, wisdom.

I will here, Sir, venture to deliver my sentiments upon the line that ought to be drawn between the supremacy of Great Britain and the dependency of the colonies. And I shall do it with the more boldness because I know it to be agreeable to the opinions of many of the warmest advocates for America, both in England and in the colonies, in the time of the Stamp Act. I imagine that if all internal taxation be vested in our own legislatures, and the right of regulating trade by duties, bounties, etc., be left in the power of the Parliament, and also the right of enacting all general laws for the good of all the colonies, that we shall have all the security for our rights, liberties and property which human policy can give us. The dependence of the colonies on the mother country will be fixed on a firm foundation; the sovereign authority of Parliament over all the dominions of the empire will be established, and the mother country and all her colonies will be knit together in one grand, firm, and compact body. . . .

ALEXANDER HAMILTON

7

from *The Farmer Refuted* (1775)

When he sat down to answer the second of Samuel Seabury's "Letters from a Westchester Farmer," Alexander Hamilton (1755–1804) was still a student at King's College (now Columbia), and just over eighteen years of age. Moreover he had been in the colonies for little more than a year–having come to New York by way of Elizabeth, New Jersey, from the British West Indies, where he was born. To say that Hamilton's A Full Vindication of the Measures of the Continental Congress *(December 15, 1774) and its sequel* The Farmer Refuted; or, A More Comprehensive and Impartial View of the Disputes between Great Britain and the Colonies *(c. March 1, 1775) were remarkable productions, given their author's age, is to understate the case; and it is small wonder that they were first attributed to older, more experienced patriots like John Jay. Not only did Hamilton ingeniously adapt his style to Seabury's audience–New York's politically uncommitted (or wavering) farmers, small merchants, and artisans–but in answering Seabury argument for argument with force, clarity, and logic, he demonstrated a mature understanding of the issues at stake. Where Seabury had ridiculed the Congress and its meas- ures, Hamilton, using the same appeal to self-interest, defended the rightness and necessity of its course of action in the stated belief that economic sanc- tions, effectively applied, would in time lead to a restoration of colonial rights and liberties.*

Following the Revolution, in which he served with distinction in the field and then as Washington's aide-de-camp, Hamilton took up the practice of law in New York City. Chosen a delegate to the Constitutional Convention, he labored hard for the ratification of the new constitution in New York as one of the three authors of the celebrated Federalist *papers (1787–88). As Wash-*

ington's secretary of the treasury (1789–95), Hamilton worked to promote his own vision of a strong, centralized government with a program calling for federal funding, a national bank, a tariff system, and the encouragement of American manufacturing. His intrusion into the bitterly partisan politics of New York brought him into collision with the volatile Aaron Burr, whose ambition Hamilton thwarted in 1800 even at the expense of advancing his political enemy Thomas Jefferson to the presidency. Hamilton's quarrel with Burr led to the fatal duel on the plains of Weehawken, New Jersey, in July of 1804, in which he was mortally wounded.

☆ ☆

Sir,

I resume my pen, in reply to the curious epistle you have been pleased to favor me with, and can assure you that, notwithstanding I am naturally of a grave and phlegmatic disposition, it has been the source of abundant merriment to me. The spirit that breathes throughout is so rancorous, illiberal, and imperious; the argumentative part of it is so puerile and fallacious; the misrepresentation of facts so palpable and flagrant; the criticisms so illiterate, trifling, and absurd; the conceits so low, sterile, and splenetic, that I will venture to pronounce it one of the most ludicrous performances which have been exhibited to public view during all the present controversy. . . .

Your envenomed pen has endeavored to sully the characters of our continental representatives with the presumptuous charges of ignorance, knavery, sedition, rebellion, treason, and tyranny—a tremendous catalog indeed! Nor have you treated their friends and adherents with any greater degree of complaisance. You have also delineated the mercantile body as entirely devoid of principle; and the several committees as bands of robbers and petty tyrants. In short, except the few who are of your own complexion and stamp, "the *virtuous* friends of order and good government," you have not hesitated to exercise your obloquy and malevolence against the whole continent.

These things being considered, it is manifest that in my answer to your *Free Thoughts* I treated you with more lenity than you had a right to expect; and did by no means observe the strict law of retaliation. None but yourself will think you can, with the least propriety, complain of abuse. . . .

The first thing that presents itself is a wish that "I had, explicitly, declared to the public my ideas of the *natural rights* of mankind. Man, in a state of nature (you say), may be considered as perfectly free from all restraint of *law* and *government;* and then, the weak must submit to the strong."

63

I shall, henceforth, begin to make some allowance for that enmity you have discovered to the *natural rights* of mankind. For, though ignorance of them, in this enlightened age, cannot be admitted as a sufficient excuse for you, yet it ought, in some measure, to extenuate your guilt. If you will follow my advice, there still may be hopes of your reformation. Apply yourself, without delay, to the study of the law of nature. I would recommend to your perusal Grotius, Pufendorf, Locke, Montesquieu, and Burlamaqui.[25] I might mention other excellent writers on this subject; but if you attend diligently to these, you will not require any others.

There is so strong a similtude between your political principles and those maintained by Mr. Hobbes that, in judging from them, a person might very easily *mistake* you for a disciple of his. His opinion was exactly coincident with yours relative to man in a state of nature. He held, as you do, that he was then perfectly free from all restraint of *law* and *government*. Moral obligation, according to him, is derived from the introduction of civil society; and there is no virtue but what is purely artificial, the mere contrivance of politicians for the maintenance of social intercourse. But the reason he ran into this absurd and impious doctrine was that he disbelieved the existence of an intelligent, superintending principle, who is the governor, and will be the final judge, of the universe.

As you sometimes swear *by Him that made you,* I conclude your sentiments do not correspond with his in that which is the basis of the doctrine you both agree in; and this makes it impossible to imagine whence this congruity between you arises. To grant that there is a Supreme Intelligence who rules the world and has established laws to regulate the actions of His creatures, and still to assert that man in a state of nature may be considered as perfectly free from all restraints of *law* and *government*, appears, to a common understanding, altogether irreconcilable.

Good and wise men in all ages have embraced a very dissimilar theory. They have supposed that the Deity, from the relations we stand in to Himself and to each other, has constituted an eternal and immutable law, which is indispensably obligatory upon all mankind, prior to any human institution whatever.

This is what is called the law of nature, "which, being coeval with mankind, and dictated by God himself, is, of course, superior in obligations to any other. It is binding over all the globe, in all countries and at all times. No human laws are of any validity if contrary to this; and such of them as are valid derive all their authority, mediately or immediately, from this original."–BLACKSTONE.[26]

Upon this law depend the natural rights of mankind: the Supreme Being gave existence to man, together with the means of preserving and beautifying that existence. He endowed him with rational faculties by the help of which to discern and pursue such things as were consistent with his duty and interest, and invested him with an inviolable right to personal liberty and personal safety.

Hence, in a state of nature no man had any *moral* power to deprive another of his life, limbs, property, or liberty, nor the least authority to command or exact obedience from him except that which arose from the ties of consanguinity.

Hence, also, the origin of all civil government, justly established, must be a voluntary compact between the rulers and the ruled, and must be liable to such limitations as are necessary for the security of the *absolute rights* of the latter; for what original title can any man, or set of men, have to govern others except their own consent? To usurp dominion over a people in their own despite, or to grasp at a more extensive power than they are willing to entrust, is to violate that law of nature which gives every man a right to his personal liberty, and can therefore confer no obligation to obedience. . . .

If we examine the pretensions of Parliament by this criterion, which is evidently a good one, we shall presently detect their injustice. First, they are subversive of our natural liberty because an authority is assumed over us which we by no means assent to. And, secondly, they divest us of that moral security for our lives and properties which we are entitled to and which it is the primary end of society to bestow. For such security can never exist while we have no part in making the laws that are to bind us, and while it may be the interest of our uncontrolled legislators to oppress us as much as possible.

To deny these principles will be not less absurd than to deny the plainest axioms. I shall not, therefore, attempt any further illustration of them.

You say: "When I assert that since Americans have not by any act of theirs empowered the British Parliament to make laws for them, it follows they can have no just authority to do it, I advance a position subversive of that dependence which all colonies must, from their very nature, have on the mother country." The premises from which I drew this conclusion are indisputable. You have not detected any fallacy in them, but endeavor to overthrow them by deducing a false and imaginary consequence. My principles admit the only dependence which can subsist, consistent with any idea of civil liberty, or with the future welfare of the British empire, as will appear hereafter.

"The dependence of the colonies on the mother country," you assert, "has ever been acknowledged. It is an impropriety of speech to talk of an independent colony. The words independent and colony convey contradictory ideas; much like *killing* and *sparing*. As soon as a colony becomes independent on the parent state it ceases to be any longer a colony, just as when you *kill* a sheep you cease to *spare* him."

In what sense the dependence of the colonies on the mother country has been acknowledged will appear from those circumstances of their political history which I shall, by and by, recite. The term colony signifies nothing more than a body of people drawn from the mother country to inhabit some distant place, or the country itself so inhabited. As to the degrees and modifications of that subordination which is due to the parent state, these must depend upon other things besides the mere act of emigration to inhabit or settle a distant country. These must be ascertained by the spirit of the constitution of the mother country, by the compacts for the purpose of colonizing, and more especially by the law of nature, and that *supreme law* of every society—*its own happiness*. . . .

Admitting that the king of Great Britain was enthroned by virtue of an act of Parliament, and that he is king of America because he is king of Great Britain, yet the act of Parliament is not the *efficient cause* of his being the king of America. It is only the *occasion* of it. He is king of America by virtue of a compact between us and the kings of Great Britain. These colonies were planted and settled by the grants and under the protection of English kings, who entered into covenants with us, for themselves, their heirs, and successors; and it is from these covenants that the duty of protection on their part, and the duty of allegiance on ours, arise. . . .

From what has been said, it is plain that we are without those checks upon the representatives of Great Britain which alone can make them answer the end of their appointment with respect to us—which is the preservation of the rights and the advancement of the happiness of the governed. The direct and inevitable consequence is *they have no right to govern us*. . . .

When I say that the authority of Parliament is confined to Great Britain, I speak of it in its primitive and original state. Parliament may acquire an incidental influence over others, but this must be by their own free consent; for, without this, any power it might exercise would be mere usurpation, and by no means a just authority.

The best way of determining disputes and of investigating truth is by descending to elementary principles. Any other method may only bewilder and misguide the understanding, but this will lead to a convincing and satisfactory crisis. By observing this method, we shall learn the following truths:

That the existence of the House of Commons depends upon the people's right to a share in the legislature, which is exercised by means of electing the members of that House. That the end and intention of this right is to preserve the life, property, and liberty of the subject from the encroachments of oppression and tyranny.

That this end is accomplished by means of the *intimate connection* of interest between those members and their constituents, the people of Great Britain.

That with respect to the people of America there is no such *intimate connection* of interest, but the contrary, and therefore that end could not be answered to them; consequently, the *end* ceasing, the *means* must cease also.

[That] the House of Commons derives all its power from its own real constituents, who are the people of Great Britain; and that, therefore, it has no power but what they *originally* had in themselves.

That they had no original right to the life, property, or liberty of Americans, nor any acquired from their own consent, and of course could give no authority over them.

That therefore the House of Commons has no such authority.

What need is there of a multiplicity of arguments or a long chain of reasoning to inculcate these luminous principles? They speak the plainest language to every man of common sense, and must carry conviction where the mental eye is not bedimmed by the mist of prejudice, partiality, ambition, or avarice. Let us now see what has been offered in opposition to them.

But, by the way, let me remark that I have levelled my battery chiefly against the authority of the House of Commons over America because if that be proved not to exist the dispute is at an end. The efficacy of acts of Parliament depends upon the due authority of the respective branches to bind the different orders and ranks of the nation.

It is said that "in every government there must be a supreme absolute authority lodged somewhere. In arbitrary governments this power is in the monarch; in aristocratical governments, the nobles; in democratical, in the people, or the deputies of their electing. Our own government being a mixture of all these kinds, the supreme authority is vested in the king, nobles, and people—i. e., the king, House of Lords, and House of Commons *elected by the people.* The supreme authority extends as far as the British dominions extend. To suppose a part of the British dominions which is not subject to the power of the British legislature is no better sense than to suppose a country at one and the same time to be, and not to be, a part of the British dominions. If, therefore, the colony of New York is a part of the British dominions, the colony of New York is subject to, and dependent on, the supreme legislative authority of Great Britain."

This argument is the most specious of any the advocates for parliamentary supremacy are able to produce; but when we come to anatomize and closely examine every part of it, we shall discover that it is entirely composed of distorted and misapplied principles, together with ambiguous and equivocal terms.

The first branch is that "in every government there must be a supreme, absolute authority lodged somewhere." This position, when properly explained, is evidently just. In every civil society there must be a supreme power to which all the members of that society are subject, for otherwise there could be no supremacy or subordination—that is, no government at all. But no use can be made of this principle beyond matter of fact. To infer from thence that unless a supreme, absolute authority be vested in one part of an empire over all the other parts there can be no government in the whole is false and absurd. Each branch may enjoy a distinct, complete legislature, and still good government may be preserved everywhere. It is in vain to assert that two or more distinct legislatures cannot exist in the same state. If by the same state be meant the same individual community, it is true. Thus, for instance, there cannot be two supreme legislatures in Great Britain, nor two in New York. But if by the same state be understood a number of individual societies or bodies politic united under one common head, then I maintain that there may be one distinct, complete legislature in each. Thus there may be one in Great Britain, another in Ireland, and another in New York; and still these several parts may form but one state. In order to do this there must indeed be some connecting, pervading principle; but this is found in the person and prerogative of the king. He it is that conjoins all these individual societies into one great body politic. He it is that is to preserve their mutual connection and dependence, and make them all cooperate to one common end—the general good. His power is equal to the purpose, and his interest binds him to the due prosecution of it.

Those who aver that the independency of America on the British Parliament implies two sovereign authorities in the same state deceive themselves, or wish to deceive others, in two ways: by confounding the idea of the same state with that of the same individual society, and by losing sight of that share which the king has in the sovereignty both of Great Britain and America. Perhaps, indeed, it may with propriety be said that the king is the only sovereign of the empire. The part which the people have in the legislature may more justly be considered as a limitation of the sovereign authority to prevent its being exercised in an oppressive and despotic manner. Monarchy is universally allowed to predominate in the constitution. In this view, there is not the least absurdity in the supposition that Americans have a right to a limitation similar to that of the people of Great Britain. At any rate, there can never be said to be two sovereign powers in the same state while *one common king* is acknowledged by every member of it. . . .

The right of colonists, therefore, to exercise a legislative power is an inherent right. It is founded upon the rights of all men to freedom and happiness. For civil liberty cannot possibly have any existence where the society for whom laws are made have no share in making them, and where the interest of their legislators is not inseparably interwoven with theirs. Before you asserted that the right of legislation was derived "from the indulgence or grant of the parent state," you should have proved two things: that all men have not a natural right to freedom, and that civil liberty is not advantageous to society.

"The position," you say, "that we are bound by no laws but those to which we have assented, either by ourselves or by our representatives, is a novel position, unsupported by any authoritative record of the British constitution, ancient or modern. It is republican in its very nature, and tends to the utter subversion of the English monarchy.

"This position has arisen from an artful change of terms. To say that an Englishman is not bound by any laws but those to which the representatives of the nation have given their consent, is to say what is true. But to say that an Englishman is bound by no laws but those to which he hath consented in person or by *his* representatives, is saying what never was true and never can be true. A great part of the people have no vote in the choice of representatives, and therefore are governed by laws to which they never consented, either by themselves or by *their* representatives."

The foundation of the English constitution rests upon this principle: that no laws have any validity or binding force without the consent and approbation of the *people*, given in the persons of *their* representatives, periodically elected by *themselves*. This constitutes the democratical part of the government.

It is also undeniably certain that no Englishman who can be deemed a *free agent* in a *political* view can be bound by laws to which he has not consented, either in person or by *his* representative. Or, in other words, every Englishman (exclusive of the mercantile and trading part of the nation) who possesses a freehold to the value of forty shillings per annum has a right to share in the legislature, which he exercises by giving his vote in the election of some person he approves of as his representative. . . .

Whatever opinion may be entertained of my sentiments and intentions, I attest that Being, whose all-seeing eye penetrates the inmost recesses of the heart, that I am not influenced (in the part I take) by any unworthy motive; that if I am in an error, it is my judgment not my heart that errs; that I earnestly lament the unnatural quarrel between the parent state and the colonies, and most ardently wish for a speedy reconciliation—a perpetual and *mutually* beneficial union; that I am a warm advocate for limited monarchy, and an unfeigned well-wisher to the present royal family.

But, on the other hand, I am inviolably attached to the essential rights of mankind and the true interests of society. I consider civil liberty, in a genuine, unadulterated sense, as the greatest of terrestrial blessings. I am convinced that the whole human race is entitled to it, and that it can be wrested from no part of them without the blackest and most aggravated guilt.

I verily believe, also, that the best way to secure a permanent and happy union between Great Britain and the colonies is to permit the latter to be as free as they desire. To abridge their liberties, or to exercise any power over them which they are unwilling to submit to, would be a perpetual source of discontent and animosity. A continual jealousy would exist on both sides. This would lead to tyranny on the one hand, and to sedition and rebellion on the other. Impositions, not really grievous in themselves, would be thought so, and the murmurs arising from thence would be considered as the effect of a turbulent, ungovernable spirit. These jarring principles would at length throw all things into disorder, and be productive of an irreparable breach and a total disunion.

That harmony and mutual confidence may speedily be restored between all the parts of the British empire is the favorite wish of one who feels the warmest sentiments of good will to mankind, who bears no enmity to you, and who is

A Sincere Friend to America.

JOSEPH WARREN

8

"Massacre Day Oration" (1775)

*Dr. Joseph Warren (1741-75), perhaps the most selfless and dedicated of
the patriot leaders, was born in Roxbury, Massachusetts. Following his
graduation from Harvard College in 1759, Warren studied medicine and then
set up a practice in Boston where he skillfully mixed medicine with politics
during the years immediately prior to the Revolution. It was Warren who
dispatched his friend Paul Revere (and William Dawes) to Concord on the
evening of April 18, 1775, to warn Sam Adams and John Hancock that the
British were on the march, and by land. The next morning, having delivered
a baby, Warren hurried off to help harass the British as they retreated from
Lexington. Two months later, on June 17, 1775, Warren, serving as a volunteer, was killed defending the American redoubt atop Breed's Hill.*

*A talented and persuasive speaker, Warren is best remembered for the
Massacre Day oration he delivered on March 5, 1775. Its setting was a dramatic one. General Thomas Gage and an army of 5,400 men had turned the
city of Boston into an armed camp. Incidents between soldiers and civilians
had multiplied of late; and, accordingly, on the day of the speech—the fifth
anniversary of the Boston Massacre—the British garrison was alerted for
trouble. So great was the concern that some forty soldiers were conspicuous-
ly positioned in the front rows of Old South Church facing the orator. And
then Dr. Warren arose to deliver the moving address that follows, in which
he reviewed the history of British-American relations and commemorated
the bloody evening five years before when soldiers fired into a Boston mob,
killing three outright and mortally wounding two others.*

☆ ☆

My ever Honored Fellow Citizens,

It is not without the most humiliating conviction of my want of ability that I now appear before you; but the sense I have of the obligation I am under to obey the calls of my country at all times, together with an animating recollection of your indulgence exhibited upon so many occasions, has induced me once more, undeserving as I am, to throw myself upon that candor which looks with kindness on the feeblest efforts of an honest mind.

You will not now expect the elegance, the learning, the fire, the enrapturing strains of eloquence which charmed you when a Lovell, a Church, or a Hancock spoke;[27] but you will permit me to say that with a sincerity equal to theirs, I mourn over my bleeding country. With them I weep at her distress, and with them deeply resent the many injuries she has received from the hands of cruel and unreasonable men.

That personal freedom is the natural right of every man, and that property, or an exclusive right to dispose of what he has honestly acquired by his own labor, necessarily arises therefrom, are truths which common sense has placed beyond the reach of contradiction. And no man or body of men can without being guilty of flagrant injustice claim a right to dispose of the persons or acquisitions of any other man or body of men, unless it can be proved that such a right has arisen from some compact between the parties in which it has been explicitly and freely granted.

If I may be indulged in taking a retrospective view of the first settlement of our country, it will be easy to determine with what degree of justice the late Parliament of Great Britain has assumed the power of giving away that property which the Americans have earned by their labor. . . .

But when at an infinite expense of toil and blood this widely extended continent had been cultivated and defended, when the hardy adventurers justly expected that they and their descendants should peaceably have enjoyed the harvest of those fields which they had sown, and the fruit of those vineyards which they had planted, this country was then thought worthy the attention of the British ministry; and the only justifiable and only successful means of rendering the colonies serviceable to Britain were adopted. By an intercourse of friendly offices, the two countries became so united in affection that they thought not of any distinct or separate interests; they found both countries flourishing and happy. Britain saw her commerce extended and her wealth increased, her lands raised to an immense value, her fleets riding triumphant on the ocean, the terror of her arms spreading to every quarter of the globe. The colonist found himself free, and thought himself secure, he dwelt under his own vine, and under his own fig tree and had none to make him afraid. . . .

These pleasing connections might have continued; these delightsome prospects might have been every day extended; and even the reveries of the most warm imagination might have been realized; but, unhappily for Britain, the madness of an avaricious minister of state has drawn a sable curtain over the charming scene, and in its stead has brought upon the stage discord, envy, hatred and revenge, with civil war close in their rear.

Some demon in an evil hour suggested to a short-sighted financier the hateful project of transferring the whole property of the king's subjects in America to his subjects in Britain. The claim of the British Parliament to tax the colonies can never be supported but by such a transfer; for the right of the House of Great Britain to originate any tax or grant money is altogether derived from their being elected by the people of Great Britain to act for them, and the people of Great Britain cannot confer on their representatives a right to give or grant anything which they themselves have not a right to give or grant personally. Therefore it follows that if the members chosen by the people of Great Britain to represent them in Parliament have, by virtue of their being so chosen, any right to give or grant American property, or to lay any tax upon the lands or persons of the colonists, it is because the lands and people in the colonies are, bona fide, owned by, and justly belonging to the people of Great Britain. But (as has been before observed) every man has a right to personal freedom, consequently a right to enjoy what is acquired by his own labor. And it is evident that the property in this country has been acquired by our own labor; it is the duty of the people of Great Britain to produce some compact in which we have explicitly given up to them a right to dispose of our persons or property. Until this is done, every attempt of theirs, or of those whom they have deputed to act for them, to give or grant any part of our property is directly repugnant to every principle of reason and natural justice. But I may boldly say that such a compact never existed, no, not even in imagination. Nevertheless, the representatives of a nation long famed for justice and the exercise of every noble virtue have been prevailed on to adopt the fatal scheme; and although the dreadful consequences of this wicked policy have already shaken the empire to its center, yet still it is persisted in. Regardless of the voice of reason—deaf to the prayers and supplication—and unaffected with the flowing tears of suffering millions, the British ministry still hugs the darling idol; and every rolling year affords fresh instances of the absurd devotion with which they worship it. Alas! how has the folly, the distraction of the British councils blasted our swelling hopes, and spread a gloom over this western hemisphere.

The hearts of Britons and Americans which lately felt the generous glow of mutual confidence and love now burn with jealousy and rage. Though but of yesterday, I recollect (deeply affected at the ill-boding change) the happy hours that passed while Britain and America rejoiced in the prosperity and greatness of each other (heaven grant those halcyon days may soon return). But now the Briton too often looks on the American with an envious eye, taught to consider his just plea for the enjoyment of his earnings as the effect of pride and stubborn opposition to the parent country. Whilst the American beholds the Briton as the ruffian, ready first to take away his property, and next, what is still dearer to every virtuous man, the liberty of his country.

When the measures of administration had disgusted the colonies to the highest degree, and the people of Great Britain had by artifice and falsehood been irritated against America, an army was sent over to enforce submission to certain acts of the British Parliament, which reason scorned to countenance, and which placemen and pensioners were found unable to support.[28]

Martial law and the government of a well-regulated city are so entirely different that it has always been considered as improper to quarter troops in populous cities; frequent disputes must necessarily arise between the citizen and the soldier, even if no previous animosities subsist. And it is further certain from a consideration of the nature of mankind as well as from constant experience that standing armies always endanger the liberty of the subject. But when the people on the one part considered the army as sent to enslave them, and the army on the other were taught to look on the people as in a state of rebellion, it was but just to fear the most disagreeable consequences. Our fears, we have seen, were but too well grounded.

The many injuries offered to the town I pass over in silence. I cannot now mark out the path which led to that unequalled scene of horror, the sad remembrance of which takes the full possession of my soul. The sanguinary theater again opens itself to view. The baleful images of terror crowd around me—and discontented ghosts, with hollow groans, appear to solemnize the anniversary of the fifth of March.

Approach we then the melancholy walk of death. Hither let me call the gay companion; here let him drop a farewell tear upon that body which so late he saw vigorous and warm with social mirth—hither let me lead the tender mother to weep over her beloved son—come widowed mourner, here satiate thy grief; behold thy murdered husband gasping on the ground, and to complete the pompous show of wretchedness bring in each hand thy infant children to bewail their father's fate—take heed, ye orphan babes, lest whilst your streaming eyes are fixed upon the ghastly corpse *your feet slide on the stones bespattered with your father's brains.* Enough! this tragedy need not be heightened by an infant weltering in the blood of him that gave it birth. Nature reluctant, shrinks already from the view, and the chilled blood rolls slowly backward to its fountain. We wildly stare about, and with amazement ask who spread this ruin round us? what wretch has dared deface the image of his God? has haughty France, or cruel Spain, sent forth her myrmidons? has the grim savage rushed again from the far distant wilderness? or does some fiend fierce from the depth of hell, with all the rancorous malice which the apostate damned can feel, twang her destructive bow and hurl her deadly arrows at our breast? No; none of these—but how astonishing! it is the hand of Britain that inflicts the wound. The arms of George, our rightful king, have been employed to shed that blood, when justice or the honor of his crown had called his subjects to the field.

But pity, grief, astonishment, with all the softer movements of the soul, must now give way to stronger passions. Say, fellow citizens, what dreadful thought now swells your heaving bosoms—you fly to arms—sharp indignation flashes from each eye—revenge gnashes her iron teeth—death grins a hideous smile, secure to drench his greedy jaws in human gore—whilst hovering furies darken all the air.

But stop, my bold adventurous countrymen, stain not your weapons with the blood of Britons. Attend to reason's voice—humanity puts in her claim —and sues to be again admitted to her wonted seat, the bosom of the brave. Revenge is far beneath the noble mind. Many, perhaps, compelled to rank among the vile assassins, do from their inmost souls detest the barbarous action. The winged death shot from your arms may chance to pierce some breast that bleeds already for your injured country.

The storm subsides—a solemn pause ensues—you spare, upon condition they depart. They go—they quit your city—they no more shall give offence. Thus closes the important drama.

And could it have been conceived that we again should have seen a British army in our land, sent to enforce obedience to acts of Parliament destructive of our liberty? But the royal ear, far distant from this western world, has been assaulted by the tongue of slander; and villains, traitorous alike to king and country, have prevailed upon a gracious prince to clothe his countenance with wrath, and to erect the hostile banner against a people ever affectionate and loyal to him and his illustrious predecessors of the house of Hanover.[29] Our streets are again filled with armed men; our harbor is crowded with ships of war; but these cannot intimidate us; our liberty must be preserved; it is far dearer than life, we hold it even dear as our allegiance; we must defend it against the attacks of friends as well as enemies; we cannot suffer even Britons to ravish it from us. . . .

But if, from past events, we may venture to form a judgment of the future, we justly may expect that the devices of our enemies will but increase the triumphs of our country. I must indulge a hope that Britain's liberty, as well as ours, will eventually be preserved by the virtue of America.

The attempt of the British Parliament to raise a revenue from America, and our denial of their right to do it, have excited an almost universal inquiry into the right of mankind in general and of British subjects in particular; the necessary result of which must be such a liberality of sentiment and such a jealousy of those in power as will, better than an adamantine wall, secure us against the future approaches of despotism.

The malice of the Boston Port Bill has been defeated in a very considerable degree by giving you an opportunity of deserving, and our brethren in this and our sister colonies an opportunity of bestowing, those benefactions which have delighted your friends and astonished your enemies, not only in America but in Europe also. And what is more valuable still, the sympathetic feelings for a brother in distress, and the grateful emotions excited in the breast of him who finds relief, must forever endear each to the other, and form those indissoluble bonds of friendship and affection on which the preservation of our rights so evidently depends.

The mutilation of our charter has made every other colony jealous for its own; for this if once submitted to by us would set on float the property and government of every British settlement upon the continent.[30] If charters are not deemed sacred, how miserably precarious is everything founded upon them.

Even the sending of troops to put these acts in execution is not without advantages to us. The exactness and beauty of their discipline inspire our youth with ardor in the pursuit of military knowledge. Charles the invincible taught Peter the Great the art of war. The battle of Pultowa convinced Charles of the proficiency Peter had made.[31]

Our country is in danger, but not to be despaired of. Our enemies are numerous and powerful—but we have many friends—determining to be free, and Heaven and earth will aid the resolution. On you depend the fortunes of America. You are to decide the important question on which rest the happiness and liberty of millions yet unborn. Act worthy of yourselves. The faltering tongue of hoary age calls on you to support your country. The lisping infant raises its suppliant hands imploring defense against the monster slavery. Your fathers look from their celestial seats with smiling approbation on their sons who boldly stand forth in the cause of virtue, but sternly frown upon the inhuman miscreant who, to secure the loaves and fishes to himself, would breed a serpent to destroy his children.

But, pardon me, my fellow citizens, I know you want not zeal or fortitude. You will maintain your rights or perish in the generous struggle. However difficult the combat, you never will decline it when freedom is the prize. An independence of Great Britain is not our aim. No, our wish is that Britain and the colonies may, like the oak and ivy, grow and increase in strength together. But whilst the infatuated plan of making one part of the empire slaves to the other is persisted in, the interest and safety of Britain, as well as the colonies, require that the wise measures, recommended by the honorable Continental Congress, be steadily pursued; whereby the unnatural contest between a parent honored and a child beloved may probably be brought to such an issue as that the peace and happiness of both may be established upon a lasting basis. But if these pacific measures are ineffectual, and it appears that the only way to safety is through fields of blood, I know you will not turn your faces from your foes, but will, undauntedly, press forward until tyranny is trodden under foot, and you have fixed your adored goddess liberty, fast by a Brunswick's side, on the American throne.

You then, who nobly have espoused your country's cause, who generously have sacrificed wealth and ease—who have despised the pomp and show of tinseled greatness—refused the summons to the festive board—been deaf to the alluring calls of luxury and mirth—who have forsaken the downy pillow to keep your vigils by the midnight lamp, for the salvation of your invaded country, that you might break the fowler's snare, and disappoint the vulture of his prey; you then will reap that harvest of renown which you so justly have deserved. Your country shall pay her grateful tribute of applause. Even the children of your most inveterate enemies, ashamed to tell from whom they sprang, while they in secret curse their stupid, cruel parents, shall join the general voice of gratitude to those who broke the fetters which their fathers forged.

Having redeemed your country, and secured the blessing to future generations who, fired by your example, shall emulate your virtues, and learn from you the heavenly art of making millions happy; with heart-felt joy—with transports all your own—you cry, the glorious work is done. Then drop the mantle to some young Elisha, and take your seats with kindred spirits in your native skies.

THOMAS PAINE

9

from *Common Sense* (1776)

"Where liberty is, there is my country," remarked Benjamin Franklin; to which Tom Paine is said to have replied, "Where liberty is not, there is mine." Such a statement, apocryphal or not, does epitomize the man; for Thomas Paine (1737–1809) spent virtually the whole of his adult life propagandizing with his pen the cause of revolution. Born in Thetford, England, Paine arrived in America on November 30, 1774, bearing with him a letter of introduction from Benjamin Franklin to his Philadelphia son-in-law. Franklin's recommendation ("an ingenious, worthy young man") is somewhat surprising, for Paine's early years—as corset maker, tobacconist, and excise officer— had not been conspicuous for their success, though Paine's efforts to improve the lot of the king's excisemen did earn him a degree of notoriety, including the attention of Dr. Franklin.

In America Paine's fortunes rapidly improved, especially after February, 1775, when he became editor of the Pennsylvania Magazine. *During the same period his growing acquaintance with many of the leaders of the Second Continental Congress and the issues involved converted him to the cause of American independence. Within months of Lexington and Concord Paine had begun work on* Common Sense, *a pamphlet which brilliantly managed to capture, distill, and crystallize the political feeling of the time. Published anonymously on January 10, 1776, it had a success both immediate and unprecedented. Within weeks the number of copies in print exceeded 100,000, and wherever it circulated, according to contemporary reports,* Common Sense *"worked a powerful change in the minds of men." In language alternating between simple directness and emotion-charged eloquence,* Common Sense *laid before colonial Americans a subject hitherto only whispered about, avoided, or denied. Paine did not so much advocate independence as assume it as an irrevocable necessity whose advantages were clear. Moreover, in openly vilifying George III ("the hardened, sullen-tempered Pharaoh of England") and ridiculing the institution of monarchy itself, Paine cut through the final fiction that America's troubles could be laid to wicked ministers and a scheming, grasping Parliament.*

Paine's second major contribution to the American Revolution was the series of Crisis *papers published periodically throughout the war, a performance that once again earned him the recognition and gratitude of George Washington and other revolutionary figures. Paine left America in 1787 for England and France, to become a propagandizer of revolutionary causes. The publication in 1791 of* The Rights of Man, *a defense of the French Revolution written in response to Edmund Burke's* Reflections on the French Revolution *(1790), made him a hero in France and a renegade in England, where his book was banned and where Paine himself was tried in absentia. Entering actively into French politics, Paine became a French citizen and an elected member of the French Convention, but when the moderate Girondist faction was swept aside by the militant Jacobins during the Reign of Terror of 1793, he was imprisoned and narrowly escaped the guillotine. It was while in prison that Paine began work on his famous deistical religious tract* The Age of Reason, *which he completed and published following his release in November of 1794. From the moment of his return to America in 1802, controversy swirled about his head. Federalists attacked him for his friendship with Jefferson and his role in the French Revolution, and the reactionary clergy for his freethinking religious ideas. Out of favor, impoverished, and in ill health, Paine lived out his final years in a small cottage in New Rochelle, New York, bestowed upon him in better days for his patriotic services.*

☆ ☆

Introduction

Perhaps the sentiments contained in the following pages are not *yet* sufficiently fashionable to procure them general favor; a long habit of not thinking a thing *wrong* gives it a superficial appearance of being *right,* and raises at first a formidable outcry in defense of custom. But the tumult soon subsides. Time makes more converts than reason.

As a long and violent abuse of power is generally the means of calling the right of it in question (and in matters, too, which might never have been thought of, had not the sufferers been aggravated into the inquiry), and as the king of England hath undertaken in his *own right* to support the Parliament in what he calls *theirs*, and as the good people of this country are grievously oppressed by the combination, they have an undoubted privilege to inquire into the pretensions of both, and equally to reject the usurpation of *either.*

In the following sheets the author hath studiously avoided everything which is personal among ourselves. Compliments as well as censure to individuals make no part thereof. The wise and the worthy need not the triumph of a pamphlet; and those whose sentiments are injudicious or unfriendly will cease of themselves, unless too much pains are bestowed upon their conversions.

The cause of America is in a great measure the cause of all mankind. Many circumstances have and will arise which are not local but universal, and through which the principles of all lovers of mankind are affected, and in the event of which their affections are interested. The laying a country desolate with fire and sword, declaring war against the natural rights of mankind, and extirpating the defenders thereof from the face of the earth, is the concern of every man to whom nature hath given the power of feeling; of which class, regardless of party censure, is

The Author

Thoughts on the Present State of American Affairs

In the following pages I offer nothing more than simple facts, plain arguments, and common sense; and have no other preliminaries to settle with the reader than that he will divest himself of prejudice and prepossession, and suffer his reason and his feelings to determine for themselves; that he will put on, or rather that he will not put off, the true character of a man, and generously enlarge his views beyond the present day.

Volumes have been written on the subject of the struggle between England and America. Men of all ranks have embarked in the controversy, from different motives, and with various designs; but all have been ineffectual, and the period of debate is closed. Arms as the last resource decide the contest; the appeal was the choice of the king, and the continent has accepted the challenge.

It hath been reported of the late Mr. Pelham[32] (who though an able minister was not without his faults) that on his being attacked in the House of Commons on the score that his measures were only of a temporary kind, replied, *"They will last my time."* Should a thought so fatal and unmanly possess the colonies in the present contest, the name of ancestors will be remembered by future generations with detestation.

The sun never shined on a cause of greater worth. 'Tis not the affair of a city, a county, a province, or a kingdom; but of a continent—of at least one-eighth part of the habitable globe. 'Tis not the concern of a day, a year, or an age; posterity are virtually involved in the contest, and will be more or less affected even to the end of time by the proceedings now. Now is the seedtime of continental union, faith and honor. The least fracture now will be like a name engraved with the point of a pin on the tender rind of a young oak; the wound would enlarge with the tree, and posterity read it in full-grown characters.

By referring the matter from argument to arms, a new era for politics is struck—a new method of thinking hath arisen. All plans, proposals, etc., prior to the nineteenth of April, i.e., to the commencement of hostilities, are like the almanacs of the last year; which though proper then, are super-seded and useless now. Whatever was advanced by the advocates on either side of the question then, terminated in one and the same point, viz., a union with Great Britain; the only difference between the parties was the method of effecting it—the one proposing force, the other friendship; but it hath so far happened that the first hath failed, and the second hath withdrawn her influence.

As much hath been said of the advantages of reconciliation, which, like an agreeable dream, hath passed away and left us as we were, it is but right that we should examine the contrary side of the argument, and inquire into some of the many material injuries which these colonies sustain, and always will sustain, by being connected with and dependent on Great Britain. To examine that connection and dependence on the principles of nature and common sense, to see what we have to trust to, if separated, and what we are to expect, if dependent.

I have heard it asserted by some that as America has flourished under her former connection with Great Britain, the same connection is necessary to-wards her future happiness, and will always have the same effect. Nothing can be more fallacious than this kind of argument. We may as well assert that because a child has thrived upon milk, it is never to have meat, or that the first twenty years of our lives is to become a precedent for the next twenty. But even this is admitting more than is true; for I answer roundly that America would have flourished as much, and probably much more, had no European power taken any notice of her. The commerce by which she hath enriched herself are the necessaries of life, and will always have a mar-ket while eating is the custom of Europe.

But she has protected us, say some. That she hath engrossed us is true, and defended the continent at our expense as well as her own is admitted; and she would have defended Turkey from the same motive, viz., for the sake of trade and dominion.

Alas! we have been long led away by ancient prejudices and made large sacrifices to superstition. We have boasted the protection of Great Britain without considering that her motive was *interest* not *attachment;* and that she did not protect us from *our enemies* on *our account*, but from *her enemies* on *her own account,* from those who had no quarrel with us on any *other account*, and who will always be our enemies on the *same account.* Let Britain waive her pretensions to the continent, or the continent throw off the dependence, and we should be at peace with France and Spain were they at war with Britain. The miseries of Hanover's last war ought to warn us against connections.

It hath lately been asserted in Parliament that the colonies have no relation to each other but through the parent country, i.e., that Pennsylvania and the Jerseys, and so on for the rest, are sister colonies by the way of England; this is certainly a very roundabout way of proving relationship, but it is the nearest and only true way of proving enmity (or enemyship, if I may so call it). France and Spain never were, nor perhaps ever will be, our enemies as *Americans,* but as our being the *subjects of Great Britain.*

But Britain is the parent country, say some. Then the more shame upon her conduct. Even brutes do not devour their young, nor savages make war upon their families. Wherefore, the assertion, if true, turns to her reproach; but it happens not to be true, or only partly so, and the phrase *parent* or *mother country* hath been jesuitically adopted by the king and his parasites, with a low papistical design of gaining an unfair bias on the credulous weakness of our minds. Europe, and not England, is the parent country of America. This new world hath been the asylum for the persecuted lovers of civil and religious liberty from *every part* of Europe. Hither have they fled, not from the tender embraces of the mother, but from the cruelty of the monster; and it is so far true of England, that the same tyranny which drove the first emigrants from home pursues their descendants still. . . .

I challenge the warmest advocate for reconciliation to show a single advantage that this continent can reap by being connected with Great Britain. I repeat the challenge; not a single advantage is derived. Our corn will fetch its price in any market in Europe, and our imported goods must be paid for buy them where we will.

But the injuries and disadvantages which we sustain by that connection are without number; and our duty to mankind at large, as well as to ourselves, instructs us to renounce the alliance: because any submission to or dependence on Great Britain tends directly to involve this continent in European wars and quarrels, and set us at variance with nations who would otherwise seek our friendship, and against whom we have neither anger nor complaint. As Europe is our market for trade, we ought to form no partial connection with any part of it. It is the true interest of America to steer clear of European contentions, which she never can do while by her dependence on Britain she is made the make-weight in the scale of British politics.

Europe is too thickly planted with kingdoms to be long at peace, and whenever a war breaks out between England and any foreign power, the trade of America goes to ruin *because of her connection with Britain.* The next war may not turn out like the last, and should it not the advocates for reconciliation now will be wishing for separation then, because neutrality in that case would be a safer convoy than a man-of-war. Everything that is right or reasonable pleads for separation. The blood of the slain, the weeping voice of nature cries, "'Tis time to part." Even the distance at which the Almighty hath placed England and America is a strong and natural proof that the authority of the one over the other was never the design of Heaven. The time likewise at which the continent was discovered adds weight to the argument, and the manner in which it was peopled increases the force of it. The Reformation was preceded by the discovery of America: as if the Almighty graciously meant to open a sanctuary to the persecuted in future years, when home should afford neither friendship nor safety.

The authority of Great Britain over this continent is a form of government which sooner or later must have an end. And a serious mind can draw no true pleasure by looking forward under the painful and positive conviction that what he calls "the present constitution" is merely temporary. As parents, we can have no joy knowing that this government is not sufficiently lasting to insure anything which we may bequeath to posterity. And by a plain method of argument, as we are running the next generation into debt, we ought to do the work of it, otherwise we use them meanly and pitifully. In order to discover the line of our duty rightly, we should take our children in our hand, and fix our station a few years farther into life; that eminence will present a prospect which a few present fears and prejudices conceal from our sight.

Though I would carefully avoid giving unnecessary offense, yet I am inclined to believe that all those who espouse the doctrine of reconciliation may be included within the following descriptions. Interested men, who are not to be trusted, weak men who *cannot* see, prejudiced men who will not see, and a certain set of moderate men who think better of the European world than it deserves; and this last class, by an ill-judged deliberation, will be the cause of more calamities to this continent than all the other three.

It is the good fortune of many to live distant from the scene of present sorrow; the evil is not sufficiently brought to their doors to make them feel the precariousness with which all American property is possessed. But let our imaginations transport us a few moments to Boston; that seat of wretchedness will teach us wisdom, and instruct us forever to renounce a power in whom we can have no trust. The inhabitants of that unfortunate city, who but a few months ago were in ease and affluence, have now no other alternative than to stay and starve, or turn out to beg. Endangered by the fire of their friends if they continue within the city, and plundered by the soldiery if they leave it, in their present situation they are prisoners without the hope of redemption, and in a general attack for their relief they would be exposed to the fury of both armies.

Men of passive tempers look somewhat lightly over the offenses of Great Britain, and, still hoping for the best, are apt to call out, *Come, come, we shall be friends again for all this.* But examine the passions and feelings of mankind, bring the doctrine of reconciliation to the touchstone of nature, and then tell me whether you can hereafter love, honor, and faithfully serve the power that hath carried fire and sword into your land? If you cannot do all these, then are you only deceiving yourselves, and by your delay bringing ruin upon posterity. Your future connection with Britain, whom you can neither love nor honor, will be forced and unnatural, and being formed only on the plan of present convenience, will in a little time fall into a relapse more wretched than the first. But if you say, you can still pass the violations over, then I ask, Hath your house been burnt? Hath your property been destroyed before your face? Are your wife and children destitute of a bed to lie on, or bread to live on? Have you lost a parent or a child by their hands, and yourself the ruined and wretched survivor? If you have not, then are you not a judge of those who have. But if you have, and can still shake hands with the murderers, then are you unworthy the name of husband, father, friend, or lover, and whatever may be your rank or title in life, you have the heart of a coward, and the spirit of a sycophant.

This is not inflaming or exaggerating matters, but trying them by those feelings and affections which nature justifies, and without which we should be incapable of discharging the social duties of life, or enjoying the felicities of it. I mean not to exhibit horror for the purpose of provoking revenge, but to awaken us from fatal and unmanly slumbers, that we may pursue determinately some fixed object. 'Tis not in the power of Britain or of Europe to conquer America if she doth not conquer herself by delay and timidity. The present winter is worth an age if rightly employed, but if lost or neglected the whole continent will partake of the misfortune; and there is no punishment which that man doth not deserve, be he who, or what, or where he will, that may be the means of sacrificing a season so precious and useful.

'Tis repugnant to reason, to the universal order of things, to all examples from former ages, to suppose that this continent can long remain subject to any external power. The most sanguine in Britain doth not think so. The utmost stretch of human wisdom cannot, at this time, compass a plan, short of separation, which can promise the continent even a year's security. Reconciliation is *now* a fallacious dream. Nature hath deserted the connection, and art cannot supply her place. For, as Milton wisely expresses, "Never can true reconcilement grow where wounds of deadly hate have pierced so deep."

Every quiet method for peace hath been ineffectual. Our prayers have been rejected with disdain, and hath tended to convince us that nothing flatters vanity or confirms obstinacy in kings more than repeated petitioning— and nothing hath contributed more than that very measure to make the kings of Europe absolute. Witness Denmark and Sweden. Wherefore, since nothing but blows will do, for God's sake let us come to a final separation, and not leave the next generation to be cutting throats under the violated unmeaning names of parent and child. . . .

I am not induced by motives of pride, party, or resentment to espouse the doctrine of separation and independence; I am clearly, positively, and conscientiously persuaded that it is the true interest of this continent to be so; that everything short of *that* is mere patchwork, that it can afford no lasting felicity—that it is leaving the sword to our children, and shrinking back at a time when a little more, a little further, would have rendered this continent the glory of the earth.

As Britain hath not manifested the least inclination towards a compromise, we may be assured that no terms can be obtained worthy the acceptance of the continent, or any ways equal to the expense of blood and treasure we have been already put to.

The object contended for ought always to bear some just proportion to the expense. The removal of North,[33] or the whole detestable junto, is a matter unworthy the millions we have expended. A temporary stoppage of trade was an inconvenience which would have sufficiently balanced the repeal of all the acts complained of, had such repeals been obtained; but if the whole continent must take up arms, if every man must be a soldier, 'tis scarcely worth our while to fight against a contemptible ministry only. Dearly, dearly do we pay for the repeal of the acts, if that is all we fight for; for, in a just estimation, 'tis as great a folly to pay a Bunker-hill price for law as for land. As I have always considered the independency of this continent as an event which sooner or later must arrive, so from the late rapid progress of the continent to maturity, the event cannot be far off. Wherefore, on the breaking out of hostilities, it was not worth the while to have disputed a matter which time would have finally redressed, unless we meant to be in earnest; otherwise it is like wasting an estate on a suit at law, to regulate the trespasses of a tenant whose lease is just expiring. No man was a warmer wisher for a reconciliation than myself before the fatal nineteenth of April, 1775, but the moment the event of that day was made known, I rejected the hardened, sullen-tempered Pharaoh of England forever; and disdain the wretch that with the pretended title of Father of His people can unfeelingly hear of their slaughter, and composedly sleep with their blood upon his soul. . . .

Ye that tell us of harmony and reconciliation, can ye restore to us the time that is past? Can ye give to prostitution its former innocence? Neither can ye reconcile Britain and America. The last cord now is broken, the people of England are presenting addresses against us. There are injuries which nature cannot forgive; she would cease to be nature if she did. As well can the lover forgive the ravisher of his mistress, as the continent forgive the murders of Britain. The Almighty hath implanted in us these unextinguishable feelings for good and wise purposes. They are the guardians of his image in our hearts. They distinguish us from the herd of common animals. The social compact would dissolve and justice be extirpated from the earth, or have only a casual existence, were we callous to the touches of affection. The robber and the murderer would often escape unpunished did not the injuries which our tempers sustain provoke us into justice.

O ye that love mankind! Ye that dare oppose not only the tyranny but the tyrant, stand forth! Every spot of the old world is overrun with oppression. Freedom hath been hunted round the globe. Asia and Africa have long expelled her. Europe regards her like a stranger, and England hath given her warning to depart. O receive the fugitive, and prepare in time an asylum for mankind. . . .

To conclude, however strange it may appear to some, or however unwilling they may be to think so, matters not, but many strong and striking reasons may be given to show that nothing can settle our affairs so expeditiously as an open and determined declaration for independence. Some of which are:

First—It is the custom of nations, when any two are at war, for some other powers, not engaged in the quarrel, to step in as mediators and bring about the preliminaries of a peace. But while America calls herself the subject of Great Britain, no power, however well disposed she may be, can offer her mediation. Wherefore, in our present state we may quarrel on forever.

Secondly—It is unreasonable to suppose that France or Spain will give us any kind of assistance if we mean only to make use of that assistance for the purpose of repairing the breach, and strengthening the connection between Britain and America, because those powers would be sufferers by the consequences.

Thirdly—While we profess ourselves the subjects of Britain, we must, in the eyes of foreign nations, be considered as rebels. The precedent is somewhat dangerous to their peace, for men to be in arms under the name of subjects; we, on the spot, can solve the paradox, but to unite resistance and subjection requires an idea much too refined for common understanding.

Fourthly—Were a manifesto to be published and despatched to foreign courts setting forth the miseries we have endured and the peaceful methods which we have ineffectually used for redress; declaring at the same time that, not being able any longer to live happily or safely under the cruel disposition of the British court, we had been driven to the necessity of breaking off all connections with her; at the same time assuring all such courts of our peaceable disposition towards them, and of our desire of entering into trade with them: such a memorial would produce more good effects to this continent than if a ship were freighted with petitions to Britain.

Under our present denomination of British subjects, we can neither be received nor heard abroad; the custom of all courts is against us, and will be so until by an independence we take rank with other nations.

These proceedings may at first seem strange and difficult, but like all other steps which we have already passed over will in a little time become familiar and agreeable; and until an independence is declared, the continent will feel itself like a man who continues putting off some unpleasant business from day to day, yet knows it must be done, hates to set about it, wishes it over, and is continually haunted with the thoughts of its necessity.

THOMAS JEFFERSON

10

The Declaration of Independence (1776)

Though the delegates to the Second Continental Congress convening at the State House in Philadelphia on May 10, 1775, exhibited a spirit of unity and solidarity seldom before witnessed in colonial America, there seemed to be no general realization that a protracted war had already begun and certainly no consensus on the steps that the delegates themselves should take. Even against an increasingly ominous background which included Lexington, Concord, Bunker Hill, and the Montgomery-Arnold invasion of Canada, many still held out hope that reconciliation on some unspecified basis might yet be effected through the timely intervention of a benevolent king. It was precisely this hope that inspired John Dickinson's "olive branch" petition of July, 1775, expressing directly to George III the desire of Americans for the cessation of hostilities and the restoration of harmony. Slowly, however, yielding to the inevitability of events, the conservatives lost ground. In November news arrived that the king not only refused to receive the Dickinson petition but accompanied that refusal by declaring the colonies in a state of armed rebellion. Popular reaction followed apace. Each setback of the conservatives and moderates meant, of course, a corresponding increase in Congress in the influence of the independence-minded radicals. The publication of Paine's Common Sense *in January of 1776 increased this momentum, as did the discovery that the long-awaited peace commissioners, Richard and William Howe, offered not conciliation but a demand for unconditional submission.*

On June 7, 1776, Virginia's Richard Henry Lee introduced into Congress a series of three resolutions, the first of which declared that "these United Colonies are, and of right ought to be, free and independent States." Four days later, on June 11, a committee composed of Thomas Jefferson, John Adams, Benjamin Franklin, Roger Sherman, and Robert R. Livingston was appointed to "prepare a declaration to the effect of the said first resolution," should it, in fact, be adopted. To Thomas Jefferson (see pp. 37–38) fell the task of preparing the first draft, which, as amended by Adams and Franklin, was reported to Congress on June 28. Following the adoption of Lee's resolution on July 2, Congress turned its attention to Jefferson's declaration which it adopted and announced two days later, on July 4, 1776.

The rhetorical purpose of the Declaration of Independence *(a title, incidentally, which appears nowhere in the original document itself) is clear: to lay before "a candid" and startled world the moral and legal justification for independence and revolution. Jefferson's method is twofold. First, he constructs out of the materials of eighteenth-century liberal philosophy a theory of government that makes rebellion, under certain circumstances, not only justifiable but a necessary "duty." Second, having established the right of revolution, Jefferson then proceeds to show "cause" through a bill of particulars cataloging the "repeated Injuries and Usurpations" by means of which George III has attempted to establish "an absolute Tyranny" over the colonies.*

The text below follows the so-called Dunlap Broadside printed at Philadelphia by John Dunlap on the evening of July 4, 1776, rather than the more familiar parchment copy bearing the signers' autographs now on permanent display in the Library of Congress. The Dunlap Broadside, printed by order of Congress and under the supervision of the drafting committee, is generally regarded as the most authoritative version. The spelling, capitalization, and punctuation are those of the original.

In CONGRESS, July 4, 1776.
A DECLARATION
By the REPRESENTATIVES of the
UNITED STATES OF AMERICA,
In GENERAL CONGRESS assembled.

When in the Course of human Events, it becomes necessary for one People to dissolve the Political Bands which have connected them with another, and to assume among the Powers of the Earth, the separate and equal Station to which the Laws of Nature and of Nature's God entitle them, a decent Respect to the Opinions of Mankind requires that they should declare the causes which impel them to the Separation.

We hold these Truths to be self-evident, that all Men are created equal, that they are endowed by their Creator with certain unalienable Rights, that among these are Life, Liberty, and the Pursuit of Happiness—That to secure these Rights, Governments are instituted among Men, deriving their just Powers from the Consent of the Governed, that whenever any Form of Government becomes destructive of these Ends, it is the Right of the People to alter or to abolish it, and to institute new Government, laying its Foundation on such Principles, and organizing its Powers in such Form, as to them shall seem most likely to effect their Safety and Happiness. Prudence, indeed, will dictate that Governments long established should not be changed for light and transient Causes; and accordingly all Experience hath shewn, that Mankind are more disposed to suffer, while Evils are sufferable, than to right themselves by abolishing the Forms to which they are accustomed. But when a long Train of Abuses and Usurpations, pursuing invariably the same Object, evinces a Design to reduce them under absolute Despotism, it is their Right, it is their Duty, to throw off such Government, and to provide new Guards for their future Security. Such has been the patient Sufferance of these Colonies; and such is now the Necessity which constrains them to alter their former Systems of Government. The History of the present King of Great-Britain is a History of repeated Injuries and Usurpations, all having in direct Object the Establishment of an absolute Tyranny over these States. To prove this, let Facts be submitted to a candid World.

He has refused his Assent to Laws, the most wholesome and necessary for the public Good.

He has forbidden his Governors to pass Laws of immediate and pressing Importance, unless suspended in their Operation till his Assent should be obtained; and when so suspended, he has utterly neglected to attend to them

He has refused to pass other Laws for the Accommodation of large Districts of People, unless those People would relinquish the Right of Representation in the Legislature, a Right inestimable to them, and formidable to Tyrants only.

He has called together Legislative Bodies at Places unusual, uncomfortable and distant from the Depository of their public Records, for the sole Purpose of fatiguing them into Compliance with his Measures.

He has dissolved Representative Houses repeatedly, for opposing with manly Firmness his Invasions on the Rights of the People.

He has refused for a long Time, after such Dissolutions, to cause others to be elected; whereby the Legislative Powers, incapable of Annihilation, have returned to the People at large for their exercise; the State remaining in the mean time exposed to all the Dangers of Invasion from without, and Convulsions within.

He has endeavoured to prevent the Population of these States; for that Purpose obstructing the Laws for Naturalization of Foreigners; refusing to pass others to encourage their Migration hither, and raising the Conditions of new Appropriations of Lands.

He has obstructed the Administration of Justice, by refusing his Assent to Laws for establishing Judiciary Powers.

He has made Judges dependent on his Will alone, for the Tenure of their Offices, and the Amount and Payment of their Salaries.

He has erected a Multitude of new Offices, and sent hither Swarms of Officers to harrass our People, and eat out their Substance.

He has kept among us, in Times of Peace, Standing Armies, without the consent of our Legislatures.

He has affected to render the Military independent of and superior to the Civil Power.

He has combined with others to subject us to a Jurisdiction foreign to our Constitution, and unacknowledged by our Laws; giving his Assent to their Acts of pretended Legislation:

For quartering large Bodies of Armed Troops among us:

For protecting them, by a mock Trial, from Punishment for any Murders which they should commit on the Inhabitants of these States:

For cutting off our Trade with all Parts of the World:

For imposing Taxes on us without our Consent:

For depriving us, in many Cases, of the Benefits of Trial by Jury:

For transporting us beyond Seas to be tried for pretended Offences:

For abolishing the free System of English Laws in a neighbouring Province, establishing therein an arbitrary Government, and enlarging its Boundaries, so as to render it at once an Example and fit Instrument for introducing the same absolute Rule into these Colonies:

For taking away our Charters, abolishing our most valuable Laws, and altering fundamentally the Forms of our Governments:

For suspending our own Legislatures, and declaring themselves invested with Power to legislate for us in all Cases whatsoever.

He has abdicated Government here, by declaring us out of his Protection and waging War against us.

He has plundered our Seas, ravaged our Coasts, burnt our Towns, and destroyed the Lives of our People.

He is, at this Time, transporting large Armies of foreign Mercenaries to compleat the Works of Death, Desolation, and Tyranny, already begun with circumstances of Cruelty and Perfidy, scarcely paralleled in the most barbarous Ages, and totally unworthy the Head of a civilized Nation.

He has constrained our fellow Citizens taken Captive on the high Seas to bear Arms against their Country, to become the Executioners of their Friends and Brethren, or to fall themselves by their Hands.

He has excited domestic Insurrections amongst us, and has endeavoured to bring on the Inhabitants of our Frontiers, the merciless Indian Savages, whose known Rule of Warfare, is an undistinguished Destruction, of all Ages, Sexes and Conditions.

In every stage of these Oppressions we have Petitioned for Redress in the most humble Terms: Our repeated Petitions have been answered only by repeated Injury. A Prince, whose Character is thus marked by every act which may define a Tyrant, is unfit to be the Ruler of a free People.

Nor have we been wanting in Attentions to our British Brethren. We have warned them from Time to Time of Attempts by their Legislature to extend an unwarrantable Jurisdiction over us. We have reminded them of the Circumstances of our Emigration and Settlement here. We have appealed to their native Justice and Magnanimity, and we have conjured them by the Ties of our common Kindred to disavow these Usurpations, which, would inevitably interrupt our Connections and Correspondence. They too have been deaf to the Voice of Justice and of Consanguinity. We must, therefore, acquiesce in the Necessity, which denounces our Separation, and hold them, as we hold the rest of Mankind, Enemies in War, in Peace, Friends.

We, therefore, the Representatives of the UNITED STATES OF AMERICA, in GENERAL CONGRESS, Assembled, appealing to the Supreme Judge of the World for the Rectitude of our Intentions, do, in the Name, and by Authority of the good People of these Colonies, solemnly Publish and Declare, That these United Colonies are, and of Right ought to be, FREE AND INDEPENDENT STATES; that they are absolved from all Allegiance to the British Crown, and that all political Connection between them and the State of Great-Britain, is and ought to be totally dissolved; and that as FREE AND INDEPENDENT STATES, they have full Power to levy War, conclude Peace, contract Alliances, establish Commerce, and to do all other Acts and Things which INDEPENDENT STATES may of right do. And for the support of this Declaration, with a firm Reliance on the Protection of divine Providence, we mutually pledge to each other our Lives, our Fortunes, and our sacred Honor.

Signed by Order *and in* Behalf *of the* Congress,
JOHN HANCOCK, President.

Attest.

CHARLES THOMSON, Secretary.

11

SONGS AND BALLADS

Songs and ballads have always been an important index of popular feeling and mood at any given moment of time. The American Revolution was no exception. As the newspapers of the day attest, hardly an important event of the escalating dispute between England and America and then of the war itself was allowed to pass uncelebrated. Though the literary merit of such productions, on the whole, was not particularly high, and though the role they played as a shaper of public opinion was probably not very extensive, songs and ballads do provide one of the most interesting bodies of revolutionary literature. Characteristically, most of the extant songs and ballads of the Revolution were written to old tunes already familiar to colonial Americans, many of which were of course imported from England where balladry was a very important part of eighteenth-century popular culture.

Printed in the newspapers and circulated in broadside (sometimes with illustrations), most of the compositions were either anonymous or written by minor figures now long forgotten. But not exclusively so. Perhaps the most popular song of the day, "Liberty Song," was the work of John Dickinson, the author of the celebrated Letters from a Farmer in Pennsylvania. *Published in the* Boston Gazette *on July 18, 1768, and written to the tune of David Garrick's enormously popular "Hearts of Oak" (1759), Dickinson's song quickly became a model for imitation and even parody as the selections below indicate. Joseph Warren, Benjamin Franklin, and Thomas Paine also wrote songs during the prewar period.*

☆ ☆

The Liberty Song (1768)[34]

Come join hand in hand, brave Americans all,
And rouse your bold hearts at fair Liberty's call;
No tyrannous acts shall suppress your just claim,
Or stain with dishonor America's name.
  In freedom we're born, and in freedom we'll live;
    Our purses are ready,
    Steady, friends, steady,
  Not as *slaves,* but as *freemen* our money we"ll give.

Our worthy forefathers—let's give them a cheer—
To climates unknown did courageously steer;
Thro' oceans to deserts, for freedom they came,
And, dying, bequeath'd us their freedom and fame.

Their generous bosoms all dangers despis'd,
So highly, so wisely, their birthrights they priz'd;
We'll keep what they gave, we will piously keep,
Nor frustrate their toils on the land or the deep.

The Tree their own hands had to Liberty rear'd,
They lived to behold growing strong and rever'd;
With transport then cried, "Now our wishes we gain,
For our children shall gather the fruits of our pain."

How sweet are the labors that freemen endure,
That they shall enjoy all the profit, secure,—
No more such sweet labors Americans know,
If Britons shall reap what Americans sow.

Swarms of placemen and pensioners soon will appear,
Like locusts deforming the charms of the year:
Suns vainly will rise, showers vainly descend,
If we are to drudge for what others shall spend.

Then join hand in hand brave Americans all,
By uniting we stand, by dividing we fall;
In so righteous a cause let us hope to succeed,
For Heaven approves of each generous deed.

All ages shall speak with amaze and applause,
Of the courage we'll show in support of our laws;
To die we can bear, but to serve we disdain,
For shame is to freemen more dreadful than pain.

This bumper I crown for our sovereign's health,
And this for Britannia's glory and wealth;
That wealth, and that glory immortal may be,
If she is but just, and we are but free.
    In freedom we're born, etc.

A New Song (1774)[35]

As near beauteous Boston lying,
    On the gently swelling flood,
Without jack or pendant flying,
    Three ill-fated tea-ships rode.

Just as glorious Sol was setting,
    On the wharf a numerous crew,
Sons of freedom, fear forgetting,
    Suddenly appeared in view.

Armed with hammers, axe and chisels,
    Weapons new for warlike deed,
Towards the herbage-freighted vessels
    They approached with dreadful speed.

O'er their heads aloft in mid-sky,
    Three bright angel forms were seen;
This was Hampden, that was Sidney,[36]
    With fair Liberty between.

"Soon," they cried, "your foes you'll banish,
    Soon the triumph shall be won;
Scarce shall setting Phoebus vanish,
    Ere the deathless deed be done."

Quick as thought the ships were boarded,
    Hatches burst and chests displayed;
Axes, hammers help afforded;
    What a glorious crash they made.

Squash into the deep descended,
    Cursed weed of China's coast;
Thus at once our fears were ended;
    British rights shall ne'er be lost.

Captains! once more hoist your streamers,
    Spread your sails, and plough the wave;
Tell your masters they were dreamers,
    When they thought to cheat the brave.

Gage's Proclamation (1774)[37]

America! thou fractious nation,
Attend thy master's proclamation!
Tremble! for know, I, Thomas Gage,
Determin'd came the war to wage.

With the united powers sent forth
Of Bute, of Mansfield, and of North;[38]
To scourge your insolence, my choice,
While England mourns and Scots rejoice!

Bostonia first shall feel my power,
And gasping midst the dreadful shower
Of ministerial rage, shall cry,
Oh, save me, Bute! I yield! and die.

Then shall my thundering cannons rattle,
My hardy veterans march to battle
Against Virginia's hostile land,
To humble that rebellious band.

At my approach her trembling swains
Shall quit well-cultivated plains,
To seek the inhospitable wood;
Or try, like swine of old, the flood.

Rejoice! ye happy Scots rejoice!
Your voice lift up, a mighty voice,
The voice of gladness on each tongue,
The mighty praise of Bute be sung.

The praise of Mansfield, and of North,
Let next your hymns of joy set forth,
Nor shall the rapturous strain assuage,
Till sung's your own proclaiming Gage.

Whistle ye pipes! ye drones drone on.
Ye bellows blow! Virginia's won!
Your Gage has won Virginia's shore,
And Scotia's sons shall mourn no more.

Hail Middlesex! oh happy county!
Thou too shalt share thy master's bounty,
Thy sons obedient, naught shall fear,
Thy wives and widows drop no tear.

Thrice happy people, ne'er shall feel
The force of unrelenting steel;
What brute would give the ox a stroke
Who bends his neck to meet the yoke?

To Murray bend the humble knee;
He shall protect you under me;
His generous pen shall not be mute,
But sound your praise thro' Fox[39] to Bute.

By Scotchmen lov'd, by Scotchmen taught,
By all your country Scotchmen thought;
Fear Bute, fear Mansfield, North and me,
And be as blest as slaves can be.

Banks of the Dee (1775)[40]

'Twas winter, and blue Tory noses were freezing,
As they march'd o'er the land where they ought not to be;
The valiants complain'd at the fifers' curs'd wheezing,
And wish'd they'd remain'd on the banks of the Dee.
Lead on, thou paid captain! tramp on, thou proud minions!
Thy ranks, basest men, shall be strung like ripe onions,
For here thou hast found heads with warlike opinions,
On the shoulders of nobles who ne'er saw the Dee.

Prepare for war's conflict; or make preparation
For peace with the rebels, for they're brave and glee;
Keep mindful of dying, and leave the foul nation
That sends out its armies to brag and to flee.
Make haste, now, and leave us, thou miscreant Tories!
To Scotland repair! there court the sad houris,
And listen once more to their plaints and their stories
Concerning the "glory and pride of the Dee."

Be quiet and sober, secure and contented:
Upon your own land, be valiant and free;
Bless God, that the war is so nicely prevented,
And till the green fields on the banks of the Dee.
The Dee then will flow, all its beauty displaying,
The lads on its banks will again be seen playing,
And England thus honestly taxes defraying,
With natural drafts from the banks of the Dee.

Liberty Tree (1775)[41]

In a chariot of light from the regions of day,
    The Goddess of Liberty came;
Ten thousand celestials directed the way,
    And hither conducted the dame.
A fair budding branch from the gardens above,
    Where millions with millions agree,
She brought in her hand as a pledge of her love,
    And the plant she named *Liberty Tree.*

The celestial exotic struck deep in the ground,
    Like a native it flourish'd and bore;
The fame of its fruit drew the nations around,
    To seek out this peaceable shore.
Unmindful of names or distinctions they came,
    For freemen like brothers agree;
With one spirit endued, they one friendship pursued,
    And their temple was *Liberty Tree.*

Beneath this fair tree, like the patriarchs of old,
    Their bread in contentment they ate,
Unvex'd with the troubles of silver and gold,
    The cares of the grand and the great.
With timber and tar they Old England supply'd,
    And supported her pow'r on the sea;
Her battles they fought, without getting a groat,
    For the honor of *Liberty Tree.*

But hear, O ye swains, 'tis a tale most profane,
    How all the tyrannical powers,
Kings, Commons and Lords, are uniting amain,
    To cut down this guardian of ours;
From the east to the west blow the trumpet to arms,
    Thro' the land let the sound of it flee,
Let the far and the near all unite with a cheer,
    In defense of our *Liberty Tree.*

Part Two

The Literature of Revolution, 1775-83
The Patriots

JOHN TRUMBULL

12

from *M'Fingal* (1776, 1782)

Of all the verse satires written during the American Revolution, none is better better known than John Trumbull's mock epic M'Fingal, *published in two parts in 1776 and 1782.*[42] *It deserves its fame. Trumbull succeeded brilliantly in his immediate purpose of holding up to ridicule and contempt the point of view of the American Tory, and in the process produced one of the few genuinely noteworthy works of early American literature. In four cantos, totaling slightly more than 3,000 iambic tetrameter lines,* M'Fingal *tells the story of a pompous and bombastic Massachusetts squire and his futile attempts to persuade his neighbors to submit to the authority of Parliament and George III. Not only is Squire M'Fingal bested in debate by his Whig opponent Honorius in cantos 1 and 2 (M'Fingal's self-condemnatory and self-satirizing speeches only serve, in fact, to caricature M'Fingal himself); but his efforts to remove the local Liberty Pole in canto 3 end with the voluble squire being tarred, feathered, and ingloriously paraded through the village by his patriotic townsmen. In canto 4 the clandestine meeting of Squire M'Fingal and his fellow Tories gives way to a lengthy vision of the course of the Revolution and the rising glory of America, after which M'Fingal makes good his escape, leaving "his constituents in the lurch." Trumbull's rollicking humor and burlesque, in which he manages, as he afterwards noted, to satirize "the follies and extravagancies of his countrymen, as well as of their enemies," is unsurpassed in revolutionary verse, though it is true that much of the poem's popularity and reputation came after 1782 and its appearance in complete and final form. Despite the surface humor of the poem, its underlying issues are serious ones; they are precisely the issues that divided colonial Americans in 1775–76 and during the war that followed.*

John Trumbull (1750–1831) was born in Waterbury, Connecticut, into a family of deep-rooted New Englanders. Precocious as a child (he learned to read by the age of two, and had read the Bible by four), Trumbull passed the entrance examinations for Yale College at the age of seven, though his clergyman father wisely held him back from college for another six years. Trumbull received his B.A. in 1767, an M.A. in 1770, and then remained at Yale for three years as a tutor, during which period he wrote and published The Progress of Dullness *(1772–73), a verse satire on contemporary collegiate education. Admitted to the Connecticut bar in November, 1773, Trumbull then entered the Boston law office of John Adams, where he unavoidably became swept up in revolutionary politics. During his year in Boston Trumbull published a number of poems on political subjects, including "An Elegy on the Times" (1774), occasioned by the Boston Port Bill. Trumbull returned to Connecticut in 1774, where he was to practice law for the next half century, serving his state as a judge on the supreme court and the supreme court of errors. Cautious and conservative by nature, Trumbull was only mildly patriotic in comparison to a Thomas Paine or a Philip Freneau (as* M'Fingal *shows, Trumbull instinctively feared lest freedom become a cloak for license). Following the Revolution he became a member of the Hartford circle of writers known as the Connecticut Wits, who mixed verse, Federalist politics, and religious conservatism in an attempt to check and turn back the ideas associated with Jeffersonian liberalism.*

The Liberty Pole

> Now warm with ministerial ire,
> Fierce sallied forth our loyal 'Squire,
> And on his striding steps attends
> His desperate clan of Tory friends.
> When sudden met his wrathful eye
> A pole ascending through the sky,
> Which numerous throngs of Whiggish race
> Were raising in the marketplace.
> Not higher schoolboys's kites aspire,
> Or royal mast, or country spire;
> Like spears at Brobdignagian tilting,
> Or Satan's walking-staff in Milton.

And on its top, the flag unfurl'd
Waved triumph o'er the gazing world,
Inscribed with inconsistent types
Of Liberty and thirteen stripes.
Beneath, the crowd without delay
The dedication rites essay,
And gladly pay, in ancient fashion,
The ceremonies of libation;
While briskly to each patriot lip
Walks eager round the inspiring flip:[43]
Delicious draught! whose powers inherit
The quintessence of public spirit;
Which whoso tastes, perceives his mind
To nobler politics refined;
Or roused to martial controversy,
As from transforming cups of Circe;
Or warm'd with Homer's nectar'd liquor,
That fill'd the veins of gods with ichor.
At hand for new supplies in store,
The tavern opes its friendly door,
Whence to and fro the waiters run,
Like bucket men at fires in town.
Then with three shouts that tore the sky,
'Tis consecrate to Liberty
To guard it from th' attacks of Tories,
A grand committee call'd of four is;
Who foremost on the patriot spot,
Had brought the flip and paid the shot.
    By this, M'Fingal with his train
Advanced upon th' adjacent plain,
And full with loyalty possesst,
Pour'd forth the zeal, that fired his breast.
    "What mad-brain'd rebel gave commission
To raise this Maypole of sedition?
Like Babel, rear'd by bawling throngs,
With like confusion too of tongues,
To point at heaven and summon down
The thunders of the British crown?
Say, will this paltry pole secure
Your forfeit heads from Gage's power? . . .
    "Ye dupes to every factious rogue
And tavern-prating demagogue,

105

Whose tongue bur rings, with sound more full,
On th' empty drumhead of his skull;
Behold you not what noisy fools
Use you, worse simpletons, for tools?
For Liberty, in your own by-sense,
Is but for crimes a patent license,
To break of law th' Egyptian yoke,
And throw the world in common stock;
Reduce all grievances and ills
To Magna Charta of your wills;
Establish cheats and frauds and nonsense,
Framed to the model of your conscience;
Cry justice down, as out of fashion,
And fix its scale of depreciation;
Defy all creditors to trouble ye,
And keep new years of Jewish jubilee;
Drive judges out, like Aaron's calves,
By jurisdiction of white staves,
And make the bar and bench and steeple
Submit t' our sovereign lord, the People;
By plunder rise to power and glory,
And brand all property as Tory;
Expose all wares to lawful seizures
By mobbers or monopolizers;
Break heads and windows and the peace
For your own interest and increase;
Dispute and pray and fight and groan
For public good, and mean your own;
Prevent the law by fierce attacks
From quitting scores upon your backs;
Lay your old dread, the gallows, low,
And seize the stocks, your ancient foe,
And turn them to convenient engines
To wreak your patriotic vengeance;
While all, your rights who understand,
Confess them in their owner's hand;
And when by clamors and confusions,
Your freedom's grown a public nuisance,
Cry 'Liberty,' with powerful yearning,
As he does 'Fire!' whose house is burning;
Though he already has much more
Than he can find occasion for.

While every clown that tills the plains,
Though bankrupt in estate and brains,
By this new light transform'd to traitor,
Forsakes his plow to turn dictator,
Starts an haranguing chief of Whigs,
And drags you by the ears, like pigs.
All bluster, arm'd with factious license,
Newborn at once to politicians.
Each leather-apron'd dunce, grown wise,
Presents his forward face t' advise,
And tatter'd legislators meet,
From every workshop through the street.
His goose the tailor finds no use in,
To patch and turn the Constitution;
The blacksmith comes with sledge and grate
To iron-bind the wheels of state;
The quack forbears his patients' souse,
To purge the Council and the House;
The tinker quits his moulds and doxies,
To cast assemblymen and proxies.
From dunghills deep of blackest hue,
Your dirt-bred patriots spring to view,
To wealth and power and honors rise,
Like new-wing'd maggots changed to flies,
And fluttering round in high parade,
Strut in the robe, or gay cockade. . . .
For in this ferment of the stream
The dregs have work'd up to the brim,
And by the rule of topsy-turvies,
The scum stands foaming on the surface.
You've caused your pyramid t' ascend,
And set it on the little end.
Like Hudibras,[44] your empire's made,
Whose crupper had o'ertopp'd his head.
You've push'd and turn'd the whole world up-
Side down, and got yourselves at top,
While all the great ones of your state
Are crush'd beneath the popular weight;
Nor can you boast, this present hour,
The shadow of the form of power.
For what's your Congress or its end?
A power t' advise and recommend;

To call forth troops, adjust your quotas—
And yet no soul is bound to notice. . . .
Yet with republics to dismay us,
You've call'd up Anarchy from chaos,
With all the followers of her school,
Uproar and Rage and wild Misrule:
For whom this rout of Whigs distracted,
And ravings dire of every crack'd head;
These new-cast legislative engines
Of country meetings and conventions:
Committees vile of correspondence,
And mobs, whose tricks have almost undone 's:
While reason fails to check your course,
And Loyalty's kick'd out of doors,
And Folly, like inviting landlord,
Hoists on your poles her royal standard;
While the king's friends, in doleful dumps,
Have worn their courage to the stumps,
And leaving George in sad disaster,
Most sinfully deny their master.
What furies raged when you, in sea,
In shape of Indians, drown'd the tea;[45]
When your gay sparks, fatigued to watch it,
Assumed the moccasin and hatchet,
With wampum'd blankets hid their laces,
And like their sweethearts, primed their faces:
While not a redcoat dared oppose,
And scarce a Tory show'd his nose;
While Hutchinson, for sure retreat,
Maneuvered to his country seat,
And thence affrighted, in the suds,
Stole off bareheaded through the woods.[46]
    "Have you not roused your mobs to join,
And make mandamus men resign,
Call'd forth each duffle-dressed curmudgeon
And dirty trousers and white bludgeon,
Forced all our councils through the land
To yield their necks at your command;
While paleness marks their late disgraces,
Through all their rueful length of faces?
    Have you not caused as woeful work
In our good city of New York,

When all the rabble, well cockaded,
In triumph through the streets paraded,
And mobb'd the Tories, scared their spouses,
And ransack'd all the custom houses:
Made such a tumult, bluster, jarring,
That mid the clash of tempests warring,
Smith's weathercock, in veers forlorn,
Could hardly tell which way to turn?[47]
Burn'd effigies of higher powers
Contrived in planetary hours;
As witches with clay images
Destroy or torture whom they please:
Till fired with rage, th' ungrateful club
Spared not your best friend, Beelzebub,
O'erlook'd his favors, and forgot
The reverence due his cloven foot,
And in the selfsame furnace frying,
Stew'd him, and North, and Bute, and Tryon?[48]
Did you not, in as vile and shallow way,
Fright our poor Philadelphian, Galloway,
Your Congress, when the loyal ribald
Belied, berated, and bescribbled?
What ropes and halters did you send,
Terrific emblems of his end,[49]
Till lest he'd hang in more than effigy,
Fled in a fog the trembling refugee? . . ."

    This said, our Squire, yet undismay'd,
Call'd forth the constable to aid,
And bade him read, in nearer station,
The riot act and proclamation.
He swift, advancing to the ring,
Began, "Our Sovereign Lord, the King"—
When thousand clam'rous tongues he hears,
And clubs and stones assail his ears.
To fly was vain; to fight was idle;
By foes encompass'd in the middle,
His hope in stratagems he found,
And fell right craftily to ground;
Then crept to seek a hiding place,
'Twas all he could, beneath a brace;
Where soon the conqu'ring crew espied him,
And where he lurk'd, they caught and tied him.

At once with resolution fatal,
Both Whigs and Tories rush'd to battle.
Instead of weapons, either band
Seized on such arms as came to hand.
And as famed Ovid paints th' adventures
Of wrangling Lapithae and Centaurs,
Who at their feast, by Bacchus led,
Threw bottles at each other's head;
And these arms failing in their scuffles,
Attack'd with andirons, tongs, and shovels:
So clubs and billets, staves, and stones
Met fierce, encountering every sconce,
And cover'd o'er with knobs and pains
Each void receptacle for brains;
Their clamors rend the skies around,
The hills rebellow to the sound;
And many a groan increas'd the din
From batter'd nose and broken shin.
M'Fingal, rising at the word,
Drew forth his old militia sword;
Thrice cried "King George," as erst in distress
Knights of romance invoked a mistress;
And brandishing the blade in air,
Struck terror through th' opposing war.
The Whigs, unsafe within the wind
Of such commotion, shrunk behind.
With whirling steel around address'd,
Fierce through their thickest throng he press'd
(Who roll'd on either side in arch,
Like Red Sea waves in Israel's march),
And like a meteor rushing through,
Struck on their pole a vengeful blow.
Around, the Whigs, of clubs and stones
Discharged whole vollies, in platoons,
That o'er in whistling fury fly;
But not a foe dares venture nigh.
And now perhaps with glory crown'd
Our 'Squire had fell'd the pole to ground,
Had not some pow'r, a Whig at heart,
Descended down and took their part
(Whether 'twere Pallas, Mars, or Iris,
'Tis scarce worth while to make inquiries),

Who at the nick of time alarming,
Assumed the solemn form of chairman,
Address'd a Whig, in every scene
The stoutest wrestler on the green,
And pointed where the spade was found,
Late used to set their pole in ground,
And urged, with equal arms and might,
To dare our 'Squire to single fight.
The Whig thus arm'd, untaught to yield,
Advanced tremendous to the field:
Nor did M'Fingal shun the foe,
But stood to brave the desp'rate blow;
While all the party gazed, suspended
To see the deadly combat ended;
And Jove in equal balance weigh'd
The sword against the brandish'd spade.
He weigh'd; but lighter than a dream,
The sword flew up, and kick'd the beam.
Our 'Squire on tiptoe rising fair
Lifts high a noble stroke in air,
Which hung not, but like dreadful engines,
Descended on his foe in vengeance,
But ah! in danger, with dishonor
The sword perfidious fails its owner;
That sword, which oft had stood its ground,
By huge trainbands encircled round;
And on the bench, with blade right royal,
Had won the day at many a trial,
Of stones and clubs had braved th' alarms,
Shrunk from these new Vulcanian arms.
The spade so temper'd from the sledge,
Nor keen nor solid harm'd its edge,
Now met it, from his arm of might,
Descending with steep force to smite;
The blade snapp'd short—and from his hand,
With rust embrown'd the glittering sand.
Swift turn'd M'Fingal at the view,
And call'd to aid th' attendant crew,
In vain; the Tories all had run,
When scarce the fight was well begun. . . .
At once the crew, at this dread crisis,
Fall on, and bind him, ere he rises;

And with loud shouts and joyful soul,
Conduct him prisoner to the pole.
When now the mob in lucky hour
Had got their en'mies in their power,
They first proceed by grave command,
To take the constable in hand.
Then from the pole's sublimest top
The active crew let down the rope,
At once its other end in haste bind,
And make it fast upon his waistband;
Till like the earth, as stretch'd on tenter,
He hung self-balanced on his center.
Then upwards, all hands hoisting sail,
They swung him like a keg of ale,
Till to the pinnacle in height
He vaulted like balloon or kite.
As Socrates of old at first did
To aid philosophy get hoisted,
And found his thoughts flow strangely clear,
Swung in a basket in mid-air:
Our culprit thus, in purer sky,
With like advantage raised his eye,
And looking forth in prospect wide,
His Tory errors clearly spied,
And from his elevated station,
With bawling voice began addressing.

    "Good gentlemen and friends and kin,
For heaven's sake hear, if not for mine!
I here renounce the pope, the Turks,
The king, the devil and all their works;
And will, set me but once at ease,
Turn Whig or Christian, what you please;
And always mind your rules so justly,
Should I live long as old Methus'lah,
I'll never join in British rage,
Nor help Lord North nor Gen'ral Gage;
Nor lift my gun in future fights,
Nor take away your charter rights;
Nor overcome your new-raised levies,
Destroy your towns, nor burn your navies;
Nor cut your poles down while I've breath,
Though raised more thick than hatchet teeth:

But leave King George and all his elves
To do their conqu'ring work themselves."
  This said, they lower'd him down in state,
Spread at all points, like falling cat;
But took a vote first on the question,
That they'd accept this full confession,
And to their fellowship and favor
Restore him on his good behavior.
  Not so our 'Squire submits to rule.
But stood, heroic as a mule.
"You'll find it all in vain," quoth he,
"To play your rebel tricks on me.
All punishments the world can render,
Save only to provoke th' offender;
The will gains strength from treatment horrid,
As hides grow harder when they're curried.
No man e'er felt the halter draw,
With good opinion of the law;
Or held in method orthodox
His love of justice in the stocks:
Or fail'd to lose by sheriff's shears
At once his loyalty and ears. . . .
Has Rivington[50] in dread of stripes,
Ceased lying since you stole his types?
And can you think my faith will alter,
By tarring, whipping or the halter?
I'll stand the worst; for recompense
I trust King George and Providence.
And when with conquest gain'd I come,
Array'd in law and terror home,
Ye'll rue this inauspicious morn,
And curse the day, when ye were born,
In Job's high style of imprecations,
With all his plagues, without his patience."
  Meanwhile beside the pole, the guard
A bench of justice had prepared,
Where sitting round in awful sort
The grand committee hold their court;
While all the crew, in silent awe,
Wait from their lips the lore of law.
Few moments with deliberation
They hold the solemn consultation;

When soon in judgment all agree,
And clerk proclaims the dread decree;
"That 'Squire M'Fingal having grown
The vilest Tory in the town,
And now in full examination
Convicted by his own confession,
Finding no tokens of repentance,
This court proceeds to render sentence:
That first the mob slipknot single
Tie round the neck of said M'Fingal,
And in due form do tar him next,
And feather, as the law directs;
Then through the town attendant ride him
In cart with constable beside him,
And having held him up to shame,
Bring to the pole, from whence he came."
    Forthwith the crowd proceed to deck
With halter'd noose M'Fingal's neck,
While he in peril of his soul
Stood tied half-hanging to the pole;
Then lifting high the ponderous jar,
Pour'd o'er his head the smoking tar.
With less profusion once was spread
Oil on the Jewish monarch's head,
That down his beard and vestments ran,
And cover'd all his outward man. . . .
    Then on the fatal cart, in state
They raised our grand Duumvirate.
And as at Rome a like committee,
Who found an owl within their city,
With solemn rites and grave processions
At every shrine perform'd lustrations;
And lest infection might take place
From such grim fowl with feather'd face,
All Rome attends him through the street
In triumph to his country seat:
With like devotion all the choir
Paraded round our awful 'Squire;
In front the martial music comes
Of horns and fiddles, fifes and drums,
With jingling sound of carriage bells,
And treble creak of rusted wheels.

Behind, the crowd, in lengthen'd row
With proud procession, closed the show.
And at fit periods every throat
Combined in universal shout;
And hail'd great Liberty in chorus.
Or bawl'd "confusion to the Tories."
Not louder storm the welkin braves
From clamors of conflicting waves;
Less dire in Lybian wilds the noise
When rav'ning lions lift their voice;
Or triumphs at town meetings made,
On passing votes to regulate trade.

Thus having borne them round the town,
Last at the pole they set them down;
And to the tavern take their way
To end in mirth the festal day.

And now the mob, dispersed and gone,
Left 'Squire and constable alone. . . .
"Ah, Mr. Constable, in vain
We strive 'gainst wind and tide and rain!
Behold my doom! this feathery omen
Portends what dismal times are coming.
Now future scenes, before my eyes,
And second-sighted forms arise.
I hear a voice, that calls away,
And cries 'The Whigs will win the day.'
My beck'ning genius gives command,
And bids me fly the fatal land;
Where changing name and constitution,
Rebellion turns to revolution,
While loyalty, oppress'd in tears,
Stands trembling for its neck and ears.

"Go, summon all our brethren, greeting,
To muster at our usual meeting;
There my prophetic voice shall warn 'em
Of all things future that concern 'em,
And scenes disclose on which, my friend,
Their conduct and their lives depend.
There!—but first 'tis more of use
From this vile pole to set me loose;
Then go with cautious steps and steady,
While I steer home and make all ready. . . ."

13

The Battle of Bunkers-Hill
(1776)

Hugh Henry Brackenridge (1748–1816), author of The Battle of Bunkers-Hill, *was born in Scotland and raised on a Pennsylvania farm where his family settled following their emigration to America in 1753. Brackenridge was educated at the College of New Jersey (Princeton), then, under the presidency of John Witherspoon, a center of liberal Whig political philosophy. His college friends included James Madison and Philip Freneau, and with the latter Brackenridge collaborated on a long patriotic poem "The Rising Glory of America," recited at their commencement exercises in 1771. Though he intended to stay on at the college to study for the ministry, an attractive offer to head an academy in Somerset County, Maryland, intervened, and it was there, in late 1775, that Brackenridge wrote* The Battle of Bunkers-Hill.

The following year, 1776, Brackenridge gave up his teaching to serve with the American army in the capacity of chaplain (though he had never been ordained). It was during this period that Brackenridge wrote and published his second revolutionary play, The Death of General Montgomery, *at the Siege of Quebec (1777). In 1778, intent on pursuing a literary career, Brackenridge went to Philadelphia; there he founded and edited the* United States Magazine, *a venture of less than six months. He then returned to Maryland to study law. In 1781 he established a practice at Pittsburgh, quickly rising to legal prominence, especially after 1800 when he became a justice on the Pennsylvania supreme court. But Brackenridge never gave up his literary aspirations. Between 1792 and 1815 he published and republished with additions his sprawling satiric novel* Modern Chivalry, *which in picaresque fashion recounts the many adventures of Captain John Ferrago and his servant Teague O'Regan through contemporary Pennsylvania.*

The Battle of Bunkers-Hill, *published anonymously at Philadelphia in 1776, was apparently written, or so its dedicatory note indicates, as "an Exercise in Oratory" for Brackenridge's academy students, rather than as a drama to be staged. That it was intended to be read rather than acted is borne out by the play itself, for* The Battle of Bunkers-Hill *is devoid of action (all blood is shed offstage) and consists of set speeches, delivered in a tone of high seriousness by the major participants. Its controlling theme is patriotism; its argument, that the American defeat at Bunker Hill was in fact a moral victory that served to demonstrate to all the world the courage and fighting ability of the American soldier. As Sir William Howe declares in act 5,*

> *E'en in an enemy I honor worth,*
> *And valor eminent. The vanquish'd foe*
> *In feats of prowess show their ancestry*
> *And speak their birth legitimate....*

Interestingly enough, there are, with the exception of Gage, who is pictured as a cowardly "old drinking man," no real villains in Brackenridge's verse drama. One must remember, however, that in 1775 Gage alone was a familiar figure to Americans: Howe, Clinton, and Burgoyne remained, as yet, largely unknown quantities. Within two years, however, all the British principals would be accorded much rougher treatment, especially John Burgoyne, who (as Livingston's "Proclamation" illustrates) was to become a special target of American ridicule and satire.

Dramatis Personae[51]

Warren
Putnam   } *American officers*
Gardner

Gage
Howe
Burgoyne } *British officers*
Clinton
Lord Pigot

Sherwin, *Aide-de-camp to General Howe*

Soldiers, etc.

Act I

Camp at Cambridge

Enter WARREN, PUTNAM, *and* GARDNER.

Warren

    Why thus, brave Putnam, shall we still encamp
Inactive here; and with this gentle flood,
By Cambridge murmuring, mix briny tears?
Salt tears of grief by many a parent shed,
For sons detain'd, and tender innocents
In yon fair city famishing for bread;
For not fond mothers or their weeping babes
Can move the hard heart of relentless Gage.
Perfidious man! Who pledg'd his oath so late,
And word of honor to those patriots
Yet in his power, that yielding him their arms,
They should receive permission to depart,
And join once more their valiant countrymen;
But now detains as hostages these men
In low damp dungeons, and in gaols chain'd down
While grief and famine on their vitals prey.
Say, noble Putnam, shall we hear of this,
And let our idle swords rust in the sheath,
While slaves of royal power impeach our worth
As vain, and call our patience cowardice?

Putnam

    Not less, bold Warren, have I felt the pangs
Of woe severe in this calamity:
And could I with my life redeem the times,
The richest blood that circles round my heart
Should hastily be shed. But what avails
The genuine flame and vigor of the soul,
When nature's self, and all the strength of art,
Opposes every effort in our power?
These sons of slavery dare not advance,
And meet in equal fight our hostile arms.
For yet they well remember Lexington,
And what they suffer'd on that rueful day,
When wantoning in savage rage, they march'd
Onward to Concord, in a firm array,
Mock music playing, and the ample flag
Of tyranny display'd; but with dire loss
And infamy drove back, they gain'd the town,
And under cover of their ships of war,
Retir'd, confounded and dismay'd. No more
In mirthful mood to combat us, or mix
Their jocund music with the sounds of war.
To tempt no more unequal fight with men,
Who to oppose dire arbitrary sway,
Have grasp'd the sword; and resolute to brave
Death in a thousand dreary shapes, can know,
In the warm breast, no sentiment of fear.

Gardner

    The free born spirit of immortal fire
Is stranger to ignoble deeds, and shuns
The name of cowardice. But well thy mind,
Sage and matur'd by long experience, weighs
The perilous attempt to storm the town,
And rescue thence the suff'ring citizens.
For but one pass to that peninsula
On which the city stands, on all sides barr'd.
And here what numbers can supply the rage
Of the all devouring, deep mouth'd cannon, plac'd
On many a strong redoubt; while on each side
The ships of war, moor'd in the winding bay,

Can sweep ten thousand from the level beach,
"And render all access impregnable."

Warren

    True, valiant Gardner, the attempt is vain
To force that entrance to the sea-girt town;
Which while we hop'd for peace, and in that view
Kept back our swords, we saw them fortify.
But what if haply, with a chosen few
Led through the midnight shades, yon heights were gain'd,
And that contiguous hill, whose grassy foot
By Mystic's gentle tide is wash'd. Here rais'd,
Strong batt'ries jutting o'er the level sea
With everlasting thunder shall annoy
Their navy far beneath; and in some lucky hour,
When dubious darkness on the land is spread,
A chosen band may pierce their sep'rate fleet,
And in swift boats across the narrow tide
Pour like a flame on their unguarded ranks,
And wither them, as when an angel smote
The Assyrian camp. The proud Sennacherib,
With impious rage, against the hill of God,
Blasphem'd. Low humbl'd, when the dawning light
Saw all his host dead men. So yet I trust,
The God of battles will avouch our cause,
And those proud champions of despotic power
Who turn our fasting to their mirth, and mock
Our prayers, naming us the saints, shall yet
Repay with blood the tears and agonies
Of tender mothers, and their infant babes,
Shut up in Boston.

Putnam

                Heaven, smile on us then,
And favor this attempt. Now from our troops
Seven hundred gallant men, and skill'd in arms,
With speed select, choice spirits of the war.
By you led on, brave Gardner, to the heights,
Ere yet the morn with dawning light breaks forth,
Intrench on Bunkers-Hill; and when the day
First o'er the hilltop rises, we shall join

United arms against the assailing foe,
Should they attempt to cross the narrow tide
In deep battalion to regain the hill.

Gardner

    The thought is perilous, and many men,
In this bold enterprise, must strew the ground.
But since we combat in the cause of God,
I draw my sword, nor shall the sheath again
Receive the shining blade till on the heights
Of Charlestown, and Bunker's pleasant Hill,
It drinks the blood of many a warrior slain.

Act II

Boston

Enter GAGE, HOWE, *and* BURGOYNE

Burgoyne

    How long, brave gen'rals, shall the rebel foe,
In vain arrangements and mock siege, display
Their haughty insolence? Shall in this town
So many thousands of Britannia's troops,
With watch incessant, and sore toil oppress'd,
Remain besieg'd? A vet'ran army pent
In the enclosure of so small a space
By a disorder'd herd untaught, unofficer'd
Let not, sweet Heav'n, the envious mouth of fame,
With breath malignant, o'er the Atlantic wave
Bear this to Europe's shores, or tell to France
Or haughty Spain of Lexington's retreat.
Who could have thought it, in the womb of time,
That British soldiers in this latter age,
Beat back by peasants and in flight disgrac'd,
Could tamely brook the base discomfiture;
Nor sallying out, with spirit reassum'd,
Exact due tribute of their victory?
Drive back the foe, to Allegheny hills,
In woody valleys, or on mountain tops,
To mix with wolves and kindred savages?

Gage

   This mighty paradox will soon dissolve.
Hear first, Burgoyne, the valor of these men,
Fir'd with the zeal of fiercest liberty,
No fear of death, so terrible to all,
Can stop their rage. Gray-headed clergymen,
With holy Bible and continual prayer,
Bear up their fortitude—and talk of Heav'n,
And tell them, that sweet soul who dies in battle
Shall walk with spirits of the just. These words
Add wings to native rage, and hurry them
Impetuous to war. Nor yet in arms
Unpractised. The day of Lexington
A sad conviction gave our soldiery,
That these Americans were not that herd
And rout ungovern'd which we painted them.

Howe

   Not strange to your maturer thought, Burgoyne,
This matter will appear. A people brave,
Who never yet of luxury or soft
Delights, effeminate and false, have tasted.
But, through hate of chains and slav'ry, suppos'd,
Forsake their mountaintops and rush to arms.
Oft have I heard their valor published:
Their perseverance, and untamable
Fierce mind, when late they fought with us, and drove
The French, encroaching on their settlements,
Back to their frozen lakes. Or when with us
On Cape Breton they stormed Louisburg.
With us in Canada they took Quebec;
And at the Havana,[52] these New England men,
Led on by Putnam, acted gallantly.
I had a brother once, who in that war
With fame commanded them, and when he fell,
Not unlamented; for these warriors,
So brave themselves, and sensible of merit,
Erected him a costly monument;
And much it grieves me that I draw my sword
For this late insurrection and revolt,
To chastise them. Would to Almighty God

The task unnatural had been assign'd
Elsewhere. But since by Heaven determined,
Let's on, and wipe the day of Lexington,
Thus soil'd, quite from our soldiers' memories.
This reinforcement, which with us have fail'd,
In many a transport from Britannia's shores
Will give new vigor to the royal arms,
And crush rebellion in its infancy.
Let's on, and from this siege calamitous
Assert our liberty; nay, rather die,
Transfix'd in battle, by their bayonets,
Than thus remain, the scoff and ridicule
Of gibing wits and paltry gazetteers,
On this, their madding continent, who cry,
Where is the British valor: that renown
Which spoke in thunder to the Gallic shores?
That spirit is evaporate, that fire,
Which erst distinguish'd them, that flame
And gen'rous energy of soul which fill'd
Their Henrys, Edwards, thunderbolts of war;
Their Hampdens, Marlboroughs, and the immortal Wolfe[53]
On the Abraham heights victorious.
Britannia's genius is unfortunate,
And flags, say they, when royal tyranny
Directs her arms. This let us then disprove
In combat speedily, and take from them
The wantonness of this fell pride and boasting.

Gage

Tho' much I dread the issue of the attempt,
So full of hazard and advent'rous spirit;
Yet since your judgment, and high skill in arms,
From full experience boldly prompts you on,
I give my voice, and when one day hath pass'd,
In whose swift hours may be wrought, highly up,
The resolution of the soldiery,
With soothing words, and ample promises
Of rich rewards in lands and settlements,
From the confiscate property throughout
These rebel colonies, at length subdu'd;
Then march we forth, beat up their drowsy camp,

And with the sun to this safe capital
Return, rich with the triumphs of the war.
And be our plan that which brave Haldiman,
Ere yet recall'd, advis'd to us.[54] Let first
Brave Howe and Clinton on that western point
Land with the transports, and meantime Burgoyne,
With the artillery, pour sharp cannonade
Along the neck, and sweep the beachy plain
Which lies to Roxborough, where yon western stream,
Flowing from Cambridge, mixes with the Bay.
Thus, these Americans shall learn to dread
The force of discipline, and skill in arms.

Act III

Bunkers-Hill

Enter GARDNER, *with seven hundred men*

Gardner

   This is the hill, brave countrymen, whose brow
We mean to fortify. A strong redoubt,
With salient angles and embrasures deep
Be speedily thrown up. Let each himself,
Not undeserving, of our choice approve,
For out of thousands I have challeng'd you
To this bold enterprise as men of might
And valor eminent, and such this day,
I trust, will honor you. Let each his spade
And pickaxe, vig'rously, in this hard soil
Where I have laid the curved line, exert.
For now the morning star, bright Lucifer,
Peers on the firmament, and soon the day,
Flush'd with the golden sun, shall visit us.
Then gallant countrymen, should faithless Gage
Pour forth his lean and half-starv'd myrmidons,
We'll make them taste our cartridges, and know
What rugged steel our bayonets are made of;
Or if o'ercharg'd with numbers, bravely fall,
Like those three hundred at Thermopylae,
And give our country credit in our deaths.

Act IV

SCENE I. Boston

GAGE, *solus*

Oh, sweet tranquillity and peace of soul
That in the bosom of the cottager
Tak'st up thy residence—cannot the beams
Of royal sunshine call thee to my breast?
Fair honor waits on thee, renown abroad,
And high dominion o'er this continent,
Soon as the spirit of rebellious war
Is scourg'd into obedience. Why then, ye gods,
This inward gnawing and remorse of thought,
For perfidy and breach of promises!
Why should the spouse, or weeping infant babe,
Or meek-ey'd virgin with her sallow cheek,
The rose by famine wither'd out of it;
Or why the father, or his youthful son,
By me detain'd from all their relatives
And in low dungeons and in gaols chain'd down,
Affect my spirit, when the mighty cause
Of George and Britain, is endangered?
For nobly struggling in the cause of kings,
We claim the high, the just prerogative,
To rule mankind, and with an iron rod
Exact submission due, tho' absolute.
What tho' they style me villain, murderer,
And imprecate from Heaven dire thunderbolts
To crush my purposes—Was that a gun
Which thunders o'er the wave? or is it guilt,
That plays the coward with my trembling heart,
And cools the blood with frightful images?
Oh guilt, thy blackness hovers on the mind,
Nor can the morning dissipate thy shades.
Yon ruddy morn, which over Bunkers-Hill
Advancing slowly, blushes to the Bay,
And tips with gold the spires of Charlestown.

Enter BURGOYNE

The rebel foe, grown yet more insolent

By that small loss, or rout, at Lexington,
Prevent our purpose, and the night by-past
Have push'd intrenchments and some flimsy works
With rude achievement on the rocky brow
Of that tall hill. A ship-boy, with the day,
From the tall masthead of the Admiral,
Descry'd their aim, and gave the swift alarm.
Our glasses mark but one small regiment there,
Yet, ev'ry hour we languish in delay
Inspires fresh hope, and fills their pigmy souls
With thoughts of holding it. Your hear the sound
Of spades and pickaxes, upon the hill,
Incessant, pounding like old Vulcan's forge
Urg'd by the Cyclops.

Enter HOWE

To your alarm posts, officers; come, gallant souls,
Let's out, and drive them from that eminence,
On which the foe doth earth himself.
I relish not such haughty neighborhood.
Give orders, swiftly, to the Admiral,
That some stout ship heave up the narrow bay,
And pour indignant, from the full-tide wave,
Fierce cannonade across the isthmus point,
That no assistance may be brought to them.
If but seven hundred, we can treat with them.
Yes, strew the hill with death and carcasses,
And offer up this band, a hecatomb,
To Britain's glory, and the cause of kings.
                              Exeunt Burgoyne and Howe.

GAGE, *solus*

May Heaven protect us from their rage, I say.
When but a boy, I dream'd of death in bed,
And ever since that time I hated things
Which put him, like a pair of spectacles,
Before my eyes. The thought lies deep in fate,
Nor can a mortal see the bottom of it.
'Tis here—'tis there—I could philosophize—
Eternity is like a winding sheet—
The seven commandments like—I think there's seven—

I scratch my head—but yet in vain I scratch—
Oh Bute, and Dartmouth,[55] knew ye what I feel,
You sure would pity an old drinking man,
That has more heartache than philosophy.

Exeunt.

SCENE II. HOWE *with the British army*

Howe

The day at length propitious shows itself,
And with full beams of majesty the sun
Hath bless'd its fair nativity; when Heaven,
Brave soldiers, and the cause of kings,
Calls on the spirit of your loyalty
To chastise this rebellion, and tread down
Such foul ingratitude—such monstrous shape
Of horrid liberty, which spurns that love—
That fond maternal tenderness of soul,
Which on this dreary coast first planted them:
Restrain'd the rage of murdering savages,
Which, with fierce inroad, on their settlements
Made frequent war—struck down the arm of France,
Just rais'd, to crush them in their infancy:
And since that time have bade their cities grow
To marts of trade: call'd fair-ey'd commerce forth
To share dominion on the distant wave,
And visit every clime and foreign shore.
Yet this, brave soldiers, is the proud return,
For the best blood of England, shed for them.
Behold yon hill, where fell rebellion rears
Her snake-stream'd ensign, and would seem to brave
With scarce seven hundred this sea-bounded camp,
Where may be counted full ten thousand men
That in the war with France so late, acquir'd
Loud fame, and shook the other continent.
Come on, brave soldiers, seize your gleaming arms,
And let this day in after times be held
As Minden[56] famous, and each hostile field
Where British valor shone victorious.
The time moves slow, which enviously detains
Our just resentment from these traitors' heads.
Their richest farms and cultur'd settlements,

By winding river or extensive bay,
Shall be your first reward. Our noble king
As things confiscate holds their property,
And in rich measure will bestow on you,
Who face the frowns and labor of this day.
He that outlives this battle shall ascend,
In titled honor to the height of state.
Dukedoms, and baronies, midst these our foes,
In tributary vassalage kept down,
Shall be your fair inheritance. Come on,
Beat up th' heroic sound of war. The word
Is George our sov'reign, and Britannia's arms.

Act V

SCENE I. Bunkers-Hill

WARREN *with the American army*

Warren

 To arms, brave countrymen, for see the foe
Comes forth to battle, and would seem to try,
Once more, their fortune in decisive war.
Three thousand 'gainst seven hundred rang'd this day,
Shall give the world an ample specimen
What strength, and noble confidence, the sound
Of Liberty inspires. That Liberty,
Which, not the thunder of Bellona's voice,
With fleets, and armies, from the British shore,
Shall wrest from us. Our noble ancestors
Out-brav'd the tempests of the hoary deep,
And on these hills, uncultivate and wild,
Sought an asylum from despotic sway;
A short asylum, for that envious power,
With persecution dire, still follows us.
At first they deem'd our charters forfeited.
Next our just rights in government abridg'd.
Then thrust in viceroys and bashaws, to rule
With lawless sovereignty. Now added force
Of standing armies, to secure their sway.
Much have we suffer'd from the licens'd rage

Of brutal soldiery in each fair town.
Remember March, brave countrymen, that day
When Boston's streets ran blood.[57] Think on that day,
And let the memory, to revenge, stir up
The temper of your souls. There might we still
On terms precarious and disdainful liv'd,
With daughters ravished and butcher'd sons,
But Heaven forbade the thought. These are the men
Who in firm phalanx threaten us with war,
And aim this day to fix forever down,
The galling chains which tyranny has forg'd for us.
These count our lands and settlements their own,
And in their intercepted letters speak
Of farms and tenements, secured for friends,
Which, if they gain, brave soldiers, let with blood,
The purchase be seal'd down. Let every arm
This day be active in fair freedom's cause,
And shower down from the hill, like Heav'n in wrath,
Full store of lightning, and fierce iron hail,
To blast the adversary. Let this ground,
Like burning Aetna or Vesuvius top,
Be wrapt in flame—The word is Liberty,
And Heaven smile on us in so just a cause.

SCENE II. Bunkers-Hill

GARDNER, *leading up his men to the engagement*

Fear not, brave soldiers, tho' their infantry,
In deep array, so far outnumbers us.
The justness of our cause will brace each arm,
And steel the soul with fortitude; while they,
Whose guilt hangs trembling on their consciences,
Must fail in battle, and receive that death
Which, in high vengeance, we prepare for them.
Let then each spirit, to the height wound up,
Show noble vigor, and full force this day.
For on the merit of our swords is plac'd
The virgin honor and true character
Of this whole continent; and one short hour
May give complexion to the whole event,
Fixing the judgment whether as base slaves

We serve these masters, or more nobly live,
Free as the breeze that on the hilltop plays
With these sweet fields and tenements, our own.
Oh fellow soldiers, let this battle speak
Dire disappointment to the insulting foe,
Who claim our fair possessions, and set down
These cultur'd-farms, and bowry-hills, and plains,
As the rich prize of certain victory.
Shall we, the sons of Massachusetts Bay,
New Hampshire, and Connecticut, shall we
Fall back, dishonor'd, from our native plains,
Mix with the savages, and roam for food
On western mountains, or the desert shores
Of Canada's cold lakes? or state more vile,
Sit down, in humble vassalage, content
To till the ground for these proud conquerors?
No, fellow soldiers, let us rise this day,
Emancipate from such ignoble choice.
And should the battle ravish our sweet lives,
Late time shall give an ample monument,
And bid her worthies emulate our fame.

SCENE III. Boston

The British army being repuls'd, Sherwin *is dispatch'd to* General Gage *for assistance.*

SHERWIN, GAGE, BURGOYNE, *and* CLINTON

Sherwin

    Our men advancing have receiv'd dire loss
In this encounter, and the case demands,
In swift crisis of extremity,
A thousand men to reinforce the war

Gage

    Do as you please, Burgoyne, in this affair,
I'll hide myself in some deep vault beneath.

                              Exit.

Burgoyne

    'Tis yours, brave Clinton, to command these men.

Embark them speedily. I see our troops,
Stand on the margin of the ebbing flood
(The flood affrighted at the scene it views),
And fear once more to climb the desp'rate hill
Whence the bold rebel show'rs destruction down.

Exeunt.

SCENE IV

Warren, *mortally wounded, falling on his right knee, covering his
breast with his right hand, and supporting himself with his firelock
in his left.*

A deadly ball hath limited my life,
And now to God I offer up my soul.
But Oh my countrymen, let not the cause,
The sacred cause of liberty, with me
Faint or expire. By the last parting breath
And blood of this your fellow soldier slain,
Be now adjur'd never to yield the right,
The grand deposit of all-giving Heaven,
To man's free nature that he rule himself.
With these rude Britons wage life-scorning war,
Till they admit it, and like hell fall off
With ebbing billows from this troubl'd coast,
Where but for them firm concord, and true love,
Should individual hold their court and reign.
Th' infernal engin'ry of state, resist
To death, that unborn times may be secure,
And while men flourish in the peace you win,
Write each fair name with worthies of the earth.
Weep not your gen'ral, who is snatch'd this day
From the embraces of a family,
Five virgin daughters young, and unendow'd,
Now with the foe left lone and fatherless.
Weep not for him who first espous'd the cause,
And risking life have met the enemy
In fatal opposition—but rejoice—
For now I go to mingle with the dead,
Great Brutus, Hampden, Sidney,[58] and the rest
Of old or modern memory, who liv'd
A mound to tyrants, and strong hedge to kings,

Bounding the inundation of their rage
Against the happiness and peace of man.
I see these heroes where they walk serene,
By crystal currents on the vale of Heaven,
High in full converse of immortal acts,
Achiev'd for truth and innocence on earth.
Meantime the harmony and thrilling sound
Of mellow lutes, sweet viols, and guitars,
Dwell on the soul and ravish ev'ry nerve.
Anon the murmur of the tight-brac'd drum,
With finely varied fifes to martial airs,
Wind up the spirit to the mighty proof
Of siege and battle, and attempt in arms.
Illustrious group! They beckon me along,
To ray my visage with immortal light,
And bind the amarinth around my brow.
I come, I come, ye first-born of true fame.
Fight on, my countrymen, be free, be free.

SCENE V. Charlestown

*The reinforcement landed, and orders given to burn Charlestown,
that they may march up more securely under the smoke,* General
Howe *rallies his repuls'd and broken troops.*

Howe

    Curse on the fortune of Britannia's arms,
That plays the jilt with us. Shall these few men
Beat back the flower and best half of our troops,
While on our side so many ships of war
And floating batt'ries from the Mystic tide
Shake all the hill and sweep its ridgy top?
Oh gods! no time can blot its memory out.
We've men enough upon the field today
To bury this small handful with the dust
Our march excites—back to the charge—close ranks,
And drive these wizards from th' enchanted ground.
The reinforcement, which bold Clinton heads,
Gives such superiority of strength,
That let each man of us but cast a stone,
We cover this small hill with these few foes,
And overhead erect a pyramid.

The smoke, you see, enwraps us in its shade.
On, then, my countrymen, and try once more
To change the fortune of the inglorious day.

SCENE VI. Bunkers-Hill

GARDNER, *to the American army*

You see, brave soldiers, how an evil cause,
A cause of slavery and civil death,
Unmans the spirit and strikes down the soul.
The gallant Englishman, whose fame in arms
Through every clime shakes terribly the globe,
Is found this day shorn of his wonted strength,
Repuls'd, and driven from the flaming hill.
Warren is fallen, on fair honor's bed,
Pierc'd in the breast, with ev'ry wound before.
'Tis ours now tenfold to avenge his death,
And offer up a reg'ment of the foe,
Achilles-like, upon the hero's tomb.
See, reinforc'd they face us yet again,
And onward move in phalanx to the war.
Oh noble spirits, let this bold attack
Be bloody to their host. God is our aid,
Give then full scope to just revenge this day.

SCENE VII. The Bay shore

The British army once more repuls'd, Howe *again rallies his
flying troops.*

Howe
But that so many mouths can witness it,
I would deny myself an Englishman,
And swear this day that with such cowardice
No kindred or alliance has my birth.
Oh base degen'rate souls, whose ancestors
At Cressy, Poitiers, and at Agincourt[59]
With tenfold numbers combated, and pluck'd
The budding laurels from the brows of France,
Back to the charge once more, and rather die
Burn'd up, and wither'd on this bloody hill,

133

Than live the blemish of your country's fame,
With everlasting infamy oppress'd.
Their ammunition, as you hear, is spent,
So that unless their looks and visages,
Like fierce-ey'd basilisks, can strike you dead,
Return, and rescue yet, sweet countrymen,
Some share of honor on this hapless day.
Let some brave officers stand on the rear,
And with the small sword and sharp bayonet
Drive on each coward that attempts to lag,
That thus, sure death may find the villain out
With more dread certainty than him who moves
Full in the van to meet the wrathful foe.

SCENE VIII. Bunkers-Hill

Gardner, *desperately wounded and borne from the field by two
soldiers.*

Gardner

A musket-ball, death-wing'd, hath pierc'd my groin,
And widely op'd the swift curr'nt of my veins.
Bear me then, soldiers, to that hollow space
A little hence, just in the hill's decline.
A surgeon there may stop the gushing wound,
And gain a short respite to life, that yet
I may return and fight one half hour more.
Then shall I die in peace, and to my God
Surrender up the spirit which He gave.

SCENE IX

PUTNAM, *to the American army*

Swift-rising fame on early wing mounts up
To the convexity of bending Heaven,
And writes each name who fought with us this day,
In fairest character amidst the stars.
The world shall read it, and still talk of us,
Who, far outnumber'd, twice drove back the foe,
With carnage horrid, murm'ring to their ships.
The ghost of Warren says enough—I see
One thousand veterans, mingled with the dust.

Now, for our sacred honor, and the wound
Which Gardner feels, once more we charge—once more,
Dear friends, and fence the obscur'd hill
With hecatombs of slain. Let every piece
Flash, like the fierce-consuming fire of Heaven,
And make the smoke in which they wrap themselves,
"A darkness visible."—Now, once again
Receive the battle, as a shore of rock
The ocean wave. And if at last we yield,
Leave many a death amidst their hollow ranks,
To damp the measure of their dear-bought joy.

SCENE X and Last. Bunkers-Hill

The American army overpower'd by numbers are obliged to retreat.

Enter HOWE, PIGOT, *and* CLINTON *with the British army.*

RICHARDSON, *a young officer, on the parapet*

The day is ours, huzza, the day is ours,
This last attack has forc'd them to retreat.

Clinton
'Tis true, full victory declares for us,
But we have dearly, dearly purchas'd it.
Full fifteen hundred of our men lie dead,
Who, with their officers, do swell the list
Of this day's carnage—on the well-fought hill
Whole ranks cut down lie struggling with their wounds,
Or close their bright eyes in the shades of night.
No wonder! such incessant musketry
And fire of cannon from the hilltop pour'd,
Seem'd not the agency of mortal men,
But Heaven itself, with snares and vengeance arm'd,
T' oppose our gaining it. E'en when was spent
Their ammunition, and fierce Warren slain,
Huge stones were hurled from the rocky brow,
And war renew'd by these inveterate;
Till Gardner wounded, the left wing gave way,
And with their shatter'd infantry the whole,
Drawn off by Putnam, to the causeway fled,
When from the ships, and batt'ries on the wave

They met deep loss, and strew'd the narrow bridge
With lifeless carcasses. Oh, such a day,
Since Sodom and Gomorrah sunk in flames,
Hath not been heard of by the ear of man,
Nor hath an eye beheld its parallel.

Lord Pigot

    The day is ours, but with heart-piercing loss
Of soldiers slain and gallant officers.
Old Abercrombie on the field lies dead.
Pitcairn and Sherwin, in sore battle slain.[60]
The gallant reg'ment of Welsh fusiliers
To seventeen privates is this day reduc'd.
The grenadiers stand thinly on the hill,
Like the tall fir-trees on the blasted heath,
Scorch'd by the autumnal burnings, which have rush'd
With wasting fire fierce through its leafy groves.
Should ev'ry hill by the rebellious foe,
So well defended, cost thus dear to us,
Not the united forces of the world
Could master them, and the proud rage subdue
Of these Americans.

Howe

    E'en in an enemy I honor worth,
And valor eminent. The vanquish'd foe
In feats of prowess show their ancestry,
And speak their birth legitimate;
The sons of Britons, with the genuine flame
Of British heat and valor in their veins.
What pity 'tis, such excellence of mind
Should spend itself in the fantastic cause
Of wild-fire liberty. Warren is dead,
And lies unburied on the smoky hill;
But with rich honors he shall be inhum'd,
To teach our soldiery how much we love,
E'en in a foe, true worth and noble fortitude.
Come then, brave soldiers, and take up the dead,
Majors and col'nels, which are this day slain,
And noble captains of sweet life bereft.
Fair flowers shall grow upon their grassy tombs,

And fame in tears shall tell their tragedy
To many a widow and soft weeping maid,
Or parent woeful for an only son,
Through mourning Britain and Hibernia's isle.

Enter BURGOYNE *from Boston*

Oft have I read, in the historic page,
And witnessed myself, high scenes in war:
But this rude day, unparallel'd in time,
Has no competitor—the gazing eye,
Of many a soldier, from the chimney-tops
And spires of Boston, witnessed when Howe,
With his full thousands moving up the hill,
Receiv'd the onset of the impetuous foe.
The hill itself, like Ida's burning mount,
When Jove came down in terrors to dismay
The Grecian host, enshrouded in thick flames;
And round its margin, to the ebbing wave,
A town on fire, and rushing from its base,
With ruin hideous and combustion down.
Meantime, deep thunder from the hollow sides
Of the artill'ry, on the hilltop heard,
With roar of thunder and loud mortars play'd,
From the tall ships and batt'ries on the wave,
Bade yon blue ocean and wide heaven resound.
A scene like which, perhaps, no time shall know,
Till Heav'n with final ruin fires the ball,
Burns up the cities and the works of men,
And wraps the mountains in one gen'ral blaze.

Exeunt.

The End

14

from *The Crisis, No. 1* (1776)

Following the publication of Common Sense *in January, 1776, Paine joined the American army. He served briefly at Amboy, New Jersey, with the Flying Camp, an irregular brigade of Pennsylvania troops under the command of Brigadier General Daniel Roberdeau, a wealthy Philadelphia merchant. In September, his short-term enlistment up, Paine left the Flying Camp and became a volunteer aide-de-camp to General Nathanael Greene, then stationed at Fort Lee, New Jersey, an outpost overlooking the Hudson. Paine was at Fort Lee in mid-November when Cornwallis launched a surprise attack just before the evening meal, forcing Greene's troops into hurried retreat. Subsequently, an unidentified British soldier noted dutifully in his journal that "... the rebels fled like scared rabbits, leaving some poor pork, a few greasy proclamations, and some of that scoundrel* Common Sense *man's letters; which we can read at our leisure, now that we have got one of the 'impregnable redoubts' of Mr. Washington to quarter in." By November 22 Washington's bedraggled and ill-equipped army had retreated through New Jersey to Newark, the British still in pursuit, and from there, in December, Paine made his way to Philadelphia, where on December 19, 1776, he published in the* Pennsylvania Journal *the first of his celebrated* Crisis *papers.*

The Crisis *papers, sixteen in number (thirteen regular and three "extraordinary" issues), appeared periodically between December, 1776, and April, 1783, timed to coincide with the critical points of the war. In one sense, the* Crisis *papers constituted but a continuation of the central themes of* Common Sense: *the essential rightness of independence, the corruptness of the king and his ministers, the ineffectuality of the British constitution. Paine's specific purposes, of course, varied with each issue. In the first, for example, he is intent on flushing out and discrediting American Tories and their sympathizers, whose numbers, wealth, and influence posed such a threat to American independence. Throughout the series he labored hard to maintain the ideological level of American patriotism in the face of fatigue, demoralization, and a periodically bleak military picture. Here, using the skillful rhetoric and passionate language of* Common Sense, *Paine was at his best, minimizing losses (retreats invariably became strategic withdrawals), emphasizing victories, and holding out the promise of inevitable success as the reward for perseverance and redoubled effort.*

☆ ☆

These are the times that try men's souls. The summer soldier and the sunshine patriot will, in this crisis, shrink from the service of their country; but he that stands it *now* deserves the love and thanks of man and woman. Tyranny, like hell, is not easily conquered; yet we have this consolation with us, that the harder the conflict, the more glorious the triumph. What we obtain too cheap, we esteem too lightly; it is dearness only that gives everything its value. Heaven knows how to put a proper price upon its goods; and it would be strange indeed if so celestial an article as freedom should not be highly rated. Britain, with an army to enforce her tyranny, has declared that she has a right (*not only to tax*) but "to *bind us in all cases whatsoever*"[61] and if being *bound in that manner* is not slavery, then is there not such a thing as slavery upon earth. Even the expression is impious, for so unlimited a power can belong only to God.

Whether the independence of the continent was declared too soon or delayed too long I will not now enter into as an argument; my own simple opinion is that had it been eight months earlier, it would have been much better. We did not make a proper use of last winter, neither could we while we were in a dependent state. However, the fault, if it were one, was all our own; we have none to blame but ourselves. But no great deal is lost yet. All that Howe has been doing for this month past is rather a ravage than a conquest, which the spirit of the Jerseys, a year ago, would have quickly repulsed, and which time and a little resolution will soon recover.

I have as little superstition in me as any man living, but my secret opinion has ever been, and still is, that God Almighty will not give up a people to military destruction, or leave them unsupportedly to perish, who have so earnestly and so repeatedly sought to avoid the calamities of war by every decent method which wisdom could invent. Neither have I so much of the infidel in me as to suppose that He has relinquished the government of the world and given us up to the care of devils; and as I do not, I cannot see on what grounds the king of Britain can look up to heaven for help against us; a common murderer, a highwayman, or a housebreaker has as good a pretense as he.

'Tis surprising to see how rapidly a panic will sometimes run through a country. All nations and ages have been subject to them. Britain has trembled like an ague at the report of a French fleet of flat-bottomed boats; and in the fourteenth[62] century the whole English army, after ravaging the kingdom of France, was driven back like men petrified with fear; and this brave exploit was performed by a few broken forces collected and headed by a woman, Joan of Arc. Would that heaven might inspire some Jersey maid to spirit up her countrymen and save her fair fellow sufferers from ravage and ravishment! Yet panics, in some cases, have their uses; they produce as much good as hurt. Their duration is always short; the mind soon grows through them, and acquires a firmer habit than before. But their peculiar advantage is that they are the touchstones of sincerity and hypocrisy, and bring things and men to light which might otherwise have lain forever undiscovered. In fact, they have the same effect on secret traitors which an imaginary apparition would have upon a private murderer. They sift out the hidden thoughts of man, and hold them up in public to the world. Many a disguised Tory has lately shown his head that shall penitentially solemnize with curses the day on which Howe arrived upon the Delaware.

As I was with the troops at Fort Lee and marched with them to the edge of Pennsylvania, I am well acquainted with many circumstances which those who live at a distance know but little or nothing of. Our situation there was exceedingly cramped, the place being a narrow neck of land between the North River and the Hackensack. Our force was inconsiderable, being not one-fourth so great as Howe could bring against us. We had no army at hand to have relieved the garrison, had we shut ourselves up and stood on our defense. Our ammunition, light artillery, and the best part of our stores had been removed, on the apprehension that Howe would endeavor to penetrate the Jerseys, in which case Fort Lee could be of no use to us; for it must occur to every thinking man, whether in the army or not, that these kind of field forts are only for temporary purposes, and last in use no longer than the enemy directs his force against the particular object which such forts are raised to defend. Such was our situation and condition at Fort Lee on the morning of the 20th of November, when an officer arrived with information that the enemy with 200 boats had landed about seven miles above. Major General Greene, who commanded the garrison, immediately ordered them under arms, and sent express to General Washington at the town of Hackensack, by the way of the ferry six miles. Our first object was to secure the bridge over the Hackensack, which lay up the river between the enemy and us, about six miles from us, and three from them. General Washington arrived in about three-quarters of an hour, and marched at the head of the troops towards the bridge, which place I expected we should have a brush for; however, they did not choose to dispute it with us, and the greatest part of our troops went over the bridge, the rest over the ferry, except some which passed at a mill on a small creek, between the bridge and the ferry, and made their way through some marshy grounds up to the town of Hackensack and there passed the river. We brought off as much baggage as the wagons could contain; the rest was lost. The simple object was to bring off the garrison and march them on till they could be strenghtened by the Jersey or Pennsylvania militia, so as to be enabled to make a stand. We stayed four days at Newark, collected our outposts with some of the Jersey militia, and marched out twice to meet the enemy, on being informed that they were advancing, though our numbers were greatly inferior to theirs. Howe, in my little opinion, committed a great error in generalship in not throwing a body of forces off from Staten Island through Amboy, by which means he might have seized all our stores at Brunswick and intercepted our march into Pennsylvania; but if we believe the power of hell to be limited, we must likewise believe that their agents are under some providential control.

I shall not now attempt to give all the particulars of our retreat to the Delaware; suffice it for the present to say that both officers and men, though greatly harassed and fatigued, frequently without rest, covering, or provision —the inevitable consequences of a long retreat—bore it with a manly and martial spirit. All their wishes centered in one, which was that the country would turn out and help them to drive the enemy back. Voltaire has remarked that King William never appeared to full advantage but in difficulties and in action;[63] the same remark may be made on General Washington, for the character fits him. There is a natural firmness in some minds which cannot be unlocked by trifles, but which, when unlocked, discovers a cabinet of fortitude; and I reckon it among those kind of public blessings, which we do not immediately see, that God hath blessed him with uninterrupted health, and given him a mind that can even flourish upon care.

I shall conclude this paper with some miscellaneous remarks on the state of our affairs; and shall begin with asking the following question: Why is it that the enemy have left the New England provinces, and made these middle ones the seat of war? The answer is easy: New England is not infested with Tories, and we are. I have been tender in raising the cry against these men and used numberless arguments to show them their danger, but it will not do to sacrifice a world either to their folly or their baseness. The period is now arrived in which either they or we must change our sentiments, or one or both must fall. And what is a Tory? Good God! what is he? I should not be afraid to go with a hundred Whigs against a thousand Tories, were they to attempt to get into arms. Every Tory is a coward; for servile, slavish, self-interested fear is the foundation of Toryism, and a man under such influence, though he may be cruel, never can be brave.

But before the line of irrecoverable separation be drawn between us, let us reason the matter together. Your conduct is an invitation to the enemy, yet not one in a thousand of you has heart enough to join him. Howe is as much deceived by you as the American cause is injured by you. He expects you will all take up arms and flock to his standard, with muskets on your shoulders. Your opinions are of no use to him unless you support him personally, for 'tis soldiers and not Tories that he wants.

I once felt all that kind of anger which a man ought to feel against the mean principles that are held by the Tories: a noted one, who kept a tavern at Amboy, was standing at his door with as pretty a child in his hand, about eight or nine years old, as I ever saw, and after speaking his mind as freely as he thought was prudent, finished with this unfatherly expression, "*Well! give me peace in my day.*" Not a man lives on the continent but fully believes that a separation must some time or other finally take place, and a generous parent should have said, "*If there must be trouble, let it be in my day, that my child may have peace;*" and this single reflection, well applied, is sufficient to awaken every man to duty. Not a place upon earth might be so happy as America. Her situation is remote from all the wrangling world, and she has nothing to do but to trade with them. A man can distinguish himself between temper and principle, and I am as confident as I am that God governs the world that America will never be happy till she gets clear of foreign dominion. Wars without ceasing will break out till that period arrives, and the continent must in the end be conqueror; for though the flame of liberty may sometimes cease to shine, the coal can never expire.

America did not nor does not want force, but she wanted a proper application of that force. Wisdom is not the purchase of a day, and it is no wonder that we should err at the first setting off. From an excess of tenderness, we were unwilling to raise an army, and trusted our cause to the temporary defense of a well-meaning militia. A summer's experience has now taught us better; yet with those troops, while they were collected, we were able to set bounds to the progress of the enemy, and, thank God! they are again assembling. I always considered militia as the best troops in the world for a sudden exertion, but they will not do for a long campaign. Howe, it is probable, will make an attempt on this city.[64] Should he fail on this side of the Delaware, he is ruined; if he succeeds, our cause is not ruined. He stakes all on his side against a part on ours; admitting he succeeds, the consequence will be that armies from both ends of the continent will march to assist their suffering friends in the middle states; for he cannot go everywhere, it is impossible. I consider Howe as the greatest enemy the Tories have; he is bringing a war into their country, which, had it not been for him and partly for themselves, they had been clear of. Should he now be expelled, I wish with all the devotion of a Christian that the names of Whig and Tory may never more be mentioned; but should the Tories give him encouragement to come, or assistance if he comes, I as sincerely wish that our next year's arms may expel them from the continent, and the Congress appropriate their possessions to the relief of those who have suffered in well-doing. A single successful battle next year will settle the whole. America could carry on a two-years war by the confiscation of the property of disaffected persons, and be made happy by their expulsion. Say not that this is revenge, call it rather the soft resentment of a suffering people who, having no object in view but the *good* of *all,* have staked their *own all* upon a seemingly doubtful event. Yet it is folly to argue against determined hardness; eloquence may strike the ear, and the language of sorrow draw forth the tear of compassion, but nothing can reach the heart that is steeled with prejudice.

Quitting this class of men, I turn with the warm ardor of a friend to those who have nobly stood and are yet determined to stand the matter out. I call not upon a few, but upon all—not on *this* state or *that* state, but on *every* state—up and help us; lay your shoulders to the wheel; better have too much force than too little when so great an object is at stake. Let it be told to the future world that in the depth of winter, when nothing but hope and virtue could survive, the city and the country, alarmed at one common danger, came forth to meet and to repulse it. Say not that thousands are gone, turn out your tens of thousands; throw not the burden of the day upon Providence, but "*show your faith by your works,*" that God may bless you. It matters not where you live, or what rank of life you hold, the evil or the blessing will reach you all. The far and the near, the home counties and the back, the rich and the poor, will suffer or rejoice alike. The heart that feels not now, is dead; the blood of his children will curse his cowardice who shrinks back at a time when a little might have saved the whole and made *them* happy. I love the man that can smile in trouble, that can gather strength from distress, and grow brave by reflection. 'Tis the business of little minds to shrink; but he whose heart is firm, and whose conscience approves his conduct, will pursue his principles unto death. My own line of reasoning is to myself as straight and clear as a ray of light. Not all the treasures of the world, so far as I believe, could have induced me to support an offensive war, for I think it murder; but if a thief breaks into my house, burns and destroys my property, and kills or threatens to kill me, or those that are in it, and to "*bind me in all cases whatsoever*" to his absolute will, am I to suffer it? What signifies it to me, whether he who does it is a king or a common man; my countryman or not my countryman; whether it be done by an individual villain or an army of them? If we reason to the root of things, we shall find no difference; neither can any just cause be assigned why we should punish in the one case and pardon in the other. Let them call me rebel and welcome, I feel no concern from it; but I should suffer the misery of devils were I to make a whore of my soul by swearing allegiance to one whose character is that of a sottish, stupid, stubborn, worthless brutish man. I conceive likewise a horrid idea in receiving mercy from a being who at the last day shall be shrieking to the rocks and mountains to cover him, and fleeing with terror from the orphan, the widow, and the slain of America. . . .

I thank God that I fear not. I see no real cause for fear. I know our situation well, and can see the way out of it. While our army was collected, Howe dared not risk a battle, and it is no credit to him that he decamped from the White Plains, and waited a mean opportunity to ravage the defenseless Jerseys; but it is great credit to us that, with a handful of men, we sustained an orderly retreat for near a hundred miles, brought off our ammunition, all our field pieces, the greatest part of our stores, and had four rivers to pass. None can say that our retreat was precipitate, for we were near three weeks in performing it, that the country might have time to come in. Twice we marched back to meet the enemy, and remained out till dark. The sign of fear was not seen in our camp, and had not some of the cowardly and disaffected inhabitants spread false alarms through the country, the Jerseys had never been ravaged. Once more we are again collected and collecting; our new army at both ends of the continent is recruiting fast, and we shall be able to open the next campaign with sixty thousand men, well armed and clothed. This is our situation, and who will may know it. By perseverance and fortitude we have the prospect of a glorious issue; by cowardice and submission, the sad choice of a variety of evils—a ravaged country, a depopulated city, habitations without safety and slavery without hope, our homes turned into barracks and bawdy-houses for Hessians, and a future race to provide for whose fathers we shall doubt of. Look on this picture and weep over it! and if there yet remains one thoughtless wretch who believes it not, let him suffer it unlamented.

Common Sense

PHILIP FRENEAU

15

Of all those who supported the cause of America with their pens, none was more unrelenting and bitter in his attack than the poet Philip Freneau. Freneau's patriotism was fierce, if somewhat doctrinaire; his capacity for outrage and anger great; his poetic skills considerable. The result was a poetry filled with satire, invective, and the poet's passionate anglophobia, a deep and abiding hatred of the British that the passage of time and Freneau's own experience only confirmed and increased. Freneau's popularity (and notoriety) as a political poet has long been recognized in the sobriquet "poet of the Revolution," a judgment that in retrospect seems fair enough. Though the quality of Freneau's revolutionary verse is uneven, what it lacks as poetry is more than made up for by the force and vigor of its sentiments.

Philip Freneau (1752–1832) was born in New York City, and educated at the College of New Jersey (Princeton), where he and Hugh Henry Brackenridge became good friends and poetic collaborators. Uncertain of vocation, a problem which he never really solved, Freneau first tried school-teaching, on Long Island and then at the Maryland academy where Brackenridge served as headmaster, but by the spring of 1775 was back in New York City, publishing the first of his satiric thrusts at the British and their American sympathizers. Then, strangely enough, having tested the political waters, Freneau set sail for the island of Santa Cruz (St. Croix) in the West Indies as the guest of a prominent planter, a visit that lasted nearly three years. Returning home in July of 1778, Freneau spent the next two years alternately writing poetry, serving with the New Jersey militia, and running cargoes to and from the West Indies. Then in May of 1780 came the fateful voyage aboard the Aurora, a Pennsylvania privateer out of Philadelphia, which was *taken off the American coast by the British frigate* Isis. *Though traveling as a passenger, Freneau found himself a prisoner, and when the* Isis *arrived at New York Freneau was transferred with the rest of the* Aurora's *crew to the decks of the infamous British prison ship* Scorpion, *moored in the Hudson. Freneau subsequently memorialized his captivity aboard the* Scorpion, *and his fever-filled weeks aboard the hospital ship* Hunter, *in "The British Prison Ship" (1781), as savage and bitter a poem as the Revolution produced. Following his release and recovery, Freneau once more took up his pen in America's defense, now understanding more than ever the meaning of freedom.*

Following the war (1784–90), Freneau served as the master of a succession of cargo vessels, until his marriage returned him to the land. In 1791 Freneau accepted a "clerkship for foreign languages" in Jefferson's State Department, a position that soon expanded (possibly by prearrangement) into the editorship of the National Gazette, *a decidedly pro-Jefferson, anti-Federalist newspaper. For nearly two years Freneau threw himself into the violently partisan political wars of the 1790s. "That rascal Freneau," Washington called him, a remark that adequately attests to the controversial figure that Freneau became. In 1793, disenchanted, Freneau retired to his New Jersey estate Mount Pleasant to begin a lengthy retirement, punctuated by brief periods of business, literary, and journalistic activity, and against a background of increasingly serious financial problems. Freneau died of exposure in 1832, having lost his way home in a snowstorm.*

☆ ☆

A Political Litany
(1775)

Libera nos, Domine—Deliver us, O Lord, not only from British
dependence, but also

From a junto that labor with absolute power,
Whose schemes disappointed have made them look sour,
From the lords of the council, who fight against freedom,
Who still follow on where delusion shall lead them.

From the group at St. James's,[65] who slight our petitions,
And fools that are waiting for further submissions—
From a nation whose manners are rough and severe,
From scoundrels and rascals,—do keep us all clear.

From pirates sent out by command of the king
To murder and plunder, but never to swing.
From Wallace and Greaves, and *Vipers* and *Roses,*[66]
Whom, if heaven pleases, we'll give bloody noses.

From the valiant Dunmore, with his crew of banditti,
Who plunder Virginians at Williamsburg city,[67]
From hot-headed Montagu,[68] mighty to swear,
The little fat man with his pretty white hair.

From bishops in Britain, who butchers are grown,
From slaves that would die for a smile from the throne,
From assemblies that vote against Congress proceedings,
(Who now see the fruit of their stupid misleadings.)

From Tryon the mighty, who flies from our city,[69]
And swelled with importance disdains the committee:
(But since he is pleased to proclaim us his foes,
What the devil care we where the devil he goes.)

From the caitiff Lord North, who would bind us in chains,
From a royal king Log, with his tooth-full of brains,
Who dreams, and is certain (when taking a nap)
He has conquered our lands, as they lay on his map.

From a kingdom that bullies, and hectors, and swears,
We send up to heaven our wishes and prayers
That we, disunited, may freemen be still,
And Britain go on—to be damned if she will.

Sir Harry's Invitation
(1779)[70]

Come, gentlemen Tories, firm, loyal, and true,
Here are axes and shovels, and something to do!
  For the sake of our king,
  Come, labor and sing;
You left all you had for his honor and glory,

And he will remember the suffering Tory:
  We have, it is true,
  Some small work to do;
  But here's for your pay
  Twelve coppers a day,
And never regard what the rebels may say,
But throw off your jerkins and labor away.

To raise up the rampart, and pile up the wall,
To pull down old houses and dig the canal,
  To build and destroy—
  Be this your employ,
In the day time to work at our fortifications,
And steal in the night from the rebels your rations:
  The king wants your aid,
  Not empty parade;
  Advance to your places
  Ye men of long faces,
Nor ponder too much on your former disgraces,
This year, I presume, will quite alter your cases.

Attend at the call of the fifer and drummer,
The French and the rebels are coming next summer,
  And forts we must build
  Though Tories are kill'd—
Then courage, my jockies, and work for your king,
For if you are taken no doubt you will swing—
  If York we can hold
  I'll have you enroll'd;
  And after you're dead
  Your names shall be read
As who for their monarch both labor'd and bled,
And ventur'd their necks for their beef and their bread.

'Tis an honor to serve the bravest of nations,
And be left to be hang'd in their capitulations—
  Then scour up your mortars
  And stand to your quarters,
'Tis nonsense for Tories in battle to run,
They never need fear sword, halberd, or gun;
  Their hearts should not fail 'em,
  No balls will assail 'em,

Forget your disgraces
And shorten your faces,
For 'tis true as the gospel, believe it or not,
Who are born to be hang'd, will never be shot.

From **"The British Prison Ship"**
(1781)[71]

Canto II—The Prison Ship

The various horrors of these hulks to tell,
These prison ships where pain and horror dwell,
Where death in tenfold vengeance holds his reign,
And injur'd ghosts, yet unaveng'd, complain;
This be my task—ungenerous Britons, you
Conspire to murder those you can't subdue.
Weak as I am, I'll try my strength today
And my best arrows at these hell-hounds play,
To future years one scene of death prolong,
And hang them up to infamy, in song.
That Britain's rage should dye our plains with gore,
And desolation spread through every shore,
None e'er could doubt, that her ambition knew,
This was to rage and disappointment due;
But that those monsters whom our soil maintain'd,
Who first drew breath in this devoted land,
Like famish'd wolves, should on their country prey,
Assist its foes, and wrest our lives away,
This shocks belief—and bids our soil disown
Such friends, subservient to a bankrupt crown.
By them the widow mourns her partner dead,
Her mangled sons to darksome prisons led;
By them—and hence my keenest sorrows rise—
My friend, my guardian, my Orestes dies;
Still for that loss must wretched I complain,
And sad Ophelia mourn her favorite swain.
Ah! come the day when from this bloody shore
Fate shall remove them to return no more—
To scorch'd Bahama shall the traitors go
With grief and rage, and unremitting woe,

On burning sands to walk their painful round,
And sigh through all the solitary ground,
Where no gay flower their haggard eyes shall see,
And find no shade but from the cypress tree.

So much we suffer'd from the tribe I hate,
So near they shov'd me to the brink of fate,
When two long months in these dark hulks we lay,
Barr'd down by night, and fainting all the day
In the fierce fervors of the solar beam,
Cool'd by no breeze on Hudson's mountain-stream;
That not unsung these threescore days shall fall
To black oblivion that would cover all!

No masts or sails these crowded ships adorn,
Dismal to view, neglected and forlorn!
Here, mighty ills oppress the imprison'd throng,
Dull were our slumbers, and our nights too long—
From morn to eve along the decks we lay
Scorch'd into fevers by the solar ray;
No friendly awning cast a welcome shade,
Once was it promis'd, and was never made;
No favors could these sons of death bestow,
'Twas endless cursing, and continual woe:
Immortal hatred doth their breasts engage,
And this lost empire swells their souls with rage.

Two hulks on Hudson's stormy bosom lie,
Two, farther south, affront the pitying eye—
There, the black *Scorpion* at her mooring rides,
There, *Strombolo* swings, yielding to the tides;
Here, bulky *Jersey* fills a larger space,
And *Hunter,* to all hospitals disgrace—
Thou, *Scorpion*—fatal to thy crowded throng,
Dire theme of horror and Plutonian song,
Requir'st my lay—thy sultry decks I know,
And all the torments that exist below!
The briny wave that Hudson's bosom fills
Drain'd through her bottom in a thousand rills,
Rotten and old, replete with sighs and groans,
Scarce on the waters she sustain'd her bones;
Here, doom'd to toil, or founder in the tide,
At the moist pumps incessantly we ply'd,
Here, doom'd to starve, like famish'd dogs we tore
The scant allowance, that our tyrants bore.

THE LITERATURE OF REVOLUTION

Remembrance shudders at this scene of fears—
Still in my view some English brute appears,
Some base-born Hessian slave walks threat'ning by,
Some servile Scot with murder in his eye
Still haunts my sight, as vainly they bemoan
Rebellions manag'd so unlike their own!
O may I never feel the poignant pain
To live subjected to such fiends again,
Stewards and mates that hostile Britain bore,
Cut from the gallows on their native shore;
Their ghastly looks and vengeance-beaming eyes
Still to my view in dismal colors rise—
O may I ne'er review these dire abodes,
These piles for slaughter, floating on the floods,—
And you, that o'er the troubled ocean go,
Strike not your standards to this miscreant foe,
Better the greedy wave should swallow all,
Better to meet the death-conducted ball,
Better to sleep on ocean's deepest bed,
At once destroy'd and number'd with the dead,
Than thus to perish in the face of day
Where twice ten thousand deaths one death delay.

When to the ocean dives the western sun,
And the scorch'd Tories fire their evening gun,
"Down, rebels, down!" the angry Scotchmen cry,
"Damn'd dogs, descend, or by our broad swords die!"

Hail, dark abode! what can with thee compare—
Heat, sickness, famine, death, and stagnant air—
Pandora's box, from whence all mischief flew,
Here real found, torments mankind anew!
Swift from the guarded decks we rush'd along,
And vainly sought repose, so vast our throng:
Three hundred wretches here, denied all light,
In crowded mansions pass the infernal night,
Some for a bed their tatter'd vestments join,
And some on chests, and some on floors recline;
Shut from the blessings of the evening air,
Pensive we lay with mingled corpses there,
Meager and wan, and scorch'd with heat below,
We loom'd like ghosts, ere death had made us so—
How could we else, where heat and hunger join'd
Thus to debase the body and the mind,

Where cruel thirst the parching throat invades,
Dries up the man, and fits him for the shades.

    No waters laded from the bubbling spring
To these dire ships the British monsters bring—
By planks and ponderous beams completely wall'd
In vain for water, and in vain, I call'd:
No drop was granted to the midnight prayer,
To Dives in these regions of despair!
The loathsome cask a deadly dose contains,
Its poison circling through the languid veins;
"Here, generous Britain, generous, as you say,
To my parch'd tongue one cooling drop convey,
Hell has no mischief like a thirsty throat,
Nor one tormentor like your David Sproat."[72]

    Dull flew the hours, till, from the East display'd,
Sweet morn dispells the horrors of the shade;
On every side dire objects meet the sight,
And pallid forms, and murders of the night;
The dead were past their pain, the living groan,
Nor dare to hope another morn their own;
But what to them is morn's delightful ray,
Sad and distressful as the close of day. . . .

    But such a train of endless woes abound,
So many mischiefs in these hulks are found,
That on them all a poem to prolong
Would swell too high the horrors of my song—
Hunger and thirst to work our woe combine,
And moldy bread, and flesh of rotten swine,
The mangled carcase, and the batter'd brain,
The doctor's poison, and the captain's cane,
The soldier's musket, and the steward's debt,
The evening shackle, and the noonday threat.

    That juice destructive to the pangs of care
Which Rome of old, nor Athens could prepare,
Which gains the day for many a modern chief
When cool reflection yields a faint relief,
That charm, whose virtue warms the world beside,
Was by these tyrants to our use denied,
While yet they deign'd that healthy juice to lade
The putrid water felt its powerful aid;
But when refus'd—to aggravate our pains—
Then fevers rag'd and revel'd through our veins;

Throughout my frame I felt its deadly heat,
I felt my pulse with quicker motions beat:
A pallid hue o'er every face was spread,
Unusual pains attack'd the fainting head,
No physic here, no doctor to assist,
My name was enter'd on the sick man's list;
Twelve wretches more the same dark symptoms took,
And these were enter'd on the doctor's book;
The loathsome *Hunter* was our destin'd place,
The *Hunter*, to all hospitals disgrace;
With soldiers sent to guard us on our road,
Joyful we left the *Scorpion's* dire abode;
Some tears we shed for the remaining crew,
Then curs'd the hulk, and from her sides withdrew.

To the Memory of the Brave Americans
(1781)

Under General Greene, in South Carolina, who fell in the action of
September 8, 1781 [73]

At Eutaw Springs the valiant died;
    Their limbs with dust are covered o'er—
Weep on, ye springs, your tearful tide;
    How many heroes are no more!

If in this wreck of ruin, they
    Can yet be thought to claim a tear,
O smite your gentle breast, and say
    The friends of freedom slumber here!

Thou, who shalt trace this bloody plain,
    If goodness rules thy generous breast,
Sigh for the wasted rural reign;
    Sigh for the shepherds, sunk to rest!

Stranger, their humble graves adorn;
    You too may fall, and ask a tear;

'Tis not the beauty of the morn
    That proves the evening shall be clear.

They saw their injured country's woe;
    The flaming town, the wasted field;
Then rushed to meet the insulting foe;
    They took the spear—but left the shield.

Led by thy conquering genius, Greene,
    The Britons they compelled to fly;
None distant viewed the fatal plain,
    None grieved, in such a cause to die—

But, like the Parthian, famed of old,
    Who, flying, still their arrows threw,
These routed Britons, full as bold,
    Retreated, and retreating slew.

Now rest in peace, our patriot band;
    Though far from nature's limits thrown,
We trust they find a happier land,
    A brighter sunshine of their own.

Epigram
(1782)

Occasioned by the title of Mr. Rivington's *New York Gazette*
being scarcely legible

Says Satan to Jemmy, "I hold you a bet
That you mean to abandon our *Royal Gazette,*
Or, between you and me, you would manage
    things better
Than the title to print on so sneaking a letter.

"Now being connected so long in the art
It would not be prudent at present to part;
And people, perhaps, would be frightened, and fret
If the devil alone carried on the *Gazette.*"

Says Jemmy to Satan (by the way of a wipe),
"Who gives me the matter should furnish the type;
And why you find fault, I can scarcely divine,
For the types, like the printer, are certainly thine.

"'Tis yours to deceive with the semblance of truth,
Thou friend of my age, and thou guide of my youth!
But, to prosper, pray send me some further supplies,
A set of new types, and a set of new lies."

Song
(1782)

On Captain Barney's Victory over the Ship *General Monk*[74]

O'er the waste of waters cruising,
Long the *General Monk* had reigned;
All subduing, all reducing,
None her lawless rage restrained:
Many a brave and hearty fellow
Yielding to this warlike foe,
When her guns began to bellow
Struck his humbled colors low.

But grown bold with long successes,
Leaving the wide watery way,
She, a stranger to distresses,
Came to cruise within Cape May:
"Now we soon (said Captain Rogers)
Shall their men of commerce meet;
In our hold we'll have them lodgers,
We shall capture half their fleet.

"Lo! I see their van appearing—
Back our topsails to the mast—
They toward us full are steering
With a gentle western blast.
"I've a list of all their cargoes,

155

All their guns, and all their men:
  I am sure these modern Argos
    Can't escape us one in ten:

"Yonder comes the *Charming Sally*
    Sailing with the *General Greene*—
First we'll fight the *Hyder Ali*,
    Taking her is taking them:
She intends to give us battle,
    Bearing down with all her sail—
Now, boys, let our cannon rattle!
    To take her we cannot fail.

"Our eighteen guns, each a nine-pounder,
    Soon shall terrify this foe;
We shall maul her, we shall wound her,
    Bringing rebel colors low."—
While he thus anticipated
    Conquests that he could not gain,
He in the Cape May channel waited
    For the ship that caused his pain.

Captain Barney then preparing,
    Thus addressed his gallant crew—
"Now, brave lads, be bold and daring,
    Let your hearts be firm and true;
"This is a proud English cruiser,
    Roving up and down the main,
We must fight her—must reduce her,
    Though our decks be strewed with slain.

"Let who will be the survivor,
    We must conquer or must die,
We must take her up the river,
    Whate'er comes of you or I:
"Though she shows most formidable
    With her eighteen pointed nines,
And her quarters clad in sable,
    Let us balk her proud designs.

"With four nine-pounders, and twelve sixes
    We will face that daring band;

Let no dangers damp your courage,
    Nothing can the brave withstand.
"Fighting for your country's honor,
    Now to gallant deeds aspire;
Helmsman, bear us down upon her,
    Gunner, give the word to fire!"

Then yardarm and yardarm meeting,
    Strait began the dismal fray,
Cannon mouths, each other greeting,
    Belched their smoky flames away:
Soon the langrage, grape and chain shot
    That from Barney's cannons flew
Swept the *Monk*, and cleared each round top,
    Killed and wounded half her crew.

Captain Rogers strove to rally,
    But they from their quarters fled,
While the roaring *Hyder Ali*
    Covered o'er his decks with dead.
When from their tops their dead men tumbled,
    And the streams of blood did flow,
Then their proudest hopes were humbled
    By their brave inferior foe.

All aghast, and all confounded,
    They beheld their champions fail,
And their captain, sorely wounded,
    Bade them quick for quarters call.
Then the *Monk's* proud flag descended,
    And her cannon ceased to roar;
By her crew no more defended,
    She confessed the contest o'er.

Come, brave boys, and fill your glasses,
    You have humbled one proud foe,
No brave action this surpasses,
    Fame shall tell the nations so—
Thus be Britain's woes completed,
    Thus abridged her cruel reign,
'Till she ever, thus defeated,
    Yields the scepter of the main.

16

"The Sale of the Hessians"
(1777)

The hoax was Benjamin Franklin's favorite satiric weapon, and nowhere did he succeed with it more brilliantly than in "The Sale of the Hessians," a purported letter from Count de Schaumbergh to Baron de Hohendorf, in which the count congratulates his commander for the conduct of his Hessians at the Battle of Trenton[75] and exhorts him to still greater expenditures of human life. By early 1777, when Franklin evidently wrote his letter, German mercenaries had already become an important factor in the balance of power between England and her former colonies. In the preceding year some eighteen thousand Hessians had been introduced into America and had distinguished themselves on Long Island, at White Plains, and in the New Jersey campaign for their excellence as soldiers and their fierceness and rigid discipline under fire. In fact, without such troops, which Lord North argued could be hired more cheaply than he could recruit soldiers at home, Britain would have been hard pressed indeed to carry the war to its rebellious colonists. Thus, as is so often the case with satire, Franklin's underlying purpose was a deadly serious one. Though England had for centuries hired foreign mercenaries to fight her wars, Franklin hoped to use the present instance of British traffic in flesh with human monsters like Count de Schaumbergh to win sympathy for the American cause before the bar of world opinion.

☆ ☆

From the Count de Schaumbergh to the Baron de Hohendorf, commanding the Hessian troops in America

Rome, 18 February, 1777

Monsieur le Baron: On my return from Naples, I received at Rome your letter of the 27th December of last year. I have learned with unspeakable pleasure the courage our troops exhibited at Trenton, and you cannot imagine my joy on being told that of the 1,950 Hessians engaged in the fight, but 345 escaped. There were just 1,605 men killed, and I cannot sufficiently commend your prudence in sending an exact list of the dead to my minister in London. This precaution was the more necessary as the report sent to the English ministry does not give but 1,455 dead. This would make 483,450 florins instead of the 643,500 which I am entitled to demand under our convention. You will comprehend the prejudice which such an error would work in my finances, and I do not doubt you will take the necessary pains to prove that Lord North's list is false and yours correct.

The court of London objects that there were a hundred wounded who ought not to be included in the list nor paid for as dead; but I trust you will not overlook my instructions to you on quitting Cassel, and that you will not have tried by human succor to recall to life the unfortunate whose days could not be lengthened but by the loss of a leg or an arm. That would be making them a pernicious present, and I am sure they would rather die than live in a condition no longer fit for my service. I do not mean by this that you should assassinate them; we should be humane, my dear Baron, but you may insinuate to the surgeons with entire propriety that a crippled man is a reproach to their profession, and that there is no wiser course than to let every one of them die when he ceases to be fit to fight.

I am about to send you some new recruits. Don't economize them. Remember glory before all things. Glory is true wealth. There is nothing degrades the soldier like the love of money. He must care only for honor and reputation, but this reputation must be acquired in the midst of dangers. A battle gained without costing the conqueror any blood is an inglorious success, while the conquered cover themselves with glory by perishing with their arms in their hands. Do you remember that of the 300 Lacedaemonians who defended the defile of Thermopylae not one returned? How happy should I be could I say the same of my brave Hessians!

It is true that their king, Leonidas, perished with them: but things have changed, and it is no longer the custom for princes of the empire to go and fight in America for a cause with which they have no concern. And besides, to whom should they pay the thirty guineas per man if I did not stay in Europe to receive them? Then, it is necessary also that I be ready to send recruits to replace the men you lose. For this purpose I must return to Hesse.

159

It is true, grown men are becoming scarce there, but I will send you boys. Besides, the scarcer the commodity, the higher the price. I am assured that the women and little girls have begun to till our lands, and they get on not badly. You did right to send back to Europe that Dr. Crumerus who was so successful in curing dysentery. Don't bother with a man who is subject to looseness of the bowels. That disease makes bad soldiers. One coward will do more mischief in an engagement than ten brave men will do good. Better that they burst in their barracks than fly in a battle and tarnish the glory of our arms. Besides, you know that they pay me as killed for all who die from disease, and I don't get a farthing for runaways. My trip to Italy, which has cost me enormously, makes it desirable that there should be a great mortality among them. You will therefore promise promotion to all who expose themselves; you will exhort them to seek glory in the midst of dangers; you will say to Major Maundorff that I am not at all content with his saving the 345 men who escaped the massacre at Trenton. Through the whole campaign he has not had ten men killed in consequence of his orders. Finally, let it be your principal object to prolong the war and avoid a decisive engagement on either side, for I have made arrangements for a grand Italian opera, and I do not wish to be obliged to give it up. Meantime I pray God, my dear Baron de Hohendorf, to have you in his holy and gracious keeping.

WILLIAM LIVINGSTON

17

"Burgoyne's Proclamation" (1777)

Perhaps no single act of the Revolution provided so much grist for the American propaganda mill as the proclamation delivered by General John Burgoyne as he set out with a lavishly appointed army on his ill-fated invasion of New York in the late spring of 1777. Burgoyne's purpose was serious enough—an attempt to neutralize the American resistance that lay in his path—but his manner was pompous and outrageous. He began his "Proclamation" by listing the flamboyant details of his own pedigree:

> *By John Burgoyne, Esquire, etc., etc., Lieutenant-General of his Majesty's Forces in America, Colonel of the Queen's Regiment of Light Dragoons, Governor of Fort William in North Britain, one of the Representatives of the Commons of Great Britain in Parliament, and commanding an army and Fleet in an Expedition from Canada, etc., etc., etc.*

After denouncing America's "unnatural rebellion" and "system of tyranny," Burgoyne proceeded to his main object: "I . . . invite and exhort all persons in all places where the progress of this army may point, and by the blessing of God I will extend it far, to maintain such a conduct as may justify me in protecting their lands, habitations and families." Though he assured his readers that his purpose was "to hold forth security, not depredation, to the country," Burgoyne concluded with the blunt warning: "I have but to give stretch to the Indian forces under my direction—and they amount to thousands—to overtake the hardened enemies of Great Britain and America: I consider them the same whereever they lurk."

As he delivered this "Proclamation," Burgoyne, the dashing "Gentleman

Johnny," had every reason to swagger; success seemed assured. Little could
he dream of the series of seemingly impossible reverses and blunders that
would result in his abject surrender at Saratoga that October.

Of all the parodies that Burgoyne's "Proclamation" called forth–and
Washington took it seriously enough to urge that it "be counteracted as
much as possible"–none was more effective or cleverer than the one which
William Livingston, governor of New Jersey, published in the New York
Journal *on September 8, 1777. Livingston (1723-90) was a member of one
of New York's most prominent colonial families. Born at Albany and educated at Yale, he studied law, and once admitted to the bar in 1748 became
one of New York City's leading lawyers, a position he occupied for nearly a
quarter of a century. In 1772 Livingston retired to Liberty Hall, his country
estate near Elizabeth, New Jersey, only to be called forth almost at once to
serve colony and country: as a member of the Continental Congress (1774-
76), as commander of the New Jersey militia, and from August, 1776, to
the time of his death, as governor of the new state of New Jersey. A man
of real literary talent–he had written and published a 700-line poem entitled
"Philosophic Solitude" at the early age of twenty-four–none knew better
than Governor Livingston of the need for propaganda in time of war; and
none practiced the art with a finer hand. Throughout the early war years
Livingston found time to deliver to the press a steady stream of contributions–he was an accomplished writer of satire and burlesque–and though
many of his efforts were published anonymously, Livingston's identity was
sufficiently well known to make him a popular subject for personal attack
by the opposition–a sure sign of his own success.*

☆ ☆

> By John Burgoyne and Burgoyne John, sir,
> And grac'd with titles still more higher,
> For I'm lieutenant general too
> Of Georgie's troops both red and blue
> On this extensive continent,
> And of Queen Charlotte's regiment
> Of eight dragoons the colonel,
> And governor eke of Castle Will
> And furthermore when I am there,
> In House of Commons there appear
> (Hoping ere long to be a peer),
> Being a member of that virtuous band

Who always vote at North's command,
Directing too the fleets and troops
From Canada as thick as hops;
And all my titles to display,
I'll end with thrice et cetera.

The troops consign'd to my command,
Like Hercules to purge the land,
Intend to act in combination
With th' other forces of the nation,
Displaying wide thro' every quarter
What Britain's justice would be after.
It is not difficult to show it,
And every mother's son must know it,
That what at first she meant to gain
By requisitions and chicane,
She's now determined to acquire
By kingly reason, sword and fire.
I can appeal to all your senses,
Your judgments, feelings, tastes and fancies;
Your ears and eyes have heard and seen
How causeless this revolt has been;
And what a dust your leaders kick up
In this rebellious civil hickup,
And how upon this curs'd foundation
Was rear'd the system of vexation
Over a stubborn generation.

But now inspired with patriot love
I come th' oppression to remove;
To free you from the heavy clog
Of every tyrant demagogue,
Who for the most romantic story
Claps into limbo loyal Tory,
All hurly burly, hot and hasty,
Without a writ to hold him fast by;
Nor suffers any living creature
(Led by the dictates of his nature)
To fight in green for Britain's cause,
Or aid us to restore her laws;
In short the vilest generation
Which in vindictive indignation

Almighty vengeance ever hurl'd
From this to the infernal world.
A Tory cannot move his tongue,
But whip, in prison he is flung,
His goods and chattels made a prey
By those vile mushrooms of a day,
He's tortur'd too, and scratch'd and bit,
And plung'd into a dreary pit;
Where he must suffer sharper doom
Than ere was hatched by Church of Rome.

These things are done by rogues, who dare
Profess to breathe in freedom's air.
To petticoats alike and breeches
Their cruel domination stretches,
For the sole crime, or sole suspicion
(What worse is done by th' inquisition?)
Of still adhering to the crown,
Their tyrants striving to kick down,
Who by perverting law and reason
Allegiance construe into treason.
Religion too is often made
A stalking horse to drive the trade,
And warring churches dare implore
Protection from th' Almighty Pow'r;
They fast and pray, in Providence
Profess to place their confidence;
And vainly think the Lord of all
Regards our squabbles on this ball;
Which would appear as droll in Britain
As any whims that one could hit on;
Men's consciences are set at naught
Nor reason valued at a groat;
And they that will not swear and fight
Must sell their all, and say good night.

By such important views they're pres't to,
I issue this, my manifesto.
I, the great knight of de la Mancha,
Without Squire Carleton my sancho,[76]
Will tear you limb from limb asunder
With cannon, blunderbuss and thunder;

And spoil your feathering and your tarring;
And cage you up for pickled herring
In front of troops as spruce as beaux,
And ready to lay on their blows;
I'll spread destruction far and near:
And when I cannot kill I'll spare,
Inviting by these presents all,
Both young and old and great and small,
And rich and poor and Whig and Tory,
In cellar deep or lofty story;
Where'er my troops at my command
Shall swarm like locusts o'er the land.
And they shall march from the North Pole,
As far at least as Pensacole,
To break off their communications,
That I can save their habitations;
For finding that Sir William's plunders[77]
Prove in the event apparent blunders,
It is my full determination
To check all kinds of depredation;
But when I've got you in my pow'r,
Favor'd is he I last devour.

From him who loves a quiet life,
And keeps at home to kiss his wife,
And drink success to King Pygmalion,
And calls all congresses rebscallion,
With neutral stomach eats his supper,
Nor deems the contest worth a copper,
I will not defalcate a groat,
Nor force his wife to cut his throat;
But with his doxy he may stay,
And live to fight another day;
Drink all the cider he has made
And have to boot a green cockade.
But as I like a good Sir Loin
And mutton chop when e'er I dine,
And my poor troops have long kept Lent,
Not for religion but for want,
Who e'er secretes cow, bull, or ox,
Or shall presume to hide his flocks,
Or with felonious hand eloign

Pig, duck, or gosling from Burgoyne,
Or dare to pull the bridges down,
My boys to puzzle or to drown;
Or smuggle hay, or plow, or harrow,
Cart, horses, wagons, or wheelbarrow;
Or 'thwart the path lay straw or switch,
As folks are wont to stop a witch,
I'll hang him as the Jews did Haman;
And smoke his carcass for a gammon.
I'll pay in coin for what I eat,
Or Continental counterfeit;
But what's more likely still, I shall
(So fare my troops) not pay at all.
With the most Christian spirit fir'd,
And by true soldiership inspir'd,
I speak as men do in a passion
To give my speech the more impression,
If any should so harden'd be
As to expect immunity,
Because *procul a fulmine,*
I will let loose the dogs of Hell,
Ten thousand Indians, who shall yell,
And foam, and tear, and grin, and roar,
And drench their moccasins in gore;
To these I'll give full scope and play
From Ticonderog to Florida;
They'll scalp your heads, and kick your shins,
And rip your guts, and flay your skins,
And of your ears be nimble croppers,
And make your thumbs tobacco stoppers.
If after all these lovely warnings,
My wishes' and my bowels' yearnings,
You shall remain as deaf as adder,
Or grow with hostile rage the madder,
I swear by George and by St. Paul
I will exterminate you all.
Subscrib'd with my manual sign
To test these presents, John Burgoyne.

FRANCIS HOPKINSON

18

"The Battle of the Kegs" (1778)

Though Francis Hopkinson was occupied throughout most of the Revolution with his official responsibilities as chairman of the Continental Navy Board (1776–78), Congress's treasurer of loans (1778–80), and admiralty judge for Pennsylvania (after 1779), he still found time, as he wrote to Franklin in 1778, to do "all the Service I could with my Pen—throwing in my Mite at Times in Prose and Verse, serious & satirical Essays, etc."

"The Battle of the Kegs," perhaps the best-known satirical ballad of the Revolution, was published in the Pennsylvania Packet *on March 4, 1778, towards the end of the bleak winter that saw Sir William Howe resting comfortably in Philadelphia while Washington's ragged army made the best of it among the hills of Valley Forge. It celebrates an attempt by the Americans to float kegs of gunpowder with detonation devices down the Delaware River upon British ships moored at Philadelphia. As American surgeon James Thacher later recounted the event in his* Military Journal *(1823):*

> *The kegs were in the night set adrift, to fall with the ebb on the shipping; but the proper distance could not be well ascertained, and they were set adrift at too great a distance from the vessels, by which means they were obstructed, and dispersed by the ice. They approached, however, in the day time, and one of them blew up a boat, and others exploded, which occasioned among the British seamen the greatest alarm and consternation. They actually manned the wharves and shipping at Philadelphia, and discharged their small arms and cannon at everything they could see floating in the river during the ebb tide.*

In his ballad, sung to the tune of "Yankee Doodle," Hopkinson expanded this episode into a ludicrous battle, making fun of Howe's vaunted British army.

Gallants attend, and hear a friend
  Trill forth harmonious ditty;
Strange things I'll tell, which late befell
  In Philadelphia city.[78]

'Twas early day, as poets say,
  Just when the sun was rising,
A soldier stood on a log of wood,
  And saw a thing surprising.

As in amaze he stood to gaze,
  The truth can't be denied, sir,
He spied a score of kegs or more
  Come floating down the tide, sir.

A sailor, too, in jerkin blue,
  This strange appearance viewing,
First damn'd his eyes in great surprise,
  Then said, "Some mischief's brewing.

"These kegs, I'm told, the rebels hold
  Packed up like pickled herring,
And they're come down t' attack the town,
  In this new way of ferrying."

The soldier flew, the sailor too,
  And scared almost to death, sir,
Wore out their shoes to spread the news,
  And ran till out of breath, sir.

Now up and down, throughout the town,
  Most frantic scenes were acted;
And some ran here, and others there,
  Like men almost distracted.

Some fire cried, which some denied,
  But said the earth had quaked;
And girls and boys, with hideous noise,
  Ran through the streets half-naked.

Sir William, he, snug as a flea,
  Lay all this time a-snoring;

(LLL

Nor dreamed of harm as he lay warm
   In bed with Mrs. Loring.[79]

Now in a fright he starts upright,
   Awak'd by such a clatter;
He rubs his eyes and boldly cries,
   "For God's sake, what's the matter?"

At his bedside he then espied
   Sir Erskine at command, sir,[80]
Upon one foot he had one boot,
   And t'other in his hand, sir.

"Arise! arise," Sir Erskine cries,
   "The rebels—more's the pity—
Without a boat are all afloat,
   And rang'd before the city.

"The motley crew, in vessels new,
   With Satan for their guide, sir,
Packed up in bags, or wooden kegs,
   Come driving down the tide, sir.

"Therefore prepare for bloody war;
   These kegs must all be routed,
Or surely we despis'd shall be,
   And British courage doubted."

The royal band now ready stand,
   All ranged in dread array, sir,
With stomachs stout, to see it out,
   And make a bloody day, sir.

The cannons roar from shore to shore,
   The small arms make a rattle;
Since wars began, I'm sure no man
   E'er saw so strange a battle.

The rebel dales, the rebel vales,
   With rebel trees surrounded,
The distant woods, the hills and floods,
   With rebel echoes sounded.

169

The fish below swam to and fro,
    Attack'd from every quarter;
Why sure, thought they, the devil's to pay
    'Mongst folks above the water.

The kegs, 'tis said, though strongly made
    Of rebel staves and hoops, sir,
Could not oppose their powerful foes,
    The conquering British troops, sir.

From morn till night these men of might
    Display'd amazing courage;
And when the sun was fairly down,
    Retir'd to sup their porridge.

An hundred men, with each a pen,
    Or more, upon my word, sir,
It is most true would be too few
    Their valor to record, sir.

Such feats did they perform that day,
    Against those wicked kegs, sir,
That years to come, if they get home,
    They'll make their boasts and brags, sir.

ETHAN ALLEN

19

from *A Narrative of Colonel Ethan Allen's Captivity* (1779)

Ethan Allen (1738–89), leader of the Green Mountain Boys and father of Vermont, was a legendary figure, even in his own lifetime. Born in Litchfield, Connecticut, Allen migrated by stages into the disputed area known as the Hampshire Grants (present-day Vermont), and by 1770 had assumed a role of leadership in defending New Hampshire's claims against those of New York. When the courts offered little redress, Allen and his followers, the famous Green Mountain Boys, took matters into their own hands in defending the Grants against Yorker intrusion. A man of prodigious physical power, Allen was a natural leader of the frontier variety: swaggering and boisterous, plain and direct, impetuous yet shrewd and calculating. He also had a flair for the dramatic. As George Washington once wrote: "There is an original something in him that commands admiration." By the time of the Revolution Ethan Allen and his brother Ira were pretty much running affairs in western New England.

Shortly after the news of Lexington and Concord reached the Grants (May 1775), Allen and his Green Mountain Boys, with the help of Benedict Arnold and some Massachusetts militiamen, fell upon the small British garrison at Fort Ticonderoga near the head of Lake Champlain and won an easy, and famous, victory. Allen's second revolutionary exploit was not quite so fortunate. In the fall of 1775 he accompanied Montgomery's invasion of Canada, only to be captured at Montreal when his attempt to take the city failed. As a prisoner of war, Allen was taken to Quebec and then shipped to England, where he was landed at Falmouth and for a time put on display for the curious at nearby Pendennis Castle. In October, 1776, Allen was returned to New York and lodged in the Provost Jail, though with permission to roam the city on parole during the day. Finally, in May, 1778, Allen was exchanged and returned home, where he continued to work actively for the independent existence of Vermont, even for a time secretly negotiating with the British.

A Narrative of Colonel Ethan Allen's Captivity *was first published serially in the* Pennsylvania Packet *late in the spring of 1779, and then, that same year, put out in book form by the Philadelphia printer Robert Bell. In the next two years it went through seven other editions. The popularity of Allen's* Narrative, *the most popular prose captivity narrative to come out of the Revolution, is readily understandable as one reads this colorful and fascinating tale of patriotism and endurance, designed, quite obviously, to act as a stimulus to wartime morale. With skillful writing, Allen succeeds in creating for himself a public persona worthy of admiration and his own reputation. To be sure, as historians have noted, Allen's account is not entirely objective, and there are errors and distortions—some, no doubt, deliberate, for Allen was anxious to put himself in the best light; others unintentional, for he wrote without benefit of notes. Through it all, however, comes the Allen that Alexander Graydon knew as a fellow prisoner in New York, and described in his* Memoirs *(1811):*

> *His figure was that of a robust, large-framed man, worn down by confinement and hard fare—a suit of blue clothes with a gold laced hat that had been presented him by the gentlemen of Cork enabled him to make a very passable appearance for a rebel colonel. I have seldom met a man possessing, in my opinion, a stronger mind, or whose mode of expression was more vehement and oratorical. His style was a singular compound of local barbarisms, scriptural phrases, and oriental wildness; and though unclassic and sometimes ungrammatical, it was highly animated and forcible. Notwithstanding that Allen might have something of the insubordinate lawless frontier in his composition, he appeared to me to be a man of generosity and honor.*

☆ ☆

Ever since I arrived to a state of manhood, and acquainted myself with the general history of mankind, I have felt a sincere passion for liberty. The history of nations doomed to perpetual slavery in consequence of yielding up to tyrants their natural born liberties, I read with a sort of philosophical horror; so that the first systematical and bloody attempt at Lexington to enslave America thoroughly electrified my mind, and fully determined me to take part with my country. And while I was wishing for an opportunity to signalize myself in its behalf, directions were privately sent to me from the then colony (now state) of Connecticut to raise the Green Mountain Boys, and, if possible, with them to surprise and take the fortress Ticonderoga. This enterprise I cheerfully undertook; and, after first guarding all the several passes that led thither to cut off all intelligence between the garrison and the country, made a forced march from Bennington, and arrived at the lake opposite to Ticonderoga on the evening of the ninth day of May, 1775, with two hundred and thirty valiant Green Mountain Boys; and it was with the utmost difficulty that I procured boats to cross the lake. However, I landed eighty-three men near the garrison, and sent the boats back for the rear guard commanded by Colonel Seth Warner;[81] but the day began to dawn, and I found myself under a necessity to attack the fort before the rear could cross the lake; and, as it was viewed hazardous, I harangued the officers and soldiers in the manner following: "Friends and fellow soldiers, you have for a number of years past been a scourge and terror to arbitrary power. Your valor has been famed abroad, and acknowledged, as appears by the advice and orders to me (from the General Assembly of Connecticut) to surprise and take the garrison now before us. I now propose to advance before you, and in person conduct you through the wicket gate; for we must this morning either quit our pretensions to valor or possess ourselves of this fortress in a few minutes; and, inasmuch as it is a desperate attempt (which none but the bravest of men dare undertake), I do not urge it on any contrary to his will. You that will undertake voluntarily, poise your firelocks."

The men being (at this time) drawn up in three ranks, each poised his firelock. I ordered them to face to the right, and, at the head of the center-file, marched them immediately to the wicket gate aforesaid, where I found a sentry posted, who instantly snapped his fusee at me. I ran immediately towards him, and he retreated through the covered way into the parade within the garrison, gave a halloo, and ran under a bomb-proof. My party, who followed me into the fort, I formed on the parade in such a manner as to face the two barracks which faced each other. The garrison being asleep (except the sentries), we gave three huzzas, which greatly surprised them. One of the sentries made a pass at one of my officers with a charged bayonet, and slightly wounded him. My first thought was to kill him with my sword; but, in an instant, altered the design and fury of the blow to a slight cut on the side of the head; upon which he dropped his gun and asked quarter, which I readily granted him, and demanded of him the place where the commanding officer kept. He showed me a pair of stairs in the front of a barrack, on the west part of the garrison, which led up to a second story in said barrack, to which I immediately repaired, and ordered the commander (Captain Delaplace) to come forth instantly, or I would sacrifice the whole garrison; at which the captain came immediately to the door, with his breeches in his hand, when I ordered him to deliver to me the fort instantly, who asked me by what authority I demanded it. I answered, "In the name of the great Jehovah and the Continental Congress." The authority of the Congress being very little known at that time, he began to speak again. But I interrupted him, and with my drawn sword over his head again demanded an immediate surrender of the garrison; to which he then complied, and ordered his men to be forthwith paraded without arms, as he had given up the garrison. In the meantime some of my officers had given orders, and in consequence thereof sundry of the barrack doors were beat down, and about one-third of the garrison imprisoned, which consisted of the said commander, a Lieutenant Feltham, a conductor of artillery, a gunner, two sergeants, and forty-four rank and file; about one hundred pieces of cannon, one 13-inch mortar, and a number of swivels. This surprise was carried into execution in the gray of the morning of the 10th day of May, 1775. The sun seemed to rise that morning with a superior luster, and Ticonderoga and its dependencies smiled on its conquerors, who tossed about the flowing bowl, and wished success to Congress and the liberty and freedom of America. . . .

[Following his success at Ticonderoga, Allen joined Montgomery's invasion of Canada. During the siege of St. Johns, Allen raised a small force of Canadian volunteers and then, apparently without authorization, joined with Major Jacob Brown in a plan to take Montreal. When Brown's troops failed to arrive at the appointed time, Allen was forced to stand alone and after a sharp skirmish to surrender, on September 15, 1775.]

The officer I capitulated with then directed me and my party to advance towards him, which was done. I handed him my sword, and in half a minute after, a savage, part of whose head was shaved, being almost naked and painted, with feathers intermixed with the hair of the other side of his head, came running to me with an incredible swiftness; he seemed to advance with more than mortal speed. As he approached near me, his hellish visage was beyond all description; snakes' eyes appear innocent in comparison of his; his features extorted; malice, death, murder, and the wrath of devils and damned spirits are the emblems of his countenance; and in less than twelve feet of me, presented his firelock. At the instant of his present, I twitched the officer, to whom I gave my sword, between me and the savage; but he flew round with great fury, trying to single me out to shoot me without killing the officer. But by this time I was near as nimble as he, keeping the officer in such a position that his danger was my defense; but in less than half a minute I was attacked by just such another imp of hell. Then I made the officer fly around with incredible velocity for a few seconds of time, when I perceived a Canadian (who had lost one eye, as appeared afterwards) taking my part against the savages; and in an instant an Irishman came to my assistance with a fixed bayonet, and drove away the fiends, swearing by Jasus he would kill them. This tragic scene composed my mind. The escaping from so awful a death made even imprisonment happy, the more so as my conquerors on the field treated me with great civility and politeness.

The regular officers said that they were very happy to see Colonel Allen. I answered them that I should rather choose to have seen them at General Montgomery's camp. The gentlemen replied that they gave full credit to what I said, and so I walked to the town, which was (as I should guess) more than two miles, a British officer walking at my right hand, and one of the French noblesse at my left, the latter of which in the action had his eyebrow carried away by a glancing shot, but was nevertheless very merry and facetious; and no abuse was offered me till I came to the barrackyard at Montreal, where I met General Prescott,[82] who asked me my name, which I told him. He then asked me whether I was that Colonel Allen who took Ticonderoga. I told him I was the very man. Then he shook his cane over my head, calling many hard names, among which he frequently used the word rebel, and put himself in a great rage. I told him he would do well not to cane me, for I was not accustomed to it, and shook my fist at him, telling him that that was the beetle of mortality for him if he offered to strike; upon which Captain M'Cloud of the British pulled him by the skirt, and whispered to him (as he afterwards told me) to this import: that it was inconsistent with his honor to strike a prisoner. . . .

The wounded were all put into the hospital at Montreal, and those that were not were put on board of different vessels in the river and shackled together by pairs, viz. two men fastened together by one handcuff being closely fixed to one wrist of each of them, and treated with the greatest severity, nay as criminals.

I now come to the description of the irons which were put on me. The handcuff was of a common size and form, but my leg irons (I should imagine) would weigh thirty pounds; the bar was eight feet long, and very substantial; the shackles which encompassed my ankles were very tight. I was told by the officer who put them on that it was the king's plate, and I heard other of their officers say that it would weigh forty weight. The irons were so close upon my ankles that I could not lie down in any other manner than on my back. I was put into the lowest and most wretched part of the vessel, where I got the favor of a chest to sit on. The same answered for my bed at night, and having procured some little blocks of the guard (who day and night with fixed bayonets watched over me) to lay under each end of the large bar of my leg irons, to preserve my ankles from galling while I sat on the chest, or lay back on the same, though most of the time, night and day, I sat on it. But at length, having a desire to lay down on my side, which the closeness of the irons forbid, I desired the captain to loosen them for that purpose, but was denied the favor. The captain's name was Royal, who did not seem to be an ill-natured man, but often times said that his express orders were to treat me with such severity, which was disagreeable to his own feelings; nor did he ever insult me, though many others who came on board did. One of the officers, by the name of Bradley, was very generous to me. He would often send me victuals from his own table, nor did a day fail but that he sent me a good drink of grog. . . .

I was confined in the manner I have related on board the *Gaspée* schooner about six weeks, during which time I was obliged to throw out plenty of extravagant language, which answered certain purposes (at that time) better than to grace a history.

To give an instance, upon being insulted, in a fit of anger I twisted off a nail with my teeth, which I took to be a ten-penny nail; it went through the mortise of the bar of my handcuff, and at the same time I swaggered over those who abused me, particularly a Doctor Dace, who told me that I was outlawed by New York, and deserved death for several years past; was at last fully ripened for the halter, and in a fair way to obtain it. When I challenged him, he excused himself, in consequence, as he said, of my being a criminal; but I flung such a flood of language at him that it shocked him and the spectators, for my anger was very great. I heard one say, "Damn him, can he eat iron?" After that a small padlock was fixed to the handcuff, instead of the nail, and as they were mean-spirited in their treatment to me, so it appeared to me that they were equally timorous and cowardly.

I was after sent with the prisoners taken with me to an armed vessel in the river, which lay off against Quebec, under the command of Captain M'Cloud of the British, who treated me in a very generous and obliging manner, and according to my rank. In about twenty-four hours I bid him farewell with regret; but my good fortune still continued. The name of the captain of the vessel I was put on board was Little John, who, with his officers, behaved in a polite, generous and friendly manner. I lived with them in the cabin, and fared on the best, my irons being taken off, contrary to the order he had received from the commanding officer; but Captain Little John swore that a brave man should not be used as a rascal on board his ship.

Thus I found myself in possession of happiness once more, and the evils I had lately suffered gave me an uncommon relish for it.

Captain Little John used to go to Quebec almost every day in order to pay his respects to certain gentlemen and ladies. Being there on a certain day, he happened to meet with some disagreeable treatment, as he imagined, from a lieutenant of a man-of-war, and one word brought on another till the lieutenant challenged him to a duel on the Plains of Abraham. Captain Little John was a gentleman who entertained a high sense of honor, and could do no less than accept the challenge.

At nine o'clock the next morning they were to fight. The captain returned in the evening, and acquainted his lieutenant and me with the affair. His lieutenant was a high-blooded Scotchman as well as himself, who replied to his captain that he should not want for a second. With this I interrupted him, and gave the captain to understand that since an opportunity had presented, I would be glad to testify my gratitude to him by acting the part of a faithful second, on which he gave me his hand, and said that he wanted no better man. Says he, "I am a king's officer, and you a prisoner under my care; you must therefore go with me to the place appointed in disguise;" and added further, "You must engage to me, upon the honor of a gentleman, that whether I die or live, or whatever happens, provided you live, that you will return to my lieutenant on board this ship." All this I solemnly engaged him; the combatants were to discharge each a pocket pistol, and then to fall on with their iron-hilted muckle whangers; and one of that sort was allotted for me. But some British officers, who interposed early in the morning, settled the controversy without fighting.

Now having enjoyed eight or nine days happiness from the polite and generous treatment of Captain Little John and his officers, I was obliged to bid them farewell, parting with them in as friendly a manner as we had lived together, which, to the best of my memory, was the eleventh of November, when a detachment of General Arnold's little army appeared on Point Levy, opposite Quebec, who had performed an extraordinary march through a wilderness country with design to have surprised the capital of Canada. I was then taken on board a vessel called the *Adamant,* together with the prisoners taken with me, and put under the power of an English merchant from London, whose name was Brook Watson, a man of malicious and cruel disposition, and who was probably excited in the exercise of his malevolence by a junto of Tories who sailed with him to England; among whom were Colonel Guy Johnson, Colonel Claus,[83] and their attendants and associates, to the number of about thirty.

All the ship's crew (Colonel Claus in his personal behavior excepted) behaved towards the prisoners with that spirit of bitterness which is the peculiar characteristic of Tories when they have the friends of America in their power, measuring their loyalty to the English king by the barbarity, fraud, and deceit which they exercise towards the Whigs.

A small place in the vessel, enclosed with white-oak plank, was assigned for the prisoners, and for me among the rest. I should imagine that it was no more than twenty feet one way, and twenty-two the other. Into this place we were all, to the number of thirty-four, thrust and handcuffed (two prisoners more being added to our number), and were provided with two excrement tubs. In this circumference we were obliged to eat and perform the office of evacuation during the voyage to England, and were insulted by every blackguard sailor and Tory on board in the cruelest manner. But what is the most surprising is that not one of us died in the passage. When I was first ordered to go into the filthy enclosure, through a small sort of door, I positively refused, and endeavored to reason the before-named Brook Watson out of a conduct so derogatory to every sentiment of honor and humanity; but all to no purpose, my men being forced in the den already; and the rascal who had the charge of the prisoners commanded me to go immediately in among the rest. He further added that the place was good enough for a rebel, that it was impertinent for a capital offender to talk of honor or humanity, that anything short of a halter was too good for me, and that that would be my portion soon after I landed in England, for which purpose only I was sent thither. About the same time a lieutenant among the Tories insulted me in a grievous manner, saying that I ought to have been executed for my rebellion against New York, and spit in my face. Upon which, though I was handcuffed, I sprang at him with both hands, and knocked him partly down, but he scrambled along into the cabin, and I after him; there he got under the protection of some men with fixed bayonets, who were ordered to make ready to drive me into the place aforementioned. I challenged him to fight, notwithstanding the impediments that were on my hands, and had the exalted pleasure to see the rascal tremble for fear. His name I have forgot, but Watson ordered his guard to get me into the place with the other prisoners, dead or alive; and I had almost as leave die as do it, standing it out till they environed me round with bayonets; and brutish, prejudiced, abandoned wretches they were, from whom I could expect nothing but death or wounds. However, I told them that they were good honest fellows, that I could not blame them, that I was only in a dispute with a calico merchant who knew not how to behave towards a gentleman of the military establishment. This was spoke rather to appease them for my own preservation, as well as to treat Watson with contempt; but still I found that they were determined to force me into the wretched circumstances which their prejudiced and depraved minds had prepared for me. Therefore, rather than die, I submitted to their indignities, being drove with bayonets into the filthy dungeon with the other prisoners, where we were denied fresh water, except a small allowance, which was very inadequate to our wants; and in consequence of the stench of the place, each of us was soon followed with a diarrhea and fever, which occasioned an intolerable thirst. When we asked for water, we were most commonly (instead of obtaining it) insulted and derided; and to add to all the horrors of the place, it was so dark that we could not see each other, and were overspread with body lice. We had, notwithstanding these severities, full allowance of salt provisions, and a gill of rum per day; the latter of which was of the utmost service to us, and probably was the means of saving several of our lives. About forty days we existed in this manner, when the land's end of England was discovered from the masthead; soon after which the prisoners were taken from their gloomy abode, being permitted to see the light of the sun and breathe fresh air, which to us was very refreshing. The day following we landed at Falmouth. . . .

[Allen's stay in England was brief. Perhaps because they feared reprisals if Allen was harmed, the British government decided to return him to America. He was landed in New York City in late October of 1776 and placed on parole.]

I now found myself on parole, and restricted to the limits of the city of New York, where I soon projected means to live in some measure agreeable to my rank, though I was destitute of cash. My constitution was almost worn out by such a long and barbarous captivity. The enemy gave out that I was crazy and wholly unmanned, but my vitals held sound (nor was I delirious any more than I have been from my youth up, but my extreme circumstances at certain times rendered it political to act in some measure the madman), and in consequence of a regular diet and exercise my blood recruited, and my nerves in great measure recovered their former tone, strength and usefulness, in the course of six months.

I next invite the reader to a retrospect sight and consideration of the doleful scene of inhumanity exercised by General Sir William Howe and the army under his command, towards the prisoners taken on Long Island on the 27th day of August, 1776, sundry of whom were in an inhuman and barbarous manner murdered after they had surrendered their arms, particularly a General Odel (or Woodhull)[84] of the militia, who was hacked to pieces with cutlasses (when alive) by the light horsemen, and a Captain Fellows of the Continental army, who was thrust through with a bayonet, of which wound he died instantly.

Sundry others were hanged up by the neck till they were dead, five on the limb of a white oak tree, and without any reason assigned (except that they were fighting in defense of the only blessing worth preserving). And indeed those who had the misfortune to fall into their hands at Fort Washington, in the month of November following, met with but very little better usage, except that they were reserved from immediate death to famish and die with hunger. In fine, the word rebel, applied to any vanquished persons, without regard to rank, who were in the Continental service on the 27th of August aforesaid, was thought (by the enemy) sufficient to sanctify whatever cruelties they were pleased to inflict, death itself not excepted. But to pass over particulars which would swell my narrative far beyond my design.

The private soldiers who were brought to New York were crowded into churches and environed with slavish Hessian guards, a people of a strange language who were sent to America for no other design but cruelty and desolation, and at others by merciless Britons, whose mode of communicating ideas being intelligible in this country, served only to tantalize and insult the helpless and perishing; but above all the hellish delight and triumph of the Tories over them, as they were dying by hundreds. This was too much for me to bear as a spectator, for I saw the Tories exulting over the dead bodies of their murdered countrymen. I have gone into the churches and seen sundry of the prisoners in the agonies of death, in consequence of very hunger, and others speechless and near death, biting pieces of chips; others pleading for God's sake for something to eat, and at the same time shivering with the cold. Hollow groans saluted my ears, and despair seemed to be imprinted on every [one] of their countenances. The filth of these churches (in consequence of the fluxes) was almost beyond description. The floors were covered with excrements. I have carefully sought to direct my steps so as to avoid it, but could not. They would beg for God's sake for one copper, or morsel of bread. I have seen in one of these churches seven dead at the same time, lying among the excrements of their bodies.

It was a common practice with the enemy to convey the dead from these filthy places in carts, to be slightly buried, and I have seen whole gangs of Tories making derision, and exulting over the dead, saying, "There goes another load of damned rebels." I have observed the British soldiers to be full of their blackguard jokes and vaunting on those occasions, but they appeared to me less malignant than Tories.

The provision dealt out to the prisoners was by no means sufficient for the support of life: it was deficient in quantity, and much more so in quality. The prisoners often presented me with a sample of their bread, which I certify was damaged to that degree that it was loathsome and unfit to be eaten, and I am bold to aver it (as my opinion) that it had been condemned, and was of the very worst sort. I have seen and been fed upon damaged bread (in the course of my captivity) and observed the quality of such bread as has been condemned by the enemy, among which was very little so effectually spoiled as what was dealt out to these prisoners. Their allowance of meat (as they told me) was quite trifling, and of the basest sort. I never saw any of it, but was informed (bad as it was) it was swallowed almost as quick as they got hold of it. I saw some of them sucking bones after they were speechless; others, who could yet speak, and had the use of their reason, urged me in the strongest and most pathetic manner to use my interest in their behalf. "For you plainly see," say they, "that we are devoted to death and destruction." And after I had examined more particularly into their truly deplorable condition, and had become more fully apprised of the essential facts, I was persuaded that it was a premeditated and systematical plan of the British council to destroy the youths of our land, with a view thereby to deter the country and make it submit to their despotism. . . .

The army of Britain and Heshland prevailed for a little season, as though it was ordered by Heaven to show to the latest posterity what the British would have done if they could, and what the general calamity must have been in consequence of their conquering the country, and to excite every honest man to stand forth in the defense of liberty, and to establish the independency of the United States of America forever. But this scene of adverse fortune did not discourage a Washington; the illustrious American hero remained immovable. In liberty's cause he took up his sword; this reflection was his support and consolation in the day of his humiliation, when he retreated before the enemy through New Jersey into Pennsylvania. Their triumph only roused his indignation, and the important cause of his country, which lay near his heart, moved him to cross the Delaware again and take ample satisfaction on his pursuers. No sooner had he circumvallated his haughty foes and appeared in *terrible array*, but the host of Heshland fell. This taught America the intrinsic worth of perseverance, and the generous sons of freedom flew to the standard of their common safeguard and defense, from which time the arm of American liberty hath prevailed.

20

The Irishman's Epistle
(1775)[85]

By my faith but I think ye're all makers of bulls,
With your brains in your breeches, your guts in your skulls.
Get home with your muskets, and put up your swords,
And look in your books for the meaning of words.
Ye see now my honies, how much you're mistaken,
For CONCORD by Discord can never be beaten.

How brave you went out with muskets all bright,
And thought to befrighten the folks with the sight;
But when you got there how they powder'd your pums,
And all the way home how they pepper'd your bums,
And is it not, honies, a comical farce,
To be proud in the face, and be shot in the a - - se?

How come ye to think now, they did not know how
To be after their firelocks as smartly as you.
Why ye see now, my honies, 'tis nothing at all,
But to pull at the trigger, and pop goes the ball.

And what have you got now, with all your designing,
But a town without victuals to sit down and dine in;
And to look on the ground, like a parcel of Noodles,

And sing, How the Yankees have beaten the Doodles.
I'm sure if you're wise you'll make peace for a dinner,
For fighting and fasting will soon make ye thinner.

The Yankee's Return from Camp
(Yankee Doodle, 1775)[86]

Father and I went down to camp,
    Along with Captain Gooding,
There we see the men and boys
    As thick as hasty pudding.

        Yankee Doodle, keep it up,
           Yankee Doodle, dandy;
        Mind the music and the step,
           And with the girls be handy.

And there we see a thousand men,
    As rich as 'Squire David;
And what they wasted every day,
    I wish it could be saved.

The 'lasses they eat every day,
    Would keep a house a winter;
They have as much that I'll be bound
    They eat it when they're a mind to.

And there we see a swamping gun,
    Large as a log of maple,
Upon a deuced little cart,
    A load for father's cattle.

And every time they shoot it off,
    It takes a horn of powder;
It makes a noise like father's gun,
    Only a nation louder.

I went as nigh to one myself,

As 'Siah's underpinning;
And father went as nigh again,
    I thought the deuce was in him.

Cousin Simon grew so bold,
    I thought he would have cocked it:
It scared me so, I shrinked it off,
    And hung by father's pocket.

And Captain Davis had a gun,
    He kind of clapt his hand on't,
And stuck a crooked stabbing iron
    Upon the little end on't.

And there I see a pumpkin shell
    As big as mother's basin,
And every time they touched it off,
    They scampered like the nation.

I see a little barrel too,
    The heads were made of leather,
They knocked upon't with little clubs,
    And called the folks together.

And there was Captain Washington,
    And gentlefolks about him,
They say he's grown so tarnal proud,
    He will not ride without 'em.

He got him on his meeting clothes,
    Upon a slapping stallion,
He set the world along in rows,
    In hundreds and in millions.

The flaming ribbons in his hat,
    They look'd so taring fine, ah,
I want pockily to get,
    To give to my Jemimah.

I see another snarl of men
    A-digging graves, they told me,
So tarnal long, so tarnal deep,

They 'tended they should hold me.

It scar'd me so, I hooked it off,
    Nor stopt, as I remember,
Nor turn'd about till I got home,
    Locked up in mother's chamber.

The King's Own Regulars
(1776)[87]

Since you all will have singing, and won't be said nay,
I cannot refuse when you so beg and pray;
So I'll sing you a song—as a body may say,
'Tis of the King's Regulars, who ne'er ran away.
    Oh! the old soldiers of the king, and the king's own Regulars.

At Prestonpans we met with some rebels one day,
We marshalled ourselves all in comely array;
Our hearts were all stout, and bid our legs stay,
But our feet were wrongheaded and took us away.

At Falkirk we resolved to be braver,
And recover some credit by better behavior:
We wouldn't acknowledge feet had done us a favor,
So feet swore they would stand, but—legs ran, however.

No troops perform better than we at reviews,
We march and we wheel, and whatever you choose,
George would see how we fight, and we never refuse,
There we all fight with courage—you may see't in the news.

To Monongahela, with fifes and with drums,
We marched in fine order, with cannon and bombs;
That great expedition cost infinite sums,
But a few irregulars cut us all into crumbs.

It was not fair to shoot at us from behind trees,

If they had stood open, as they ought, before our great guns,
    we should have beat them with ease,
They may fight with one another that way if they please,
But it is not *regular* to stand and fight with such rascals as these.

At Fort George and Oswego, to our great reputation,
We show'd our vast skill in fortification;
The French fired three guns—of the fourth they had no occasion;
For we gave up those forts, not through fear, but mere persuasion.

To Ticonderoga we went in a passion,
Swearing to be revenged on the whole French nation;
But we soon turned tail, without hesitation,
Because they fought behind trees, which is not the *regular* fashion.

Lord Loudoun, he was a regular general, they say;
With a great regular army he went on his way
Against Louisburg, to make it his prey,
But returned—without seeing it—for he didn't *feel bold* that day.

Grown proud at reviews, great George had no rest,
Each grandsire, he had heard, a rebellion suppressed,
He wish'd a rebellion, looked round and saw none,
So resolved a rebellion to make—of his own.

The Yankees he bravely pitched on, because he thought they
    wouldn't fight,
And so he sent us over to take away their right;
But lest they should spoil our review clothes, he cried braver
    and louder,
For God's sake, brother kings, don't sell the cowards any powder.

Our general with his council of war did advise
How at Lexington we might the Yankees surprise;
We march'd—and re-march'd—all surprised—at being beat;
And so our wise general's plan of *surprise*—was complete.

For fifteen miles they follow'd and pelted us, we scarce had time
    to pull a trigger;
But did you ever know a retreat performed with more vigor?
For we did it in two hours, which saved us from perdition;
'Twas not in *going out,* but in *returning,* consisted our expedition.

Says our general, "We were forced to take to our *arms* in our
    own defense
(For *arms* read *legs*, and it will be both truth and sense);
Lord Percy (says he) I must say something of him in civility,
And that is—'I can never enough praise him for his great—agility.' "

Of their firing from behind fences he makes a great pother;
Every fence has two sides, they made use of one, and we only
    forgot to use the other;
That we turned our backs and ran away so fast, don't let that
    disgrace us:
'Twas only to make good what Sandwich said, that the Yankees—
    could not face us.

As they could not get before us, how could they look us in the face?
We took care they shouldn't, by scampering away apace.
That they had not much to brag of, is a very plain case;
For if they beat us in the fight, we beat them in the race.

Independence
(1776)

Freemen! if you pant for glory,
If you sigh to live in story,
    If you burn with patriot zeal;
Seize this bright auspicious hour,
Chase those venal tools of power,
    Who subvert the public weal.

Huzza! Huzza! Huzza!
See Freedom her banner display,
Whilst glory and virtue your bosoms inspire,
Corruption's proud slaves shall with anguish retire.

Would traitors base with bribes beguile you,
Or with idiot scoffs revile you,
    Ne'er your sacred trusts betray;
Hancock, Adams, nobly pleading,

Never from the truth receding,
    Them, North's vengeance can't dismay.

See, their glorious path pursuing,
All Britannia's troops subduing,
    Patriots whom no threats restrain.
Lawless tyrants all confounding,
Future times their praise resounding,
    Shall their triumphs long maintain.

Nathan Hale
(1776)[88]

The breezes went steadily thro' the tall pines,
    A-saying "Oh! hu-ush!" a-saying "Oh! hu-ush!"
As stilly stole by a bold legion of horse,
    For Hale in the bush, for Hale in the bush.

"Keep still!" said the thrush as she nestled her young,
    In a nest by the road, in a nest by the road,
"For the tyrants are near, and with them appear
    What bodes us no good, what bodes us no good."

The brave captain heard it, and thought of his home
    In a cot by the brook, in a cot by the brook,
With mother and sister and memories dear
    He so gaily forsook, he so gaily forsook.

Cooling shades of the night were coming apace,
    The tattoo had beat; the tattoo had beat.
The noble one sprang from his dark lurking place,
    To make his retreat, to make his retreat.

He warily trod on the dry rustling leaves,
    As he pass'd thro' the wood, as he pass'd thro' the wood;
And silently gain'd his rude launch on the shore,
    As she play'd with the flood, as she play'd with the flood.

The guards of the camp, on that dark, dreary night,
    Had a murderous will, had a murderous will.
They took him and bore him afar from the shore,
    To a hut on the hill, to a hut on the hill.

No mother was there, nor a friend who could cheer,
    In that little stone cell, in that little stone cell.
But he trusted in love from his father above.
    In his heart, all was well; in his heart, all was well.

An ominous owl with his solemn base voice
    Sat moaning hard by, sat moaning hard by.
"The tyrant's proud minions most gladly rejoice,
    For he must soon die, for he must soon die."

The brave fellow told them, no thing he restrain'd,
    The cruel gen'ral, the cruel gen'ral,
His errand from camp, of the ends to be gain'd,
    And said that was all, and said that was all.

They took him and bound him and bore him away
    Down the hill's grassy side, down the hill's grassy side.
'Twas there the base hirelings, in royal array,
    His cause did deride, his cause did deride.

Five minutes were given, short moments, no more,
    For him to repent, for him to repent;
He pray'd for his mother, he ask'd not another,
    To Heaven he went; to Heaven he went.

The faith of a martyr the tragedy show'd,
    As he trod the last stage, as he trod the last stage.
And Britons will shudder at gallant Hale's blood,
    As his words do presage, as his words do presage.

"Thou pale king of terrors, thou life's gloomy foe,
    Go frighten the slave, go frighten the slave;
Tell tyrants, to you their allegiance they owe.
    No fears for the brave; no fears for the brave."

The Fate of John Burgoyne
(1777)[89]

When Jack, the king's commander,
    Was going to his duty,
Through all the crowd he smil'd and bow'd,
    To every blooming beauty.

The city rung with feats he'd done,
    In Portugal and Flanders,
And all the town thought he'd be crown'd
    The first of Alexanders.

To Hampton Court he first repairs,
    To kiss great George's hand, sirs,
Then to harangue on state affairs,
    Before he left the land, sirs.

The "lower house" sat mute as mouse,
    To hear his grand oration;
And "all the peers" with loudest cheers
    Proclaim'd him to the nation.

Then off he went to Canada,
    Next to Ticonderoga,
And quitting those, away he goes
    Straightway to Saratoga.

With great parade his march he made,
    To gain his wished-for station,
When far and wide his minions hied
    To spread his "Proclamation."

To such as staid he offers made
    Of "pardon on submission;
But savage bands should waste the lands
    Of all in opposition."

But ah, the cruel fate of war!
    This boasted son of Britain,
When mounting his triumphal car,
    With sudden fear was smitten.

The sons of freedom gathered round,
　　His hostile bands confounded,
And when they'd fain have turn'd their back,
　　They found themselves surrounded!

In vain they fought, in vain they fled,
　　Their chief, humane and tender,
To save the rest, soon thought it best
　　His forces to surrender.

Brave St. Clair, when he first retired,
　　Knew what the fates portended;
And Arnold and heroic Gates
　　His conduct have defended.[90]

Thus may America's brave sons
　　With honor be rewarded,
And be the fate of all her foes
　　The same as here recorded.

Volunteer Boys
(1780)[91]

Hence with the lover who sighs o'er his wine,
　　Cloes and Phillises toasting,
Hence with the slave who will whimper and whine,
　　Of ardor and constancy boasting.
　　　　Hence with love's joys,
　　　　Follies and noise,
The toast that I give is the volunteer boys.

Nobles and beauties and such common toasts,
　　Those who admire may drink, sir;
Fill up the glass to the volunteer hosts,
　　Who never from danger will shrink, sir.
　　　　Let mirth appear,
　　　　Every heart cheer,
The toast that I give is the brave volunteer.

Here's to the squire who goes to parade,
    Here's to the citizen soldier;
Here's to the merchant who fights for his trade,
    Whom danger increasing makes bolder.
        Let mirth appear,
        Union is here,
The toast that I give is the brave volunteer.

Here's to the lawyer, who, leaving the bar,
    Hastens where honor doth lead, sir,
Changing the gown for the ensigns of war,
    The cause of his country to plead, sir.
        Freedom appears,
        Every heart cheers,
And calls for the health of the law volunteers.

Here's to the soldier, though batter'd in wars,
    And safe to his farmhouse retir'd;
When called by his country, ne'er thinks of his scars,
    With ardor to join us inspir'd.
        Bright fame appears,
        Trophies uprear,
To veteran chiefs who became volunteers.

Here's to the farmer who dares to advance
    To harvests of honor with pleasure;
Who with a slave the most skilful in France
    A sword for his country would measure.
        Hence with cold fear,
        Heroes rise here;
The plowman is chang'd to the stout volunteer.

Here's to the peer, first in senate and field,
    Whose actions to titles add grace, sir;
Whose spirit undaunted would never yet yield
    To a foe, to a pension or place, sir.
        Gratitude here,
        Toasts to the peer,
Who adds to his titles "the brave volunteer."

Thus the bold bands for old Jersey's defense
    The muse hath with rapture review'd, sir;

With our volunteer boys, as our verses commence,
   With our volunteer boys they conclude, sir.
      Discord or noise
      Ne'er damp our joys,
But health and success to the volunteer boys.

The Dance
(1781)[92]

Cornwallis led a country dance,
   The like was never seen, sir,
Much retrograde and much advance,
   And all with General Greene, sir.

They rambled up and rambled down,
   Join'd hands, then off they run, sir,
Our General Greene to Charlestown,
   The Earl to Wilmington, sir.

Greene, in the South, then danc'd a set,
   And got a mighty name, sir,
Cornwallis jigg'd with young Fayette,
   But suffer'd in his fame, sir.

Then down he figur'd to the shore,
   Most like a lordly dancer,
And on his courtly honor swore,
   He would no more advance, sir.

Quoth he, my guards are weary grown
   With footing country dances,
They never at St. James's shone
   At capers, kicks or prances.

Though men so gallant ne'er were seen
   While sauntering on parade, sir,
Or wriggling o'er the park's smooth green,
   Or at a masquerade, sir.

Yet are red heels and long-lac'd skirts
    For stumps and briars meet, sir?
Or stand they chance with hunting-shirts,
    Or hardy veteran feet, sir?

Now hous'd in York he challeng'd all,
    At minuet or allemande,
And lessons for a courtly ball
    His guards by day and night conn'd.

This challenge known, full soon there came
    A set who had the bon ton,
De Grasse and Rochambeau, whose fame
    Fut brillant pour un long temps.

And Washington, Columbia's son,
    Whom easy nature taught, sir,
That grace which can't by pains be won
    Or Plutus' gold be bought, sir.

Now hand in hand they circle round
    This ever-dancing peer, sir;
Their gentle movements soon confound
    The Earl, as they draw near, sir.

His music soon forgets to play—
    His feet can no more move, sir,
And all his bands now curse the day
    They jiggèd to our shore, sir.

Now Tories all, what can ye say?
    Come—is not this a griper,
That while your hopes are danc'd away,
    'Tis you must pay the piper.

Cornwallis Burgoyned
(1781)[93]

When British troops first landed here,
    With Howe commander o'er them,

They thought they'd make us quake for fear
    And carry all before them;
With thirty thousand men or more,
    And she without assistance,
America must needs give o'er,
    And make no more resistance.

But Washington, her glorious son,
    Of British hosts the terror,
Soon, by repeated overthrows,
    Convinc'd them of their error;
Let Princeton and let Trenton tell
    What gallant deeds he's done, sir,
And Monmouth's plains where hundreds fell
    And thousands more have run, sir.

Cornwallis, too, when he approach'd
    Virginia's old dominion,
Thought he would soon her conqu'ror be;
    And so was North's opinion.
From state to state with rapid stride
    His troops had march'd before, sir,
Till quite elate with martial pride,
    He thought all dangers o'er, sir.

But our allies, to his surprise,
    The Chesapeake had enter'd;
And now too late he curs'd his fate,
    And wish'd he ne'er had ventur'd,
For Washington no sooner knew
    The visit he had paid her,
Than to his parent state he flew,
    To crush the bold invader.

When he sat down before the town,
    His Lordship soon surrender'd;
His martial pride he laid aside,
    And cas'd the British standard;
Gods! how this stroke will North provoke,
    And all his thoughts confuse, sir!
And how the peers will hang their ears
    When first they hear the news, sir.

Be peace, the glorious end of war,
　By this event effected;
And be the name of Washington
　To latest times respected;
Then let us toast America,
　And France in union with her;
And may Great Britain rue the day
　Her hostile bands came hither.

Part Three

The Literature of Revolution, 1775–83
The Loyalists

"THE BATTLE OF BROOKLYN" (1776)

21

Published Anonymously
by James Rivington

Shortly after the American defeat on Long Island (August 27, 1776), James Rivington published in New York an anonymous little two-act drama entitled The Battle of Brooklyn: A Farce. *Broadly propagandistic, defamatory, even scurrilous, throughout, it has a clear purpose: to use the occasion of the Battle of Long Island, the first full-scale military engagement of the war, to ridicule and burlesque America's generals and the cause they represent. The play has little or no action. What plot there is consists of setting up the "rebel chiefs" (Washington, Putnam, Sullivan, and Stirling) as straw men and then systematically exposing them as self-serving, licentious, and cowardly rogues. Stirling is portrayed as a drunkard and counterfeiter; Putnam as a horse thief; Washington as a lecher—and all as military incompetents who have deliberately misled their countrymen. As a bemused Washington confesses (act 1, scene 4):*

> My apprehensions from the king's troops, believe me, are trifling compared with the risk we run from the people of America at large. The tyranny that our accursed usurpation has made necessary, which they now feel, and feeling, I fear, will soon make them see through the disguise.

To which Sullivan replies:

> My dear General, the moments for reflection are elapsed and irrecoverable. Our safety is first in conquest; if that is denied to our endeavors, I am sure we can obtain better terms from our much injured Sovereign than from our more injured country. . . .

In Sullivan's speech lies, of course, the propagandist's ultimate appeal to rebellious Americans (an appeal sounded and resounded in various guises throughout the war): lay down your arms and reaffirm your allegiance to George III and to England. There are other, just slightly more subtle, propagandistic notes as well. Clark, the Connecticut rum merchant, observes in act 1, scene 2, for example, that the Maryland and Pennsylvania regiments, which "are mostly composed of Europeans, *a great majority of which are Irish and Germans," are to bear "the burden and heat" of battle in order "to spare the natives." And later (act 1, scene 5), Putnam and his Yankee chaplain Parson Snuffle discuss the desirability of using the opportunity of war to destroy American episcopacy and Quakerism and to seize the estates of wealthy Tories: "It is but cooking up some new-fangled oath which their squeamish consciences won't let them swallow; then, whip go their estates like a juggler's ninepence, and themselves to prison to be hanged as traitors to the commonwealth." While it is scarcely an overstatement that* The Battle of Brooklyn *has but little claim to literary merit, it is not without a certain cleverness and vitality. A good example of Loyalist propaganda, it remains today, as Moses Coit Tyler described it many years ago, "an authentic memorial of the very spirit and procedure of the time."*

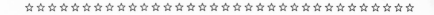

Dramatis Personae[94]

Men

Washington
Putnam } rebel chiefs
Sullivan
Stirling
Lasher, a shoemaker of New York
Clark, a retailer of rum in Connecticut } colonels
Remsen, a farmer of Newtown, Long Island
Ebenezer Snuffle, a New England parson, chaplain to General Putnam
Joe King, servant to Stirling
Noah, servant to Sullivan
Skinner, a thief employed by Putnam

Women

Lady Gates
Betty, her servant

Officers and soldiers

Scene: Partly within the rebel lines at Brooklyn and partly at Gowanus[95]

Act I

SCENE I: *An apartment at Brooklyn. Enter Stirling, as from his bedroom, rubbing his head.*

Stirling. Joe! Honest Joe!—Damn the fellow, where can this King be; (*looking at his watch*) odds, almost twelve o'clock. [*Enter King.*]

King. Why, here my lord—Devil damme, sir; pray, who do you damn so?

Stir. My dear Joe, the cares that distract and split this poor head of mine—

King. Split! Yes, by heaven! you drank *stinkabus* enough last night to split the head of an Indian!

Stir. Insolence! In future know me for your master—your lord! who has the disposal of your life.

King. [*Aside*] I must hold a candle to this devil.—My lord, I ask your pardon; I meant no harm, but only as an old acquaintance. You know, my lord, I am given to joking, and you formerly encouraged me in it, when we were concerned together in the paper manufactory.

Stir. Forgive me, honest Joe—the public cares so hang upon me that they quite destroy my constitutional good humor. The Regulars are near to us, and every moment we expect them over the hills.

King. Your lordship has so long and so uniformly wished to meet them that I thought the nearer the prospect the better you would have been pleased. You have no doubt, my lord, of spitting and roasting and pickling these redcoat fellows?

Stir. We are to meet at the church this day to determine in council what to do with them. I am for surrounding—surround! is the word with me. If they were twenty times the number, I say surround them all!—But these gripes, Joe, and my canteens are empty; you must procure me something for them.

King. O heavens, the gripes! [*Aside*] Zounds! a puncheon of Jamaica to have the gripes.—I have some peach brandy, my lord.

Stir. The best of all possible things: it so admirably fits a man for the cabinet and the field. [*A knocking at the door.*] What can that mean? Run Joe, and see who knocks.

King. I go, sir. [*As he goes, he observes Stirling's countenance. Aside*] Pale and trembling, by that august body the Congress. [*Exit.*]

Stir. These bloody fellows, I fear, are in motion. I hope to God that damn'd rascal King will be shot; he has been my evil genius ever since I was concerned with him in counterfeiting paper currency. [*Enter King.*] Dear Joe, what is the matter?

King. Nothing, but to desire you to meet the other generals in council, two hours hence, at the church.

Stir. O, is that all? I shall attend; in the meantime, go to the commissary of rum and get my canteens filled, and by all means, my good Joe, be at home when I return. [*Exit Stirling.*]

King. Canteens filled—and then thy whole soul will be in thy canteens. That is, if he has credit enough with the commissary to get his canteens filled with rum, he will belch it out of his stomach in the damn'dest lies that ever disqualified a man for the character of a gentleman: and yet Parson M'Worther bellows from his pulpit that this most *ignobleman* is a chosen vessel to execute the Lord's work.—Ill-fated country! when will this delusion end? [*Exit.*]

SCENE II: *The scene changes to a small house in a field: cattle and horses grazing. Enter Lasher and Clark.*

Clark. Behold, Colonel, these flocks and herds; with the sword of Gideon have I made them mine; and honestly collected them in the district allotted to me by our agreement.

Lasher. I rejoice with you in the acquisition. My harvest from the Wallabout is like the miraculous draught: two hundred and seven head of horned beasts, and thirty-seven horses, graze where my guards direct.

Clark. Favor has not been so amply manifested unto me; for from the farthest verge of Gowanus, even from C—ar's house, till you come to Brewer's mills, one hundred and nine horned, and twenty-eight beasts of burden, were all I could collect: nor was there compassion in my soul to spare one of the kine for milk to the offspring of a people who believe that men cannot be saved by faith alone without works.

Lasher. Impious and blasphemous tenet; destructuve of republicanism and intoleration. I doubt whether such people should be spared from the sword.—But, Brother Clark, to secure what we have thus obtained by a strong hand and mighty arm was assigned to your care and prudence.

Clark. That I am not unworthy of the trust, you are to know that nine of our sloops will this day be discharged from the Continental service: tomorrow they will be ready at the ferry to receive the spoil. Every fifth beast, by lot, is to be the wages of their safe delivery at New Haven in Connecticut, the residence of the faithful. But, we being fellow laborers, if you approve—Tabitha, the wife of my bosom, shall be charged with the care of your cattle.

Lasher. Be it as thou hast said; at her hands will I require them; and as I had allotted to myself a large brass kettle in a former division of the spoil, with the cattle let it be convey'd as a testimony of the love I bear unto her.

Clark. Whatever is in thy heart to do, that do and prosper. I hear that twelve thousand are to keep the hills today; spies proclaim some motion in the camp of the Philistines.

Lasher. What the end of these things will be, I know not; but as my soul liveth I mean not to budge a jot beyond the summit of the hill, keeping in full view and practible acquisition the fort called Greene.[96]

Clark. Know you not the wise determination of the Congress on that head; stimulated thereto by the prudence of our generals, who, I do believe, received it by inspiration?

Lasher. Ignorant have I been kept; but unfold the mighty tidings, for I already perceive they are big with joy.

Clark. Have you not observed with what address the southern militias are drawn hither?

Lasher. That they are here, I know, but am yet to learn the secret cause, if any secret cause there be.

Clark. Know, then, that the Marylanders, Pennsylvanians, and the rifle regiments are mostly composed of *Europeans,* a great majority of which are Irish and Germans.

Lasher. These things I am no stranger to but still lack information.

Clark. Which way soever the battle tends, the burden and heat of it will be theirs; for thus it is resolved to spare the *natives,* and make no account of the *expenditure* of the *Europeans;* feel you not the power of inspiration now?

Lasher. Wonderful! truly wonderful workings of wisdom indeed!

Clark. But for some twenty head of cattle, the gleanings of Gowanus, in the orchard of one Bergen, I would not go so far: these once obtained, we will be near each other. [*Enter Remsen, without a hat, his hair on end, his coat torn, and every mark of fear about him.*]

Lasher. Mercy! mercy! O Lord, where are they?

Clark. O heavens! he is wounded and out of his senses! Dear Colonel, can you speak?

Remsen. Oh! Heere Godt! what merciful scape I get this time.—Shentle-men, have you seen my *regiment?*

Clark. No, where did you leave it?—Lord help us! how near is the enemy?

Remsen. O Godt! O Godt! O Godt!—Count the bloodt out of me in any place?

Lasher. Blood, no; nor can I see anybody coming after you: your hurt, I fancy, is fear, Colonel! and your wound must be sought for in your breeches. But compose yourself, and tell us what has has happened.

Remsen. Well, I will tell you, then. I was, yust now, van the head of my regiment, close up behind Shon van Dinen's field. I keep my eye on Arian Morte's lane. I see, yust by the groundt, something creep; I say my regiment, take care of yourself boys. I peep again mit both mine eyes, and see nothing: I say, boys, 'tis close up with us now—they begin for to run; my horse he see the danger too, and carry me off: Godt knows I get here; I believe the rest is all killed or taken prisoners. [*Enter an officer.*] Godt bless you ayn-dant, where is the regment?

Officer. Where! damn them, scattered in every cover between this and the place where you started.

Remsen. Heere Godt! all killed?

Officer. Killed! no, nor any of them hurt except four or five that you rode over: why there was not a Regular within a mile when you took fright.

Lasher. O you ungodly coward! out from the presence of the brave! [*Kicks him off, and exit after him.*]

Officer. That fellow kicks as awkward as if he soon expected the same discipline; but I will go and try if possible to collect our heroes. [*Exit officer.*]

Clark. What credulous stuff these New Yorkers are made of! The bill of lading for the cattle and horses will be in my name only. Poor Lasher! not a hide of them shalt thou have to put a stich in—and then there is the kettle, too! a! ha! ha! [*Exit laughing.*]

SCENE III. *A room at Brooklyn Ferry. Enter Lady Gates and Betty.*

Betty. After council, mem, General Washington will wait of you; till then he begs your patience, as the time is near when he is to meet the rest of the generals.

Lady G. Council! a pretty collection of councillors, indeed; but since it must be so, you shall comply with your promise to me, girl, by giving me the narrative of Harrison[97] and your general: it will beguile the time.

Betty. La, mem, you so discomfit me by claiming this promise that I am a-blush all over.

Lady G. Why, Betty, you must have assumed the blushing trade lately; it was not always so with you.

Betty. Indeed, your ladyship does not make proper allowances for necessity and inexperience.—Fifty dollars, and hard ones too, with a promise of fifty times as much was irresistible: but oh! the nasty beast! I almost puke at the recollection.

Lady G. Oh! that must be affectation, for bless me, what could raise such ideas?

Betty. Why, he is such a slobbering, odious, unsavory smelling creature that I wonder any woman in the world could sleep at night by his side.

Lady G. And yet, you see, that fifty hard dollars made you put up for a night with all the inconveniency of bad smells.

Betty. A night! your ladyship wrongs me very much: why, he snored within an hour! and the first snore was a signal for my retreat. I am sure I should have been a corpse if I had been obliged to stay the night.

Lady G. Fifty dollars is a good deal of money, Betty; but did he make no claim upon you afterwards?

Betty. Indeed, mem, he stayed from Congress on purpose to tease me; why, he cried and said he was in liquor that night, and did everything, I think, that could make me despise him; but all would not do.

Lady G. And there your affairs ended with Harrison, did they not, Betty?

Betty. Not quite, my lady; for when he found that I could not abide him, he proposed to introduce General Washington to me. The general was a very pretty gentleman, and I consented to it on purpose to get rid of

Harrison.

Lady G. This I should have imagined a favorable change myself, Betty, was it not?

Betty. The general is the sweetest, meekest, melancholy fighting gentleman; and then he is such a warrior—O mem, I shall always love the general.

Lady G. And among his other qualifications, the most liberal.

Betty. Why, my lady, I will tell you honestly: his Excellency gave me a thirty-dollar bill; he assured me it would have been more, but that he was obliged to repay Harrison the fifty hard dollars that he had given me: now, mem, is not Harrison a dirty fellow in every shape that you can view him?

Lady G. No great things, girl, to be sure, from your account of him; neither is your meek, melancholy hero, from my own observation.

Betty. Lord! lord! mem, did he not make codfish of them all at Boston? And has he not seen Tory men rid upon rails at New York by the tailors and cobblers of the town! And more, my lady, did he not order the king's statue to be pulled down, and the head cut off![98] For God's sake, mem, what would you have of a hero?

Lady G. Codfish at Boston! it is really an odd term, Betty; but he did no more than that old fool Putnam would have done. His not forbidding that insult to humanity at New York was countenancing an act of barbarism; and none but a little-minded barbarian would have suffered the arts to be trampled under foot, as he did in the case of the king's statue.

Betty. You know of these things best, mem, to be sure; but I have heard the New England officers say that he should be their general no longer than he pleased them, and maybe they would have it so.

Lady G. Be you assured, girl, that if he had native dignity of heart, he would have soon convinced the rabble that they must be governed by him, notwithstanding that he may have obtained his power by a usurpation from themselves—but hark! what clamorous noise is that in the street? Run and learn. [*Exit Betty.*] There appears to be some commotion, and it grows late; I begin to despair of seeing the general. [*Enter Betty.*]

Betty. O, my lady, do not let us wait to see the general. The New England colonels are in a mutiny and say they will not fight if the boats are not all ready to carry their men off to New York when they run away. Let us go, dear mem, for I do not think we shall be safe on this side of the Allegheny Mountains.

Lady G. I will take your advice, girl. O Horatio! that you should sully your laurels in the abominable cause of republican tyrants, and smugglers in power: to be runagate for such miscreants almost distracts me. [*Exeunt.*]

SCENE IV: *The scene changes to Brooklyn Church. Washington, Putnam, Sullivan and Stirling in council.*

Wash. Gentlemen, spies from Flatbush inform that the Regulars are making a disposition to cross the hills near that place.—General Putnam's wisdom in ordering that road to be flanked with breastworks is now apparent. Lord Stirling, with his usual intrepidity and precision, has reconnoitered their numbers, which he finds to be about seven thousand. General Sullivan has appointed the hill with exquisite judgment, where the brigades under him and Lord Stirling are to take post and act as occasion may require: twelve thousand men are allotted for the service of sending them back to their ships. I with eight thousand will stay within these lines, to be called out to the slaughter and pursuit, unless our present deliberations alter this plan of operation. My lord, the council expects your opinion.

Stir. I rise to give it to the most respectable and most puissant council of general officers that this or any other age ever produced. I would not presume, gentlemen, to speak in this place without being conscious that I possess the energy and oratory of a *Burke!* or even write on the subject, but that I feel the powers and the pen of a *Junius!*[99] That I reconnoitered them is most true; and if my weak opinion has any weight in council I am for *surrounding* them, and when we have got them hemmed in, I am then for sending to our noble commander-in-chief in these lines to know what to do with them.

Sull. [*Aside.*] Pompous, slimsey, drunken fool.—The noble lord has said nothing against the disposition that the general had pointed out, and of which I approve. His Lordship's ideas are exceedingly *surrounding;* I wish the practice may be as easy as the theory, and that their numbers may not exceed seven thousand. But if the council holds the opinion of General Washington and myself, our deliberations are at an end, and we cannot be too soon at our different posts.

Put. I this morning gave the chaps another pill, and I will tell you how. You know the road to Bedford, a little on this side the house that the bandy-legged Jew lives in; well, d'ye see, there is on each side the road a stone wall near three feet high; beyond that on each side are clear fields—what do you think I have done there?

Stir. Why, something like a great officer, nobody doubts.

Put. Swamp me, if I have not hove up a breastwork right across the road from wall to wall:—but before we break up, determine, gentlemen, what I am to do with my prisoners.

Stir. Right, General; I should have gone to my post, and been at a loss on this head.

Wash. Send them to me: a great part of Fort Greene is allotted for their reception; but be sure that they are disarmed and well guarded.

Stir. O, to be sure, undoubtedly, sir, we will take care of that. I am for my post: gentlemen, farewell.

Put. A little business dispatched, and I will call upon you there. [*Exit Stirling.*] If your Excellency should have any commands for me an hour hence, I may be found upon the Flatbush road: your servant, gentlemen. [*Exit Putnam.*]

Wash. Good betide them both.—After this fustian, a little sober reasoning, General Sullivan, may fit the mind for the doubtful events of war. My apprehensions from the king's troops, believe me, are trifling compared with the risk we run from the people of America at large. The tyranny that our accursed usurpation has made necessary, which they now feel, and feeling, I fear, will soon make them see through the disguise. Their rage no doubt will be heightened by the slaughter that will probably ensue; and we, as members of the Congress, fall the first victims of it.—O Sullivan! my heart never consented to this ruin of my native country!

Sull. My dear General, the moments for reflection are elapsed and irrecoverable. Our safety is first in conquest; if that is denied to our endeavors, I am sure we can obtain better terms from our much injured sovereign than from our more injured country—but wear a less rueful countenance: it is a proberb among the troops that their general is much melted down since the fleet arrived.

Wash. Our soldiers are a standing miracle to me: they define sensibly upon matters that are unimportant to them, and resign their powers of thinking to us in a case where their all is at stake; and do not yet discover that we make them the engines of our power at the expense of all that is dear and sacred to them as men!—but avaunt reflection! Our hope, my dear Sullivan, is in you; every command of ground is ours, with a perfect knowledge of all the woods and defiles: these advantages, at the least, double the strength of our men; and if we cannot defend these, I know of no place we can.

Sull. All things that depend upon me will, I hope, meet with your approbation, and I shall aim to infuse such sentiments into the troops that our next meeting may be ushered in with greetings of congratulation; till then, my dear General, farewell. [*Exit Sullivan.*]

Wash. Greetings of congratulation!—oh! could I congratulate myself on finding my lost peace of mind!—on the restoration of my honor! O! cursed ambition! what have I sacrificed to thee? An ambition, too, of foreign growth; obtruded upon me by the most artful, insinuating villains that ever enslaved a once free and happy country. To behold myself, against my principle and better judgment, made the tool of their diabolical determinations to entail a war upon my fellow subjects of America.—Heigho! ho!

[*Looking at his watch.*] Bless me, so late and my engagement to a lady not complied with. [*Exit.*]

SCENE V: *A room in a house at Brooklyn. Enter Putnam and Snuffle.*

Snuff. My dear General, the great, the important day advances; big with the fate of empire in the united states of America.

Put. True, good sir: and I laugh to think that when we have established our power, and driven these redcoats into the sea, what ripping reformation you gentlemen will make in church affairs. Down goes episcopacy and Quakerism at least. I hope you won't leave one broad-brim on the continent.

Snuff. Why really, General, we shall be very apt to make free with those gentlemen. We have long beheld with a jealous eye the growing power of the Episcopal clergy, and considered them as the only obstacle to our becoming the heads of the church in America, a dignity that so properly belongs to the elect, and for which they have had the assurance to contend with the Lord's own people. As for the Quakers, who in general have joined the Tories against us, we shall not fail to produce an "ancient testimony" in their behalf: I mean the testimony of our forefathers; till with fines, whipping, imprisonment, and the gallows we have extirpated them from the face of the earth.

Put. In the meantime, we shall not be behind-hand with the Tories: for as the best estates in America belong to them, it is but cooking up some new-fangled oath which their squeamish consciences won't let them swallow; then, whip go their estates like a juggler's ninepence, and themselves to prison to be hanged as traitors to the commonwealth. [*Enter Skinner.*]

Snuff. Very true, my dear General: but here comes one of your officers. I will retire to offer up my prayers for the success of our arms, while you pursue the more important business of your department. [*Exit.*]

Put. Adieu, sir. Well, Skinner, what news with you?

Skin. The horses are delivered as your Excellency directed. They are, by this time, well on their way to Connecticut; and so elegant a string of nine horses are not to be picked up again on all Long Island.

Put. My letter tells me they are clever horses:—but that horse of Polhemus's[100]—O my heart was set upon that horse. You let him slip through your fingers carelessly, Skinner; or did the owner of him tempt you with a bribe to leave him—I wish to know where he is.

Skin. I know where he is, to the length of my whip.—I careless! I take a bribe!—why the general should know me better; the horse is at Harlem.

Put. At Harlem!—why what notion of deviltry could send him there? Is there anybody but us upon the lay on this island?

Skin. What's his name brought him there—damn his name. I can't remember it; he is son, however, to the governor of Rhode Island.[101]

Put. Oho! then I quite excuse you; you are too young in the business to be a match for young Fitch: he inherits his father's talents. I had expectation, though, that we should have done better with your knowledge of the country and other advantages.—I had reckoned upon twenty horses.

Skin. I myself, sir, thought that number sure, but he lay in my rear and brought off six that I had reconnoitered.

Put. Well, Skinner, as the business is over for the present, and we expect bloody noses in a few hours, there is a hundred dollars for your encouragement. [*Gives him a handful of Congress notes.*] Go over, now, and join your regiment.

Skin. I hope your Excellency will reconsider the matter, and make it more; there is not one of those horses but that is worth more than a hundred and fifty dollars—consider, sir!

Put. Consider! why, you are an unreasonable whelp! do you consider that I took you from serving drams to Negroes for your mother Foster at Rockaway and robbing the neighboring hen roosts for a livelihood! From petty larceny, you cur, I put you at the head of the procession; procured you a lieutenant's commission, and a separate command to hunt Tories on this island in order to push you forward—and dare you grumble?

Skin. I do not grumble, sir; but fifty dollars more would enable me to take the field with credit: it would make my regimentals my own.

Put. I seldom mistake my men: I knew that you had talents, Skinner, or I should not have employed you; I will therefore point out a fund for you to raise the fifty dollars more. Remember, sir, the fuzee you filched at Merrick; item, the two watches, rings, etc., etc., at several other places; you gave me no account of these, though I had an equitable demand upon you for half. There is a fifty-dollar fund for you—don't you think, young man, to catch old birds with chaff. It is near night: I must to my post, and get you over the ferry to your duty. [*Exit Putnam.*]

Skin. What a damn'd old scoundrel he is. How the devil did he know of the gun and the other things?—In future I will do business for myself. [*Exit.*]

Act II

SCENE I: *A hill at Gowanus about two miles from Brooklyn lines, with an encampment on it. Time, about three o'clock in the morning. Enter a soldier.*

Sol. Where's General Stirling?—Hollo, General Stirling!—Zounds! how dark it is. [*Enter Stirling half-dressed.*]

Stir. For God's sake! what is the matter, sentry?

Sol. Here, sir! it is I that call to inform your lordship there has been a great deal of shooting towards the Red Lion within this little while.

Stir. Dear sentry, which way did it come from?

Sol. I can hardly tell, sir; but it seemed tight work for a little while:— there! there it begins again.

Stir. It does indeed: do you think it comes anything nearer, sentry?

Sol. Rather nearer, if anything; though much in the same place.

Stir. Run, sentry, to the rear, make my respects to General Sullivan, and beg of him to come hither.

Sol. I will, my lord. There it goes again: ripping work, my lord! [*Exit soldier.*]

Stir. Now will I endeavor to get button'd up and my garters tied. [*Enter Clark.*] O Colonel Clark! from whence—from whence are you come?

Clark. From where our out-sentries are attacked.—I see you are getting ready, my lord.

Stir. But where are they attacked? Where is the enemy? Are there many of them—are they coming forward—is anybody killed,—say, dear Will?

Clark. I cannot tell you half of what you have already asked me; but I will tell you all I know. They sent a captain to relieve me: I would not be relieved by a captain, so I went to sleep at one Bergen's, from whence the out-sentries were relieved. This Bergen awaked me a while ago, and said there was shooting in his field.

Stir. God bless me! shooting in his field! was it near the house?

Clark. Very near—so I stole out, for I knew the road, dark as it was. Everything was still, as if nothing had happened; except some groans of dying men that appeared to be at a little distance. But I have seen nothing nor heard anything by the way.

Stir. Then their numbers are still a secret?

Clark. I will be bound there are not fifty of them, or there would have been some noise.

Stir. O damn it! 'tis nothing but a scouting party.—Come, Colonel, we will take a whistle from my canteens.

Clark. With all my heart, my lord.—[*Aside.*] Poison take the canteens; I have lost the cattle that were in Bergen's orchard. [*Enter five soldiers.*] What are these! who are you?

1st Sol. We are the remains of the outpost guard, your Honors.

Stir. And where are the rest of the guard, my good lads?

1st Sol. In Sarah's bosom, I hope.

2d Sol. In Abraham's bosom he means, noble General.

1st Sol. Blood-an-oons, is not she his wife? which makes it all one.

Stir. Leave off this trifling, and tell me what you know.

1st Sol. Your Honor must know that we was standing by the end of a side

211

of an Indian cornfield, up yonder a piece. We heard something rustle among the watermelon leaves, and saw something move; we bid them stand, and blazed away like brave boys.

Stir. Well, my lad, and what followed?

1st Sol. Followed! by my soul, a sharp iron thing that they call a bayonet.

Stir. And what then?

1st Sol. What then! your Honor! why to be sure, the few that could run, run away; and then all was peace and quietness.

Stir. Do you not know how many there were?

1st Sol. How many! your Honor must know that they were speechless; they carried their tongues in them damn'd bayonets, and most of our guard, I believe, are eating breakfast with their great-grandfathers!

Stir. What corps do you belong to?

1st Sol. Pennsylvanians, and please your Honor.

Stir. Go, and join your regiment. [*Exit soldiers.*] Colonel Clark, as it begins to be light, go and get intelligence. I every moment expect General Sullivan: one or other of us you will find here to make a report to.

Clark. I shall not stay long, my lord. [*Exit Clark.*]

Stir. I begin to feel easy: it has been but a scouting party, and they have gone back again. It is a devilish raw morning, and I must have something to keep the cold out. [*Exit.*]

SCENE II: *A hill, with troops drawn up, under arms. Time, broad daylight. Enter Sullivan and Stirling.*

Stir. Well, do you not think, from the examination of these fellows, that it was a mere scouting party that surprised the guard?

Sull. Their silence, my lord, with me, marks order and good conduct; besides, they do not make war by scouting parties—but here comes Colonel Clark. [*Enter Clark.*]

Clark. Gentlemen, the Regulars are in motion: they are numerous, and will be here within an hour. From yonder hill I looked down upon them.

Stir. Good Colonel, have they any artillery with them?

Clark. I know not, my lord; but I must away and join my men. [*Aside.*] O what a scrape those cattle have brought me into. I am afraid I shall be obliged to fight at last. [*Exit.*]

Sull. Well, my lord, will you make a disposition for your favorite scheme of surrounding?

Stir. For God's sake, dear General, don't mention it. I did not expect them this way. Our whole dependence is upon you, my dear General; but do not let them cut off our retreat.

Sull. Let your brigades immediately take post in the bottom, and extend from the small house below as far as the stone house upon the left; and farther, if the hill gives them cover, let them approach as near the road as possible without being discovered. The Pennsylvanians are to draw up at the foot of this hill in full view of the enemy. From their uniform they may be taken for Hessians, and the fire from the brigades be more completely surprising and effectual.

Stir. It shall be done.–Oh! it shall be done. [*Exit Stirling.*]

Sull. If they should force these brigades to the hill, we can easily maintain this post against the united force of Britain without loss: and make the retreat to our lines when we please unmolested. [*Reenter Stirling.*]

Stir. The brigades are disposed, as your Excellency directed; and the Regulars are nearly up to them; you will see their advanced guard pass the stone house, directly.

Sull. There they are, and have discovered the Pennsylvanians, for they have quitted the road, and push towards them.

Stir. I hope to God they will push back again as soon as our fire begins. O! there they go—well fired, my boys! they cannot stand this! you'll see, they will push directly, General.

Sull. I see they do push, but it is with their bayonets, and our men are scampering towards us. [*Enter a Pennsylvanian, hastily.*] Stop, soldier, you are far enough.

Pen. I will be judge of that, my dear; for by my soul, honey, you have brought old Ireland about your ears, at last; and we can find the way to eat now without asking such vermin as you for victuals. [*Exit.*]

Stir. Dear General, what shall we do now?

Sull. Ply the artillery as far as possible. [*Enter an officer.*]

Off. Towards the south an incessant firing has prevailed for half an hour, nor has it ought approached. My post is that way advanced, but I thought my duty bid me quit it to give you this information.

Sull. You have my thanks. To your post again, and let me speedily be informed if the firing approaches. [*Exit officer.*] While they are kept at bay, my lord, we are safe upon this hill.

Stir. But yet we should prepare for a retreat—for see, where they fearless climb up yonder hill.

Sull. There is nothing to obstruct us in our rear, my lord: we will retreat in good time. [*Enter Clark.*]

Clark. Lost! O Lord! undone! ruined! destroyed!

Sull. Amazement! what ails the man?

Clark. In the rear—there in our rear—no retreat! no retreat!

Sull. Too true—there is part of the royal army, indeed, between us and our lines.

Stir. O General Sullivan! General Sullivan! what do you think of it now?

Sull. This I now know, my lord, that we heaven-born generals are exceedingly apt to lead our troops to the devil.

Stir. But my dear General Sullivan, what shall we do?

Sull. Just what you please: every man is now his own general, so gentlemen, farewell. [*Exit.*]

Stir. Do not leave me also, Colonel Clark. O Lord, incline their hearts to mercy.

Clark. Amen and amen. I hope, however, we are not of consequence to be hanged. This way, my lord, this way. [*Exeunt.*]

SCENE III: *Fort Greene, in Brooklyn lines: A Sentinel on one of the merlins, looking out. Enter Washington.*

Wash. What do you look so earnestly at, sentry?

Sen. At our people, sir, that are setting fire to the houses and barns in their retreat.

Wash. What, are they retreating then?

Sen. Look this way, sir; there they run like so many deer, and will get in: but the poor souls yonder, that come across the meadow and attempt to cross the mill creek; O, what a number of them stick in the mud, and the stronger ones make a bridge of them.

Wash. All other retreat must be cut off; but I shall soon know the event, for there comes Putnam galloping. [*Enter Putnam.*] What is the disaster? What news do you bring me, General Putnam?

Put. This is no Boston work, sir; they are in earnest! Orders must be immediately issued for the boats to be in readiness to carry our people over to New York.

Wash. There is time enough for that, General Putnam, after we have defended these works; the account of the battle is what I wish to hear.

Put. Defend, sir! we cannot defend these works; our people won't defend them; if they do not see the boats, they will swim over; they won't be hemmed in to be made minc'd of. If you don't give your orders, I will give the orders myself.

Wash. If it must be so, the orders shall originate with me; and as soon as you have satisfied me on the fate of the day, proper measures shall be taken.

Put. Accursed fate, indeed, and most impious, for they took us fasting; and then they deceived us—a most devilish deception too; for they did not come any one way that we had marked out for them.

Wash. Well, but you had the woods, and the hills, and every other advantage. The riflemen did great execution from behind the trees, surely!

Put. Zounds! Sir, the Regulars did all the execution! They know that riflemen are deer killers!—Rifle guns and rifle frocks will be as cheap in their camp tomorrow as cods' heads in Newfoundland.—But the orders, sir; there is no time to be lost: they are at our heels.

Wash. Have patience, General. What is our loss? Where are the other generals?

Put. How can I tell where they are, or what our loss really is? but I am sure it is thousands. Good God, sir, let us make haste to save what is not lost.

Wash. This, General Putnam, is against my will; but I wait on you to execute yours. [*Exeunt.*]

SCENE IV: *A room at Brooklyn Ferry. Enter Noah, solus, his clothes covered with creek mud.*

Noah. Notwithstanding your dirty condition, Mr. Noah, I congratulate you on your safe arrival into your old quarters; neither hol'd by musket-balls, nor swelled up with salt water and creek mud. Thanks to my activity that I am not crab's meat with the rest. [*Enter King.*] Welcome, Joe; dripping from the creek, I see; but I am glad to see you alive!

King. Confirm it that I am really alive, for I feel some doubts about it.

Noah. Don't you know me then?

King. As well as I know myself, Noah; but are we not both in the other world?

Noah. Why, man, look about you; and you will find this to be the very room that we have inhabited for some time past.

King. My senses, good Noah, claim conviction: something, first, to cherish me, and then I may be convinced that I can, with propriety, talk upon sublunary subjects.

Noah. Behold, Joe, this pocket bottle; one-half of its contents I prescribe to your conviction and restoration.

King. [*Drinks.*] Now I return your congratulations, and am heartily glad to find you on this side of the grave—but, Noah, what has become of our generals?

Noah. Killed or taken prisoners; but I suppose the latter.—My poor general, I quite lament him.

King. Mine is under the same predicament, but I have not a pity for him: nor should I love you very much if I thought you serious in your lamentation.

Noah. Consider; he and I were brought up together. We went together to sea before the mast, and since he commenced lawyer, he maintained a suit for me against my mother, and got the cause.

King. Confound the dog! But was he really a lawyer, and did he influence you to commence an action against your mother?

215

Noah. He!—why, that fellow drank flip every night with the common people of our town of Berwick, and had art enough to influence them to all his ends.

King. And some hundreds of the common people has he influenced to their end this day.—But, for God's sake, Noah, how came a man of your understanding in the capacity of this fellow's servant?

Noah. Without doubt, I might have started with a regiment and probably have been, myself, a general by this time. But I saw through their topsy-turvy schemes; though I was obliged to float with the tide, I knew the post of honor would be the most private station. But Sullivan will be a loss to his family.

King. So will not Stirling. He will be a loss to nobody but those that find him. Had Sullivan any property?

Noah. Most excellent property, for he made a property of weakness and ignorance, and consequently had an extensive fund. But yours was a titled general, and I suppose very full of property; as he has often declared he was of principle.

King. His principle, Noah, has for years past been to withhold other people's property from them; and when all the resources of art failed, his estate was exposed to sale by virtue of an execution. But he resisted the sheriff, and declared himself a partisan of confusion because law and order would compel him to acts of justice. But do you recollect that this is the fast day?

Noah. Is it really! then it is one of the baits which the Continental Congress threw out for the people of America to bite at; and the event gives the lie to the inflaming and prophetic oratory this day resounded from the pulpits of New England. A day on which heaven has discarded them and disavowed their cause, in a remarkable manner. O King, our preachers prevented this unhappy dispute from coming to a bloodless issue.

King. It is a maxim with the Congress at Philadelphia that by the marvellous the vulgar are to be robb'd of their reason; but heaven has rejected the sacrifice, that the people may open their eyes and be no longer the dupes of their tyranny, deception and bloodshed.

Noah. From the first meeting of that *Hydra* at Philadelphia, its sixty-four mouths have all been open to devour two strangers!

King. Devouring mouths I know they are; but what strangers do you point at?

Noah. Power! and Riches!

King. True, very true—strangers indeed to most of them. The first they have amply usurped from the people, and have art enough to make use of them as instruments to confirm the usurpation.

Noah. They are, indeed, such monopolizers of liberty that they do not suffer other people to follow their inclinations. But as we know and consequently detest their machinations, let us avail ourselves of the character of servants and the confusion of retreat to lie concealed, until they are clear of the island.

King. Agreed; and in order that we may claim the mercy that our good old master has extended to his erring servants, and return to that authority which never oppressed a subject, let us renew our allegiance to the most admirable and virtuous prince that ever swayed scepter; and join our weak endeavors in supporting a constitution that has been, at once, the envy and admiration of the whole world.

Noah. I honor your sentiments because I experimentally know them to be just. And O! Almighty Disposer of human events, open the eyes of my deluded fellow subjects in this once-happy country! Encourage them to a free exercise of that reason which is the portion of every individual, that each may judge for himself. Then peace and order will smile triumphant over the rugged face of war and horror; the same hand that sows shall reap the field; and our vines and vineyards shall be our own. [*Exeunt omnes.*]

THE END

22

"The Congratulation" (1779)
from "The American Times:
A Satire" (1780)

Jonathan Odell (1737–1818), the most talented and unrelenting Loyalist party of the Revolution, was born in Newark, New Jersey, and educated at what is now Princeton University. Graduating in 1757, Odell took up the study of medicine and for a time served with the British army as a surgeon before going to London to prepare himself for the Anglican priesthood. Following his ordination in January of 1767, Odell was assigned to a parish in Burlington, New Jersey, where he continued as the confrontation between colonies and mother country drew to its climax.

Though Odell had no doubt on which side his allegiance lay, he managed to refrain from writing on political subjects until 1776. But in the spring of that year, with talk of independence in the air, he composed a song honoring the birthday of George III, which was sung on that occasion (June 4) by a number of captured British officers, including John André, being held prisoner in Burlington. When Odell's authorship became known, he was arrested as "a person suspected of being inimical to American liberty," and placed on parole with a pledge to remain in the vicinity of Burlington. By mid-December of 1776, however, the situation had become personally intolerable, and Odell fled to the safety of British-occupied New York City. Odell remained in New York for the remainder of the war, where he rendered valuable service to the British as chaplain and surgeon, as a secret agent (together with fellow poet Joseph Stansbury he handled the Arnold-André correspondence), and, most importantly, as a writer of Loyalist prose and poetry. Following the war Odell joined thousands of other American Loyalists in Nova Scotia, where he successfully built a new life for himself.

Like Philip Freneau, with whom he is often compared, Odell was a grim

*and unyielding poet who utilized his considerable talent relentlessly on be-
half of a cause to which he was unconditionally devoted. Though Odell had
no illusion that Britain's prewar taxation policies had been anything but
blunders, he drew a firm line at rebellion, and had nothing but scorn and invective for Congress and its leaders who were, he was convinced, leading
Americans down the path to perdition. For such individuals the savage bite
of his satire offered no quarter. Unfortunately, the bulk of Odell's work
was published anonymously, making it now impossible to establish the full
scope of his literary activities.*

☆ ☆

The Congratulation
(1779)[102]

Joy to great Congress, joy a hundred fold:
The grand cajolers are themselves cajol'd!
In vain has Franklin's artifice been tried,
And Louis swell'd with treachery and pride:
Who reigns supreme in heav'n deception spurns,
And on the author's head the mischief turns.
What pains were taken to procure D'Estaing!
His fleet's dispers'd, and Congress may go hang.

Joy to great Congress, joy a hundred fold:
The grand cajolers are themselves cajol'd!
Heav'n's King sends forth the hurricane and strips
Of all their glory the perfidious ships.
His ministers of wrath the storm direct;
Nor can the prince of air his French protect.
Saint George, Saint David show'd themselves true hearts;
Saint Andrew and Saint Patrick topp'd their parts.
With right eolian puffs the wind they blew;
Crack went the masts; the sails to shivers flew.
Such honest saints shall never be forgot;
Saint Dennis, and Saint Tammany, go rot.

Joy to great Congress, joy a hundred fold;
The grand cajolers are themselves cajol'd!
Old Satan holds a council in mid-air;

Hear the black dragon furious rage and swear—
Are these the triumphs of my Gallic friends?
How will you ward this blow, my trusty fiends?
What remedy for this unlucky job?
What art shall raise the spirits of the mob?
Fly swift, ye sure supporters of my realm,
Ere this ill news the rebels overwhelms.
Invent, say anything to make them mad;
Tell them the king—No, dev'ls are not so bad;
The dogs of Congress at the king let loose;
But ye, brave dev'ls, avoid such mean abuse.

Joy to great Congress, joy a hundred fold:
The grand cajolers are themselves cajol'd!
What thinks Sir Washington of this mischance;
Blames he not those who put their trust in France?
A broken reed comes pat into his mind:
Egypt and France by rushes are defin'd,
Basest of kingdoms underneath the skies,
Kingdoms that could not profit their allies.
How could the tempest play him such a prank?
Blank is his prospect, and his visage blank:
Why from West Point his armies has he brought?
Can nought be done?—sore sighs he at the thought.
Back to his mountains Washington may trot:
He take this city[103]—yes, when ice is hot.

Joy to great Congress, joy a hundred fold:
The grand cajolers are themselves cajol'd!
Ah, poor militia of the Jersey state,
Your hopes are bootless, you are come too late.
Your four hours plunder of New York is fled,
And grievous hunger haunts you in its stead.
Sorrow and sighing seize the Yankee race
When the brave Briton looks them in the face:
The brawny Hessian, the bold refugee,
Appear in arms, and lo! the rebels flee;
Each in his bowels griping *spankue* feels;
Each drops his haversack, and trusts his heels.
Scamp'ring and scouring o'er the fields they run,
And here you find a sword, and there a gun.

Joy to great Congress, joy a hundred fold;
The grand cajolers are themselves cajol'd!
The doleful tidings Philadelphia reach,
And Duffield[104] cries—The wicked make a breach!
Members of Congress in confusion meet,
And with pale countenance each other greet.
—No comfort, brother?—Brother, none at all.
Fall'n is our tower; yea, broken down our wall.
Oh brother! things are at a dreadful pass:
Brother, we sinn'd in going to the mass.
The Lord, who taught our fingers how to fight,
For this denied to curb the tempest's might:
Our paper coin refus'd for flour we see,
And lawyers will not take it for a fee.

Joy to great Congress, joy a hundred fold:
The grand cajolers are themselves cajol'd!
What caus'd the French from Parker's fleet to steal?[105]
They wanted thirty thousand casks of meal.
Where are they now—can mortal man reply?
Who finds them out must have a lynx's eye.
Some place them in the ports of Chesapeake;
Others account them bound to Martinique;
Some think to Boston they intend to go;
And some suppose them in the deep below.
One thing is certain, be they where they will,
They keep their triumph most exceeding still.
They have not even Pantagruel's luck,
Who conquer'd two old women and a duck.

Joy to great Congress, joy a hundred fold:
The grand cajolers are themselves cajol'd!
How long shall the deluded people look
For the French squadron moor'd at Sandy Hook?[106]
Of all their hopes the comfort and the stay,
This vile deceit at length must pass away.
What imposition can be thought on next,
To cheer their partisans, with doubt perplex'd?
Dollars on dollars heap'd up to the skies,
Their value sinks the more, the more they rise;
Bank notes of bankrupts, struck without a fund,
Puff'd for a season, will at last be shunn'd.

Call forth invention, ye renown'd in guile;
New falsehoods frame in matter, and in style;
Send some enormous fiction to the press;
Again prepare the circular address;
With lies, with nonsense, keep the people drunk:
For should they once reflect, your power is sunk.

Joy to great Congress, joy a hundred fold:
The grand cajolers are themselves cajol'd!
The farce of empire will be finish'd soon,
And each mock-monarch dwindle to a loon.
Mock-money and mock-states shall melt away,
And the mock-troops disband for want of pay.
Ev'n now decisive ruin is prepar'd:
Ev'n now the heart of Huntington is scar'd.[107]
Seen or unseen, on earth, above, below,
All things conspire to give the final blow.
Heaven has ten thousand thunderbolts to dart;
From Hell, ten thousand livid flames will start;
Myriads of swords are ready for the field;
Myriads of lurking daggers are conceal'd;
In injur'd bosoms dark revenge is nurst:
Yet but a moment, and the storm shall burst.

Joy to great Congress, joy a hundred fold:
The grand cajolers are themselves cajol'd!
Now War, suspended by the scorching heat,
Springs from his tent, and shines in arms complete.
Now Sickness, that of late made heroes pale,
Flies from the keenness of the northern gale.
Firmness and Enterprise, united, wait
The last command, to strike the stroke of Fate.
Now Boston trembles; Philadelphia quakes;
And Carolina to the center shakes.
There is, whose councils the just moment scan:
Whose wisdom meditates the mighty plan:
He, when the season is mature, shall speak;
All Heaven shall plaud him, and all Hell shall shriek.
At his dread fiat tumult shall retire;
Abhorr'd rebellion sicken and expire;
The fall of Congress prove the world's relief;
And deathless glory crown the god-like chief!

Joy to great Congress, joy a hundred fold:
The grand cajolers are themselves cajol'd!
What now is left of Continental brags?
Taxes unpaid, tho' payable in rags.
What now remains of Continental force?
Battalions mould'ring: waste without resource.
What rests there yet of Continental sway?
A ruin'd people, ripe to disobey.
Hate now of men, and soon to be the jest;
Such is your fate, ye monsters of the west!
Yet must on every face a smile be worn,
While every breast with agony is torn.
Hopeless yourselves, yet hope you must impart,
And comfort others with an aching heart.
Ill-fated they who, lost at home, must boast
Of help expected from a foreign coast:
How wretched is their lot, to France and Spain
Who look for succor, but who look in vain.

Joy to great Congress, joy a hundred fold:
The grand cajolers are themselves cajol'd!
Courage, my boys; dismiss your chilling fears:
Attend to me, I'll put you in your geers.
Come, I'll instruct you how to advertise
Your missing friends, your hide-and-seek allies.
O yes!—If any man alive will bring
News of the squadron of the Christian king:
If any man will find out Count D'Estaing,
With whose scrub actions both the Indies rang:
If any man will ascertain on oath
What has become of Monsieur de la Mothe:[108]
Whoever these important points explains,
Congress will nobly pay him for his pains,
Of pewter dollars, what both hands can hold,
A thimble-full of plate, a mite of gold;
The lands of some big Tory he shall get,
And start a famous colonel *en brevet:*
And last to honor him (we scorn to bribe)
We'll make him chief of the *Oneida* tribe![109]

JONATHAN ODELL

From "The American Times: A Satire"
(1780)

When Faction, pois'nous as the scorpion's sting,
Infects the people and insults the king;
When foul Sedition skulks no more conceal'd,
But grasps the sword and rushes to the field;
When Justice, Law, and Truth are in disgrace,
And Treason, Fraud, and Murder fill their place;
Smarting beneath accumulated woes,
Shall we not dare the tyrants to expose?
We will, we must—tho' mighty Laurens frown,
Or Hancock with his rabble hunt us down;[110]
Champions of virtue, we'll alike disdain
The guards of Washington, the lies of Paine;
And greatly bear, without one anxious throb,
The wrath of Congress, or its lords the mob.
Bad are the times, almost too bad to paint;
The whole head sickens, the whole heart is faint;
The state is rotten, rotten to the core,
'Tis all one bruise, one putrefying sore.
Here Anarchy before the gaping crowd
Proclaims the people's majesty aloud;
There Folly runs with eagerness about,
And prompts the cheated populace to shout;
Here paper dollars meager Famine holds,
There votes of Congress Tyranny unfolds;
With doctrines strange in matter and in dress,
Here sounds the pulpit, and there groans the press;
Confusion blows her trump—and far and wide
The noise is heard—the plow is thrown aside;
The awl, the needle, and the shuttle drops;
Tools change to swords, and camps succeed to shops;
The doctor's glister-pipe, the lawyer's quill,
Transform'd to guns, retain the power to kill;
From garrets, cellars, rushing thro' the street,
The newborn statesmen in committee meet;
Legions of senators infest the land,
And mushroom generals thick as mushrooms stand.

Ye western climes, where youthful plenty smil'd,
Ye plains just rescued from the dreary wild,

Ye cities just emerging into fame,
Ye minds new ting'd with learning's sacred flame,
Ye people wondering at your swift increase,
Sons of united liberty and peace,
How are your glories in a moment fled?
See, Pity weeps, and Honor hangs his head.

O! for some magic voice, some pow'rful spell,
To call the Furies from profoundest hell;
Arise, ye fiends, from dark Cocytus' brink;
Soot all my paper; sulfurize my ink;
So with my theme the colors shall agree,
Brimstone and black, the livery of Lee.[111]

They come, they come!—convulsive heaves the ground,
Earth opens—lo! they pour, they swarm around;
About me throng unnumber'd hideous shapes,
Infernal wolves, and bears, and hounds, and apes;
All Pandemonium stands reveal'd to sight;
Good monsters, give me leave, and let me write:
They will be notic'd—Memory, set them down,
Tho' reason stand aghast, and order frown.

Whence and what art thou, execrable form,
Rough as a bear, and roaring as a storm?
Ay, now I know thee—Livingston[112] art thou—
Gall in thy heart, and malice on thy brow;
Coward, yet cruel—zealous, yet profane;
Havoc, and spoil, and ruin are thy gain;
Go, glut like Death thy vast unhidebound maw,
Remorseless swallow liberty and law;
At one enormous stroke a nation slay,
But thou thyself shall perish with thy prey.

What fiend is this of countenance acute,
More of the knave who seems, and less of brute;
Whose words are cutting like a show'r of hail,
And blasting as the mildew in the vale?
'Tis Jay[113]—to him these characters belong:
Sure sense of right, with fix'd pursuit of wrong;
An outside keen, where malice makes abode,
Voice of a lark, and venom of a toad;

225

Semblance of worth, not substance, he puts on;
And Satan owns him for his darling son.

Flit not around me thus, pernicious elf,
Whose love of country terminates in self;
Back to the gloomy shades, detested sprite,
Mangler of rhet'ric, enemy of right;
Curs'd of thy father, sum of all that's base;
Thy sight is odious, and thy name is Chase.[114] ...

What group of wizards next salutes my eyes,
United comrades, quadruple allies?
Bostonian Cooper, with his Hancock join'd,
Adams with Adams, one in heart and mind.[115]
Sprung from the soil where witches swarm'd of yore,
They come well skill'd in necromantic lore;
Intent on mischief, busily they toil,
The magic cauldron to prepare and boil;
Array'd in sable vests and caps of fur,
With wands of ebony the mess they stir;
See! the smoke rises from the cursed drench,
And poisons all the air with horrid stench. ...

Hear thy indictment, Washington, at large;
Attend and listen to the solemn charge:
Thou hast supported an atrocious cause
Against thy king, thy country, and the laws;
Committed perjury, encourag'd lies,
Forced conscience, broken the most sacred ties;
Myriads of wives and fathers at thy hand
Their slaughter'd husbands, slaughter'd sons demand;
That pastures hear no more the lowing kine,
That towns are desolate, all—all is thine;
The frequent sacrilege that pain'd my sight;
The blasphemies my pen abhors to write;
Innumerable crimes on thee must fall—
For thou maintainest, thou defendest all. ...

What could, when half-way up the hill to fame,
Induce thee to go back, and link with shame?
Was it ambition, vanity, or spite,
That prompted thee with Congress to unite;

Or did all three within thy bosom roll,
"Thou heart of hero with a traitor's soul?"
Go, wretched author of thy country's grief,
Patron of villainy, of villains chief;
Seek with thy cursed crew the central gloom,
Ere Truth's avenging sword begin thy doom;
Or sudden vengeance of celestial dart
Precipitate thee with augmented smart.

O poet, seated on the lofty throne,
Forgive the bard who makes thy words his own;
Surpris'd I trace in thy prophetic page
The crimes, the follies of the present age;
Thy scenery, sayings, admirable man,
Portray our struggles with the dark divan.
What Michael to the first arch-rebel said,
Would well rebuke the rebel army's head;
What Satan to th' angelic Prince replied,
Such are the words of Continental pride.
I swear by Him who rules the earth and sky,
The dread event shall equally apply;
That Clinton's warfare is the war of God,
And Washington shall feel the vengeful rod. . . .

Stand forth, Taxation—kindler of the flame;
Inexplicable question, doubtful claim:
Suppose the right in Britain to be clear;
Britain was mad to exercise it here.
Call it unjust, or, if you please, unwise;
The colonists were mad in arms to rise:
Impolitic, and open to abuse,
How could it answer—what could it produce?
No need for furious demagogues to chafe;
America was jealous, and was safe.
Secure she stood in national alarms,
And Madness only would have flown to arms.
Arms could not help the tribute, nor confound:
Self-slain it must have tumbled to the ground.
Impossible the scheme should e'er succeed,
Why lift the spear against a brittle reed?

But arm they would, ridiculously brave;
Good laughter, spare me; I would fain be grave:

So arm they did—the knave led on the fool;
Good anger, spare me; I would fain be cool:
Mixtures were seen amazing in their kind;
Extravagance with cruelty was joined.
The Presbyterian with the convict march'd;
The meetinghouse was thinn'd, the gaol was search'd:
Servants were seiz'd, apprentices enroll'd;
Youth guarded not the boy, nor age the old:
Tag, rag, and bobtail issued on the foe,
Marshal'd by generals—Ewin, Roberdeau.[116]

This was not Reason—this was wildest rage,
To make the land one military stage:
The strange resolve, obtain'd the Lord knows how,
Which forc'd the farmer to forsake the plow;
Bade tradesmen mighty warriors to become,
And lawyers quit the parchment for the drum;
To fight they knew not why, they knew not what;
Was surely Madness—Reason it was not.

Next independence came, that German charm,
Of pow'r to save from violence and harm;
That curious olio, vile compounded dish. . . .

Heav'ns! how my breast has swell'd with painful throb
To view the frenzy of the cheated mob:
True sons of liberty in flattering thought;
But real slaves to basest bondage brought:
Frantic as Bacchanals in ancient times,
They rush'd to perpetrate the worst of crimes;
Chas'd peace, chas'd order from each bless'd abode;
While Reason stood abash'd, and Folly crow'd.
Now, now erect the rich triumphal gate;
The French alliance comes in solemn state:
Hail to the masterpiece of madness, hail;
The head of glory with a serpent's tail!
This seals, America, thy wretched doom:
Here, Liberty, survey thy destin'd tomb:
Behold, the temple of tyrannic sway
Is now complete—ye deep-ton'd organs, play;
Proclaim thro' all the land that Louis rules—
Worship your saint, ye giddy-headed fools.

Illustrious guardians of the laurel hill,
Excuse this warmth, these sallies of the quill:
I would be temperate, but severe disdain
Calls for the lash whene'er I check the rein:
I would be patient, but the teasing smart
Of insects makes the fiery courser start.
I wish'd for Reason in her calmest mood,
In vain—the cruel subject fires my blood.
When thro' the land the dogs of havoc roar,
And the torn country bleeds in every pore,
'Tis hard to keep the sober line of thought:
The brain turns round with such ideas fraught.
Rage makes a weapon blunt as mine to pierce,
And indignation gathers in the verse....

JOSEPH STANSBURY

23

Joseph Stansbury (1742–1809) was born in England but came to Philadelphia in October of 1767 and established himself as a merchant. A man of
urbanity and wit, Stansbury entered enthusiastically into the social life of
the city, where he soon became known as a singer and writer of humorous,
lightly satirical songs. Like so many Americans, Stansbury, though patriotic,
stopped short of independence, and in 1776 he was briefly jailed in consequence of his Loyalist sentiments. During the British occupation of the city
(September, 1777, to June, 1778), Stansbury held several minor posts, no
doubt occasioned by his usefulness as a Loyalist songster. When the British
army withdrew, he elected to stay behind and sign an oath of allegiance to
Congress. There he remained until 1780, when he was arrested and jailed
for treasonable activities (ironically, Stansbury's role as go-between in the
André-Arnold conspiracy was then undetected). In December of 1780, after
six months confinement, Stansbury finally joined the British in New York
City, and for the remainder of the war put his small subsidy to good use
turning out pro-British poetry and prose. After the war Stansbury spent two
years abroad, in Nova Scotia and England, before returning to America in
1785, where, apparently unmolested and politically reconstructed, he lived
out his remaining years.

In contrast with Odell's verse, Stansbury's poems and songs seem mild
and almost tame. Lacking Odell's intense bitterness, which could only find
outlet in stinging invective, Stansbury's genial personality displayed itself
in gay, witty, and rousing songs, patriotic but without rancor. To be sure,
Stansbury could be tough-minded. He saw the inconsistencies of Congress
and the patriot leaders and exploited them in his verse; but his Loyalism

was sufficiently clear-sighted to allow him to poke fun at the British as well, when the occasion demanded. Stansbury loved both Britain and America, and the conciliatory attitude he adopted at the beginning of the war remained with him throughout. As a result, unlike so many of his fellow Tories, Stansbury was able to proclaim at its conclusion,

> *Now this war at length is o'er;*
> *Let us think of it no more,*

and go on to rebuild his life in his adopted country.

☆ ☆

When Good Queen Elizabeth Governed the Realm
(c. 1774)[117]

When good Queen Elizabeth govern'd the realm,
And Burleigh's sage counsels directed the helm,[118]
In vain Spain and France our conquests oppos'd;
For Valor conducted what Wisdom propos'd.
    Beef and beer was their food;
    Love and Truth arm'd their band;
    Their courage was ready—
    Steady, boys, steady—
To fight and to conquer by sea and by land.

But since tea and coffee, so much to our grief,
Have taken the place of strong beer and roast beef,
Our laurels have wither'd, our trophies been torn;
And the lions of England French triumphs adorn.
    Tea and slops are their food;
    They unnerve every hand—
    Their courage unsteady
    And not always ready—
They often are conquer'd by sea and by land.

St. George views with transport our generous flame:
"My sons, rise to glory, and rival my fame.
Ancient manners again in my sons I behold
And this age must eclipse all the ages of gold."

231

> Beef and beer are our food;
> Love and Truth arm our band;
> Our courage is steady
> And always is ready
To fight and to conquer by sea and by land.

While thus we regale as our fathers of old,
Our manners as simple, our courage as bold,
May Vigor and Prudence our freedom secure
Long as rivers, or ocean, or stars shall endure.
> Beef and beer are our food;
> Love and Truth arm our band;
> Our courage is steady,
> And always is ready
To fight and to conquer by sea and by land.

Verses to the Tories[119]

Come, ye brave, by fortune wounded
More than by the vaunting foe,
Cheer your hearts, ne'er be confounded;
Trials all must undergo.
Tho' without or rhyme or reason
Hurried back thro' wilds unknown,
Virtue's smiles can make a prison
Far more charming than a throne.
Think not, tho' wretched, poor, or naked,
Your breast alone the load sustains:
Sympathizing hearts partake it—
Britain's monarch shares your pains.
This night of pride and folly over,
A dawn of hope will soon appear.
In its light you shall discover
Your triumphant day is near.

The Church-and-King Club
(1778)[120]

Come, honest Tories, a truce with your politics;
    Hoc age tells you in Latin as much:
Drink and be merry and—*à melancholy, nix!*
    'Tis de same ting do I speaks it in Dutch.
If old Diogenes lov'd altercation,
    Had he, sir, a drop of good wine in his tub?
Mirth and good humor is *our* occupation:
    Let this be the rule of the Church-and-King Club.

Well do we know the *Adelphi's* miscarriages,
    And the disasters of Johnny Burgoyne;
As to beefsteaks, no good fellow disparages
    One who in battle finds leisure to dine.

Congo[121] pretends (O good Lord, what a fibber 'tis!)
    Now to feel bold, and to fear no mischance.
As well might he say that he fights for their liberties,
    Whom he hath sold in a mortgage to France!

Soon shall you see a rebellious minority
    Blush for the part they have acted so long;
Britain shall rouse and regain her authority:
    Come then, a bumper, and call t' other song.
If old Diogenes lov'd altercation, etc.

A Pasquinade
(1780)

Has the Marquis la Fayette
Taken off all our hay yet?
Says Clinton to the wise heads around him:
    Yes, faith, great Sir Harry,
    Each stack he did carry,
And likewise the cattle—confound him!

Besides he now goes
Just under your nose,
To burn all the houses to cinder.
If that be his project,
It is not an object
Worth a great man's attempting to hinder.

For forage and house
I care not a louse;
For revenge let the Loyalists bellow.
I swear I'll not do more
To keep them in humor,
Than play on my violoncello.

Since Charlestown is taken,
'Twill sure save my bacon:
I can live a whole year on that fame, sir.
Ride about all the day;
At night, concert or play;
So a fig for those men that dare blame, sir.

If growlers complain
I inactive remain,
Will do nothing, nor let any others;
'Tis sure no new thing
To serve thus our King;
Witness Burgoyne and two famous brothers! [122]

Invitation
(1781)

Ye members of Congress and councils of state,
By rebellion who hope to become rich and great;
The project, tho' bulky, is lighter than cork,
Then quit it in time, and come hither to York.

You'll here see an army polite and well fed,
And crowds of fine folks, who lay three in a bed;

With ladies too wise to be shut up in cloisters,
Or live upon pulse when there's plenty of oysters.

If musters, fines, taxes, improv'd beyond reason,
Or loyal attachment transformed to treason,
Have wasted your means or your patience, come all
Where you'll pay, *for the present,* no taxes at all.

But first load a vessel with lumber, and send her:
'Tis true she may meet with some man-of-war's tender.
My *Shelah* fell in with the *Savage* and *Triton;*
They sold her, and left me the subject to write on.[123]

If loyal, come freely—if rebel, come too;
Only come without leave, it is all you've to do.
Take the oath, and declare you was forc'd to this push;
And if York will not suit you, repair to Flatbush.

You'll there find a country in which you may thrive;
And two dollars, from you, will go farther than five
From a poor refugee: and the reason is clear—
"It is good to provide lest the rebels come here."

Here plenty of all things for cash may be had;
If that should be wanting, your case will be bad.
Yet money's so plenty, you'll find, to your cost,
That gold, like your paper, its value has lost.

Should fortune deny you a mattress or bed,
Or a closet or hovel to shelter your head;
Conceal your chagrin, and a volunteer enter,
And swear you came here life and fortune to venture!

If this should not suit you, you may if you please
Join freely with loyal and brave refugees,
And plunder your friends and your foes, great and small;
And if you are caught, why—they'll hang you, that's all.

They'll hang you, that's all—I repeat it again:
And that, you'll confess, puts and end to your pain.
'Tis what you are used to—but here, by the Lord!
Theft, rapine and murder may smile at the cord.

But, joking apart, all the difference I find
'Twixt this place and that I left lately behind;
I lie down in peace, and in safety arise,
And Liberty's mine, an invaluable prize.

So here I enjoy, with unspeakable pleasure,
The objects for which so much bloodshed and treasure
Have idly been wasted by both sides, I fear:
And all who would taste them, should wisely come here.

If all in rebellion would take this advice,
The rupture so wide would be clos'd in a trice.
Forgetting past quarrels, we'd happily sing,
Hearts and voices united, O God Save the King!

Let Us Be Happy as Long as We Can
(1782)

I've heard in old times that a sage us'd to say
The seasons were nothing—December or May—
The heat or the cold never enter'd his plan;
That all should be happy whenever they can.

No matter what power directed the state,
He look'd upon such things as order'd by fate.
Whether govern'd by many, or rul'd by one man,
His rule was—be happy whenever you can.

He happen'd to enter this world the same day
With the supple, complying, fam'd Vicar of Bray.
Thro' both of their lives the same principle ran:
My boys, we'll be happy as long as we can.

Time-serving I hate, yet I see no good reason
A leaf from their book should be thought out of season.
When kick'd like a football from Sheba to Dan,
Egad, let's be happy as long as we can.

Since no one can tell what tomorrow may bring,
Or which side shall triumph, the Congress or king;
Since fate must o'errule us and carry her plan,
Why, let us be happy as long as we can.

Tonight let's enjoy this good wine and a song,
And relish the hour which we cannot prolong.
If evil will come, we'll adhere to our plan
And baffle misfortune as long as we can.

The United States
(1783)

Now this war at length is o'er;
Let us think of it no more.
Every party lie or name,
Cancel as our mutual shame.
Bid each wound of faction close,
Blushing we were ever foes.

Now restor'd to peace again,
Active commerce plows the main;
All the arts of civil life
Swift succeed to martial strife;
Britain now allows their claim,
Rising empire, wealth, and fame.

JOHN ANDRÉ

24

"The Cow Chace" (1780)

*The unfortunate Major John André (1751–80), who as every American
schoolboy knows paid for Benedict Arnold's treason with his life, was born
in London and educated at Geneva. Entering the British army in March of
1771, André came to America with the Royal Fusiliers some three years
later, in 1774. In November, 1775, he was captured at St. Johns in Canada,
and spent the next year on parole as an American prisoner. During the British occupation of Philadelphia (1777–78) André, now a captain, served as
aide-de-camp to General Charles Grey. This period marked André's rise to
prominence. As ambitious as he was engaging and talented, André entered
with a zest into the social life of the city. He organized dramatic performances, flirted with the lovely Peggy Shippen (soon to be the wife of Benedict Arnold), and staged, with Oliver De Lancey, Jr., the famous Mischianza
of May, 1778, an extravaganza celebrating Howe's departure as commander-
in-chief. Such abilities recommended him to Howe's successor Sir Henry
Clinton, who made André his aide-de-camp. In this capacity André took
charge of the British secret service, an assignment that slowly but inexorably
enmeshed him in the web of conspiracy surrounding Benedict Arnold. The
rest of André's story is well known: his night meeting with Arnold at Haver-
straw on the banks of the Hudson; his failure to return safely to the British
man-of-war* Vulture; *his attempt to reach New York City by an overland
route; his capture near Tarrytown with documents beneath his stockings;
his subsequent trial and execution which left only mourners in its wake.*

*André had many talents besides his military ones: he could draw, act,
direct and stage plays and pageants; and he could write. The best-known
example of his literary ability is the burlesque which he titled "The Cow
Chace," a parody of the famous English ballad "Chevy Chase," which tells
in mock epic form the story of Anthony Wayne's fruitless attempt to seize*

238

*the blockhouse at Bull's Ferry, New Jersey on July 21, 1780. "The Cow
Chace" was published in Rivington's* Royal Gazette *in three installments in
August and September, 1780. Ironically, the third canto—containing its
prophetic concluding stanza—was published on Saturday, September 23, the
very day that its author stumbled into three young militiamen near Tarrytown.*

☆ ☆

Canto I[124]

> To drive the kine one summer's morn,
>   The tanner took his way;
> The calf shall rue that is unborn
>   The jumbling of that day.
>
> And Wayne descending steers shall know,
>   And tauntingly deride;
> And call to mind in every low
>   The tanning of his hide.[125]
>
> Yet Bergen cows still ruminate,
>   Unconscious in the stall
> What mighty means were used to get
>   And loose them after all.
>
> For many heroes bold and brave,
>   From Newbridge and Tappan,
> And those that drink Passaic's wave,
>   And those who eat supaun;[126]
>
> And sons of distant Delaware,
>   And still remoter Shannon,
> And Major Lee with horses rare,
>   And Proctor with his cannon;[127]
>
> All wond'rous proud in arms they came—
>   What hero could refuse
> To tread the rugged path to fame,
>   Who had a pair of shoes?
>
> At six, the host with sweating buff
>   Arrived at Freedom's pole;[128]

When Wayne, who thought he'd time enough,
    Thus speechified the whole.

"O ye, whom glory doth unite,
    Who freedom's cause espouse;
Whether the wing that's doom'd to fight,
    Or that to drive the cows,

"Ere yet you tempt your further way,
    Or into action come,
Hear, soldiers, what I have to say,
    And take a pint of rum.

"Intemp'rate valor then will string
    Each nervous arm the better;
So all the land shall I O sing,
    And read the general's letter.[129]

"Know that some paltry refugees,
    Whom I've a mind to fight,
Are playing h—l amongst the trees
    That grow on yonder height.

"Their fort and blockhouses we'll level,
    And deal a horrid slaughter;
We'll drive the scoundrels to the devil,
    And ravish wife and daughter.

"I, under cover of attack,
    Whilst you are all at blows,
From English neighb'rhood and Nyack
    Will drive away the cows;

"For well you know the latter is
    The serious operation,
And fighting with the refugees
    Is only demonstration."

His daring words from all the crowd
    Such great applause did gain,
That every man declar'd aloud,
    For serious work with Wayne.

Then from the cask of rum once more,
    They took a heady gill;
When one and all they loudly swore
    They'd fight upon the hill.

But here the muse hath not a strain
    Befitting such great deeds;
Huzza! they cried, huzza! for Wayne,
    And shouting ———.

Canto II

Near his meridian pomp, the sun
    Had journey'd from the horizon;
When fierce the dusky tribe mov'd on
    Of heroes drunk as pison.

The sounds confus'd of boasting oaths
    Reecho'd through the wood;
Some vow'd to sleep in dead men's clothes,
    And some to swim in blood.

At Irving's nod 'twas fine to see
    The left prepare to fight;
The while the drovers, Wayne and Lee,
    Drew off upon the right.

Which Irving 'twas, fame don't relate,
    Nor can the muse assist her;
Whether 'twas he that cocks a hat,
    Or he that gives a clyster.[130]

For greatly one was signaliz'd,
    That fought on Chestnut Hill;
And Canada immortaliz'd
    The vender of the pill.[131]

Yet the attendance upon Proctor
    They both might have to boast of;
For there was business for the doctor,
    And hats to be disposed of.

JOHN ANDRÉ

Let none uncandidly infer
   That Stirling wanted spunk;
The self-made peer had sure been there,
   But that the peer was drunk.

But turn we to the Hudson's banks,
   Where stood the modest train,
With purpose firm, though slender ranks,
   Nor car'd a pin for Wayne.

For them the unrelenting hand
   Of rebel fury drove;
And tore from every genial band
   Of friendship and of love.

And some within a dungeon's gloom
   By mock tribunals laid,
Had waited long a cruel doom
   Impending o'er each head.

Here one bewails a brother's fate,
   There one a sire demands,
Cut off, alas! before their date
   By ignominious hands.

And silver'd grandsires here appear'd
   In deep distress serene,
Of reverent manners that declar'd
   The better days they'd seen.

Oh, curs'd rebellion, these are thine,
   Thine are these tales of woe;
Shall at thy dire insatiate shine
   Blood never cease to flow?

And now the foe began to lead
   His forces to the attack;
Balls whistling unto balls succeed,
   And make the blockhouse crack.

No shot could pass, if you will take
   The general's word for true;

But 'tis a d——ble mistake,
    For every shot went through.[132]

The firmer as the rebels press'd,
    The loyal heroes stand;
Virtue had nerv'd each honest breast,
    And industry each hand.

In valor's frenzy Hamilton
    Rode like a soldier big,
And secretary Harrison
    With pen stuck in his wig.[133]

But lest their chieftain Washington
    Should mourn them in the mumps,
The fate of Withrington to shun,
    They fought behind the stumps.[134]

But ah, Thaddeus Posset, why
    Should thy poor soul elope?
And why should Titus Hooper die,
    Ay, die—without a rope?

Apostate Murphy, thou to whom
    Fair Shela ne'er was cruel,
In death shalt hear her mourn thy doom,
    "Och! would you die, my jewel?"

Thee, Nathan Pumpkin, I lament,
    Of melancholy fate;
The gray goose stolen as he went,
    In his heart's blood was wet.[135]

Now, as the fight was further fought,
    And balls began to thicken,
The fray assum'd, the generals thought,
    The color of a lickin'.

Yet undismay'd the chiefs command,
    And to redeem the day,
Cry, soldiers, charge! they hear, they stand,
    They turn and run away.

JOHN ANDRÉ

Canto III

Not all delights the bloody spear,
   Or horrid din of battle;
There are, I'm sure, who'd like to hear
   A word about the cattle.

The chief whom we beheld of late
   Near Schralenburg haranguing,
At Yan Van Poop's unconscious sat
   Of Irving's hearty banging.

Whilst valiant Lee, with courage wild,
   Most bravely did oppose
The tears of woman and of child,
   Who begg'd he'd leave the cows.

But Wayne, of sympathizing heart,
   Required a relief;
Not all the blessings could impart
   Of battle or of beef.

For now a prey to female charms,
   His soul took more delight in
A lovely hamadryad's arms
   Than cow-driving or fighting.

A nymph the refugees had drove
   Far from her native tree,
Just happen'd to be on the move
   When up came Wayne and Lee.

She in mad Anthony's fierce eye
   The hero saw portray'd,
And all in tears she took him by
   —The bridle of his jade.

"Hear," said the nymph, "O, great commander!
   No human lamentations;
The trees you see them cutting yonder,
   Are all my near relations.

"And I, forlorn! implore thine aid,
    To free the sacred grove;
So shall thy prowess be repaid
    With an immortal's love."

Now some, to prove she was a goddess,
    Said this enchanting fair
Had late retired from the bodies
    In all the pomp of war.

The drums and merry fifes had play'd
    To honor her retreat;
And Cunningham[136] himself convey'd
    The lady through the street.

Great Wayne, by soft compassion sway'd,
    To no inquiry stoops,
But takes the fair afflicted maid
    Right into Yan Van Poop's.

So Roman Anthony, they say,
    Disgrac'd the imperial banner,
And for a gypsy lost a day,
    Like Anthony the tanner.

The hamadryad had but half
    Receiv'd address from Wayne,
When drums and colors, cow and calf,
    Came down the road amain.

And in a cloud of dust were seen
    The sheep, the horse, the goat,
The gentle heifer, ass obscene,
    The yearling and the shoat.

And pack-horses with fowls came by,
    Befeather'd on each side;
Like Pegasus, the horse that I
    And other poets ride.

Sublime upon his stirrups rose
    The mighty Lee behind,

245

JOHN ANDRÉ

And drove the terror-smitten cows
    Like chaff before the wind.

But sudden see the woods above
    Pour down another corps,
All helter-skelter in a drove,
    Like that I sung before.

Irving and terror in the van
    Came flying all abroad;
And cannon, colors, horse, and man
    Ran tumbling to the road.

Still as he fled, 'twas Irving's cry,
    And his example too,
"Run on, my merry men—For why?
    The shot will not go through."[137]

As when two kennels in the street,
    Swell'd with a recent rain,
In gushing streams together meet
    And seek the neighboring drain;

So met these dung-born tribes in one,
    As swift in their career,
And so to Newbridge they ran on—
    But all the cows got clear.

Poor Parson Caldwell,[138] all in wonder,
    Saw the returning train,
And mourn'd to Wayne the lack of plunder
    For them to steal again.

For 'twas his right to steal the spoil, and
    To share with each commander,
As he had done at Staten Island
    With frost-bit Alexander.[139]

In his dismay, the frantic priest
    Began to grow prophetic;
You'd swore, to see his laboring breast,
    He'd taken an emetic.

"I view a future day," said he,
    "Brighter than this day dark is;
And you shall see what you shall see,
    Ha! ha! my pretty Marquis![140]

"And he shall come to Paulus Hook,
    And great achievements think on;
And make a bow and take a look,
    Like Satan over Lincoln.

"And every one around shall glory
    To see the Frenchman caper;
And pretty Susan[141] tell the story
    In the next Chatham paper."

This solemn prophecy, of course,
    Gave all much consolation,
Except to Wayne, who lost his horse
    Upon that great occasion.

His horse that carried all his prog,
    His military speeches;
His corn-stock whiskey for his grog,
    Blue stockings and brown breeches.

And now I've clos'd my epic strain,
    I tremble as I show it,
Lest this same warrior-drover, Wayne,
    Should ever catch the poet.

LOYALIST POEMS AND SONGS

25

☆ ☆

Burrowing Yankees
(1776)

Ye Yankees who, mole-like, still throw up the earth,
And like them, to your follies are blind from your birth;
Attempt not to hold British troops at defiance,
True Britons, with whom you pretend an alliance.

Mistake not; such blood ne'er run in your veins,
'Tis no more than the dregs, the lees, or the drains:
Ye affect to talk big of your hourly attacks;
Come on! and I'll warrant, we'll soon see your backs.

Such threats of bravadoes serve only to warm
The true British hearts you ne'er can alarm;
The Lion once rous'd, will strike such a terror,
Shall show you, poor fools, your presumption and error.

And the time will soon come when your whole rebel race
Will be drove from the lands, nor dare show your face:
Here's a health to great *George,* may he fully determine,
To root from the earth all such insolent vermin.

The Congress
(1776)

Ye Tories all rejoice and sing
Success to George our gracious king;
The faithful subjects tribute bring
    And execrate the Congress.

These hardy knaves and stupid fools;
Some apish and pragmatic mules;
Some servile acquiescing tools;
    These, these compose the Congress.

When Jove resolv'd to send a curse,
And all the woes of life rehearse;
Not plague, not famine, but much worse;
    He curs'd us with a Congress.

Then peace forsook this hapless shore;
Then cannons blaz'd with horrid roar;
We hear of blood, death, wounds and gore;
    The offspring of the Congress.

Imperial Rome from scoundrels rose;
Her grandeur's hail'd in verse and prose;
Venice the dregs of sea compose;
    So sprung the mighty Congress.

When insects vile emerge to light,
They take their short inglorious flight,
Then sink again to native night:
    An emblem of the Congress.

With freemen's rights they wanton play;
At their command, we fast and pray;
With worthless paper they us pay;
    A fine device of Congress.

With poverty and dire distress,
With standing armies us oppress;
Whole troops to Pluto swiftly press,
    As victims to the Congress.

Time-serving priests to zealots preach,
Who king and Parliament impeach;
Seditious lessons to us teach
    At the command of Congress.

Good Lord! disperse this venal tribe;
Their doctrine let no fools imbibe;
Let Balaam no more asses ride
    Nor burdens bear to Congress.

With puffs, and flams, and gasconade,
With stupid jargon, they bravade:
We transports take—Quebec invade—
    With laurels crown the Congress.

Our mushroom champions they dragoon;
We cry out hero, not poltroon;
The next campaign we'll storm the moon,
    And there proclaim the Congress.

In shades below, Montgomery's ghost[142]
Is welcom'd to the Stygian coast;
Congenial traitors see and boast
    Th' unhappy dupe of Congress.

Old Catiline, and Cromwell too,
Jack Cade and his seditious crew,[143]
Hail brother rebel at first view,
    And hope to meet the Congress.

The world's amaz'd to see the pest
The tranquil land with wars infest;
Britannia puts them to the test,
    And tries the strength of Congress.

O goddess, hear our hearty prayers;
Confound the villains by the ears;
Disperse the plebeians—try the peers;
    And execute the Congress.

See, see, our hope begins to dawn;
Bold Carleton[144] scours the northern lawn;

The sons of faction sigh forlorn;
    Dejected is the Congress.

Clinton, Burgoyne, and gallant Howe,[145]
Will soon reward our conduct true,
And to each traitor give his due;
    Perdition waits the Congress.

See, noble Dunmore[146] keeps his post;
Marauds and ravages the coast;
Despises Lee[147] and all his host,
    That hair-brain tool of Congress.

There's Washington and all his men—
Where Howe had one, the goose had ten—
March'd up the hill, and down again;
    And sent returns to Congress.

Prepare, prepare, my friends prepare,
For scenes of blood, the field of war;
To royal standard we'll repair,
    And curse the haughty Congress.

Huzza! Huzza! we thrice huzza!
Return peace, harmony, and law!
Restore such times as once we saw,
    And bid adieu to Congress.

British Light Infantry
(1778)

For battle prepared in their country's just cause,
Their king to avenge and support all his laws;
As fierce as a tiger, as swift as the roe,
The British Light Infantry rush on their foe.

Though rebels unnumber'd oppose their career,
Their hearts are undaunted; they're strangers to fear;
No obstacles hinder; resistless they go,
And death and destruction attend every blow.

'Cross the deep-gullied vale, up the mountain's steep side,
Through the rough foaming river's impetuous tide,
O'er the fortified redoubt, close wedged in array,
Regardless of safety they follow their prey.

The alarm of the drum and the cannon's loud roar,
The musket's quick flash, but inflames them the more.
No dangers appal, for they fear no control,
But glory and conquest inspires every soul.

Whenever their foe stands arrang'd in their sight,
With ardor impatient they pant for the fight;
Rout, havoc, confusion they spread through the field,
And rebellion and treason are forced to yield.

Yankee Doodle's Expedition to Rhode Island
(1778)[148]

From Lewis, Monsieur Gerard[149] came,
   To Congress in this town, sir,
They bow'd to him, and he to them,
   And then they all sat down, sir.

Begar, said Monsieur, one grand coup
   You shall bientot behold, sir;
This was believ'd as gospel true,
   And Jonathan felt bold, sir.

So Yankee Doodle did forget
   The sound of British drum, sir,
How oft it made him quake and sweat,
   In spite of Yankee rum, sir.

He took his wallet on his back,
   His rifle on his shoulder,
And vow'd Rhode Island to attack,
   Before he was much older.

In dread array their tatter'd crew
Advanc'd with colors spread, sir,
Their fifes played Yankee doodle, doo,
King Hancock at their head, sir.[150]

What numbers bravely cross'd the seas,
I cannot well determine,
A swarm of rebels and of fleas,
And every other vermin.

Their mighty hearts might shrink, they tho't,
For all flesh only grass is,
A plenteous store they therefore brought
Of whiskey and molasses.

They swore they'd make bold Pigot squeak,
So did their good ally, sir,
And take him pris'ner in a week,
But that was all my eye, sir.

As Jonathan so much desir'd
To shine in martial story,
D'Estaing with politesse retir'd,[151]
To leave him all the glory.

He left him what was better yet,
At least it was more use, sir,
He left him for a quick retreat
A very good excuse, sir.

To stay, unless he rul'd the sea,
He thought would not be right, sir,
And Continental troops, said he,
On islands should not fight, sir.

Another cause with these combin'd,
To throw him in the dumps, sir,
For Clinton's name alarmed his mind,
And made him stir his stumps, sir.

The Epilogue
(1778)

Our farce is now finish'd, your sport's at an end,
But ere you depart, let the voice of a friend
By way of a chorus, the evening crown
With a song to the tune of a hey derry down,
   Derry down, down, hey derry down.

Old Shakespeare, a poet, who should not be spit on,
Altho' he was born in the island called Britain,
Hath said that mankind are all players at best,
A truth we'll admit of, for sake of the jest.

On this puny stage we've strutted our hour,
And have acted our parts to the best of our power;
That the farce hath concluded not perfectly well,
Was surely the fault of the devil in hell.

This devil, you know, out of spleen to the church,
Will oftentimes leave his best friends in the lurch,
And turn them adrift in the midst of their joy;
'Tis a difficult matter to cheat the Old Boy.

Since this is the case, we must e'en make the best
Of a game that is lost; let us turn it to jest;
We'll smile, nay, we'll laugh, we'll carouse and we'll sing,
And cheerfully drink life and health to the king.

Let Washington now from his mountains descend,
Who knows but in George he may still find a friend;
A Briton, altho' he loves bottle and wench,
Is an honester fellow than parle vous French.

Our great Independence we give to the wind,
And pray that Great Britain may once more be kind.
In this jovial song all hostility ends,
And Britons and we will forever be friends.

Boys fill me a bumper! now join in the chorus!
There is happiness still in the prospect before us,

In this sparkling glass all hostility ends,
And Britons and we will forever be friends.

Good night! my good people, retire to your houses,
Fair ladies, I beg you, convince your dear spouses
That Britons and we are united in bliss,
And ratify all with a conjugal kiss.

Once more, here's a health to the king and queen!
Confusion to him, who in rancor and spleen,
Refuses to drink with an English friend
Immutable amity to the world's end.

The Old Year and the New
(1779)[152]

What though last year be past and gone,
    Why should we grieve or mourn about it?
As good a year is now begun,
    And better too, let no one doubt it.
        'Tis New Year's morn; why should we part?
        Why not enjoy what Heaven has sent us?
    Let wine expand the social heart,
        Let friends, and mirth, and wine content us.

War's rude alarms disturb'd last year;
    Our country bled and wept around us;
But this each honest heart shall cheer;
    And peace and plenty shall surround us.
        'Tis New Year's morn, etc.

Last year King Congo, through the land,
    Display'd his thirteen stripes to fright us;
But *George's* power, in *Clinton's* hand,
    In this New Year shall surely right us.
        'Tis New Year's morn, etc.

Last year saw many honest men
   Torn from each dear and sweet connection:
But this shall see them home again,
    And happy in their king's protection.
     'Tis New Year's morn, etc.

Last year vain Frenchmen brav'd our coasts,
    And baffled Howe, and scap'd from Byron;[153]
But this shall bring their vanquish'd hosts
    To crouch beneath the British lion.
     'Tis New Year's morn, etc.

Last year rebellion proudly stood,
    Elate, in her meridian glory;
But this shall quench her pride in blood;
    George will avenge each martyr'd Tory.
     'Tis New Year's morn, etc.

Then bring us wine; full bumpers bring:
    Hail this New Year in joyful chorus:
God bless great George our gracious king,
    And crush rebellion down before us.
     'Tis New Year's morn; why should we part?
      Why not enjoy what Heaven has sent us?
     Let wine expand the social heart,
      Let friends, and mirth, and wine content us.

About Savannah
(1779)[154]

Come let us rejoice,
    With heart and with voice,
Her triumphs let loyalty show, sir,
    While bumpers go round,
    Reecho the sound,
Huzza for the king and Prevost,[155] sir.

With warlike parade,
And his Irish brigade,
His ships and his spruce Gallic host, sir,
As proud as an elf,
D'Estaing[156] came himself,
And landed on Georgia's coast, sir.

There joining a band
Under Lincoln's[157] command,
Of rebels and traitors and Whigs, sir,
'Gainst the town of Savannah
He planted his banner,
And then he felt wonderous big, sir.

With thund'ring of guns
And bursting of bombs
He thought to have frighten'd our boys, sir.
But amidst all their din
Brave Maitland push'd in,
And Moncrieff cried, "A fig for your noise," sir.[158]

Chagrined at delay,
As he meant not to stay,
The count form'd his troops in the morn,[159] sir.
Van, center, and rear
March'd up without fear,
Cocksure of success, by a storm, sir.

Though rude was the shock,
Unmov'd as a rock
Stood our firm British bands to their works, sir.
While the brave German corps
And Americans bore
Their parts as intrepid as Turks, sir.

Then muskets did rattle,
Fierce raged the battle,
Grape shot, it flew thicker than hail, sir.
The ditch fill'd with slain,
Blood dyed all the plain,
When rebels and French turned tail, sir.

See! see! how they run!
Lord! what glorious fun!
How they tumble, by cannon mow'd down, sir!
Brains fly all around,
Dying screeches resound,
And mangled limbs cover the ground, sir.

There Pulaski fell,
That imp of old Bell,
Who attempted to murder his king, sir.[160]
But now he is gone,
Whence he'll never return,
But will make hell with treason to ring, sir.

To Charleston with fear
The rebels repair;
D'Estaing scampers back to his boats, sir,
Each blaming the other,
Each cursing his brother,
And—may they cut each other's throats, sir.

Scarce three thousand men
The town did maintain,
'Gainst three times their number of foes, sir,
Who left on the plain,
Of wounded and slain
Three thousand to fatten the crows, sir.[161]

Three thousand! no less!
For the rebels confess
Some loss, as you very well know, sir.
Then let bumpers go round,
And reecho the sound.
Huzza for the king and Prevost, sir.

Song of the Volunteers of Ireland
(1780)[162]

Success to the shamrock, and all those who wear it,
    Be honor their portion wherever they go:
May riches attend them, and store of good claret,
    For how to employ them sure none better know.
Every foe surveys them with terror;
But every silk petticoat wishes them nearer:
So *Yankee* keep off, or you'll soon learn your error,
    For Paddy shall prostrate lay every foe.

This day—but the year I can't rightly determine—
    Saint Patrick the vipers did chase from his land:
Let's see if, like him, we can't sweep off the vermin,
    Who dare 'gainst the sons of the shamrock to stand.
Hand in hand! Let's carol the chorus—
"As long as the blessings of Ireland hang o'er us,
The crest of Rebellion shall tremble before us,
Like brothers while thus we march hand in hand!"

Saint George and Saint Patrick, Saint Andrew, Saint David,
    Together may laugh at all Europe in arms,
Fair Conquest her standard has o'er their head waved,
    And glory on them conferr'd all her charms.
War's alarms to us are a pleasure!
Since Honor our danger repays in full measure:
And all who join us shall find we have leisure
    To think of our sport e'en in war's alarms!

NOTES

PART I

1. JAMES OTIS

1. The French and Indian War (1756–63).

2. JOHN DICKINSON

2. The Townshend Revenue Act of 1767.
3. William Pitt (1708–78), first earl of Chatham, had led the fight in Parliament for the repeal of the Stamp Act.

3. BENJAMIN FRANKLIN

4. Frederick the Great (1712–86), who ruled as king of Prussia from 1740 to 1786.

4. THOMAS JEFFERSON

5. In the section omitted Jefferson traces the history of imperial relations down to the beginning of the reign of George III in 1760.

5. FRANCIS HOPKINSON

6. A reference to the colonial charters granted by the king and jealously guarded by Americans throughout the colonial period.
7. An allusion to the Magna Charta, the great charter of English liberties granted by King John at Runnymede in June of 1215.
8. The Stamp Act of 1765 required that a blue government stamp be affixed to newspapers, almanacs, pamphlets, broadsides, legal documents, and various other kinds of papers.
9. In 1216, at the command of Henry III, archbishops, bishops, and parish priests were required to read the Magna Charta in church twice a year and receive an oath from their congregations not to subvert its spirit or letter.
10. Throughout the summer of 1765 clandestine groups known as the Sons of Liberty organized to oppose the Stamp Act. So successful were their efforts, which not infrequently included violence and mob action, that by November 1, the

261

date upon which the Stamp Act was to go into effect, all the stamp agents in the colonies had resigned.

11. The Stamp Act was repealed on March 18, 1766.

12. On March 18, 1766, having repealed the Stamp Act, Parliament passed the Declaratory Act asserting its authority in the colonies "in all cases whatsoever."

13. The Townshend Acts of June 17, 1767, which placed importation duties on such items as glass, lead, paints, paper, and tea.

14. Nonimportation agreements, utilized to combat the Stamp Act, were revived in an attempt to bring to bear the weight of economic sanction.

15. On April 12, 1770, the Townshend Acts were repealed *except* for the tax on tea (water gruel). One of Lord North's reasons for moving for repeal was the pressure exerted by British merchants.

16. Parliament passed the Tea Act on May 10, 1773, giving the nearly bankrupt East India Company exclusive monopoly to sell its huge surplus of tea (seventeen million pounds worth), free of export duties, directly to agents in the American colonies.

17. Tea ships arriving in New York and Philadelphia were turned back to England with their cargoes intact; in Charleston, however, the tea agents having been forced to resign, the tea was landed for nonpayment of taxes and stored in government warehouses.

18. Massachusetts.

19. The famous Boston Tea Party on the evening of December 16, 1773.

20. Retaliation for the Boston Tea Party came in the form of the "Coercive Acts," the first of which, the Boston Port Bill, closed Boston Harbor as of June 1, 1774, until such time as the destroyed tea was paid for.

21. The Massachusetts Government Act (passed on May 20, 1774) all but revoked the Massachusetts charter by empowering the governor to select the members of his council and the leading justices of the colony, and requiring that town meetings have the governor's consent.

22. By an act of April 21, 1774, the murder trials of royal officials were transferred to England as were the trials and punishment of all those charged with treason against the government.

23. Coincidental with the closing of Boston Harbor, General Thomas Gage (1719–87), commander of the British army in North America, became governor of Massachusetts. From that moment on the entire colony lay under what amounted to martial law.

24. "The rest is wanting."

7. ALEXANDER HAMILTON

25. Hugo Grotius (1583–1645), Samuel Pufendorf (1632–94), John Locke (1632–1704), Baron de Montesquieu (1689–1755), and Jean Jacques Burlamaqui (1694–1748) were political philosophers much admired—and often quoted—by colonial American writers. Thomas Hobbes (1588–1679), referred to in the next paragraph, who argued that natural man can survive and escape anarchy only by surrendering, irreversibly, his rights to an absolute monarch (a Leviathan), was naturally opposed by those who believed that man was capable of self-government.

26. Sir William Blackstone (1723–80), one of England's great legal minds and the author of *Commentaries on the Laws of England* (1765), was frequently quoted by colonial Americans on the rights they enjoyed as Englishmen.

8. JOSEPH WARREN

27. James Lovell (1737–1814), Benjamin Church (1734–77), and John Hancock (1737–93), three well-known Boston patriots, delivered the anniversary addresses in 1771, 1773, and 1774 respectively.

28. A British garrison was established at Boston early in October of 1768.
29. Between 1714 and 1901 the British throne was occupied by scions of the Prussian house of Hanover.
30. See note 21 above.
31. An allusion to the so-called Northern War (1700–21) in which Russia's Peter the Great, reversing his early defeats at the hands of Charles II of Sweden, routed him at Poltava in 1709.

9. THOMAS PAINE

32. An allusion, apparently, to Thomas Pelham Holles (1693–1768), the Duke of Newcastle, who served as secretary of state for some thirty years.
33. Lord Frederick North (1732–92), the British prime minister.

11. SONGS AND BALLADS, 1768–75

34. By John Dickinson (1732–1808); first published in the *Boston Gazette*, July 18, 1768. To the tune of the very popular British song "Hearts of Oak," composed in 1759 by Dr. William Boyce, with words by David Garrick, the celebrated actor.
35. The event celebrated is, of course, the Boston Tea Party of December 16, 1773. Intended to be sung to the tune of "Hosier's Ghost" (or "Cease, Rude Boreas," as it is now more commonly known), an air used for many sea songs.
36. John Hampden (1594–1643) and Sir Algernon Sidney (1622–83) were venerated by colonial Americans as champions of political liberty: Hampden refused to submit to a tax levied by Charles I in 1636; Sidney challenged monarchial absolutism in his *Discourses Concerning Government* (1683), for which he was put to death.
37. General Thomas Gage (1719–87) replaced Thomas Hutchinson as royal governor of Massachusetts in the spring of 1774, with the task of implementing and enforcing the Coercive Acts. Though Gage was an able administrator whose caution and good sense undoubtedly delayed the outbreak of hostilities, he had a penchant for making proclamations denouncing patriot activity and upholding royal authority. These proclamations, parodied in verse and widely circulated, became grist for the mills of American propagandists. This particular version first appeared in the *Virginia Gazette*, hence the allusions to Middlesex County, Virginia (which had passed a resolution of loyalty to the crown early in 1774), and to John Murray (Lord Dunmore), the royal governor.
38. Frederick Lord North (1732–92), who became prime minister in 1770, was held responsible for the Boston Port Bill. North's name was often linked by American propagandists (apparently without reason) with the name of John Stuart (1713–92), the third Earl of Bute, who served as tutor to George III and later as his prime minister. Bute was long believed by Americans to be the secret power behind the throne. William Murray, first Earl of Mansfield (1705–93), as lord chief justice was a leading advocate of parliamentary supremacy and a staunch defender of the government. Throughout the eighteenth century the English people manifested great dislike and hatred for the deposed House of Stuart and its Catholicism, an onus that was borne to a certain degree by the Scottish people as well, especially after the aborted uprising of 1745 under Bonnie Prince Charlie. Suspicions of Jacobite (Stuart) influence were greatly aroused, therefore (and nowhere more greatly than in America) when two Scotsmen, Bute and Mansfield, rose to power and authority.
39. Charles James Fox (1749–1806), a brilliant orator, was a defender of the American cause in the House of Commons.
40. A parody of a song of the same title that was very popular in both England and the colonies. Attributed to Oliver Arnold of Norwich, Connecticut. The first stanza of the original reads as follows:

'Twas summer, and softly the breezes were blowing,
And sweetly the nightingale sang from the tree.
At the foot of a hill, where the river was flowing,
I sat myself down on the banks of the Dee.
Flow on, lovely Dee, flow on, thou sweet river,
Thy banks, purest stream, shall be dear to me ever,
For there I first gain'd the affection and favor
Of Jamie, the glory and pride of the Dee.

41. Written by Thomas Paine to the tune "The Gods of the Greeks" and first published in the *Pennsylvania Magazine* in July, 1775. The liberty tree was a majestic elm in Boston's South End that first became a rallying point during the Stamp Act crisis of August, 1765, when it was used to suspend the effigy of Andrew Oliver, one of the designated stamp distributors. Thereafter, until it was cut down by the British in 1774, it served as a rendezvous for the Sons of Liberty. This early icon of the Revolution had its counterparts elsewhere. New York City had its Liberty Pole, and liberty trees were consecrated in Charlestown and Lexington, Massachusetts, Providence, Rhode Island, and Charleston, South Carolina.

PART II

12. JOHN TRUMBULL

42. The first part of *M'Fingal* (one half of the final poem) was published anonymously in Philadelphia in January of 1776, the same month as Paine's *Common Sense*. A second edition appeared in Philadelphia in 1776, and a London edition appeared the same year. No further editions, apparently, were published between 1776 and 1782, when Trumbull divided the original poem into two cantos and added two more to complete the work. Some seven editions appeared during the decade that followed.

43. Flip, a hot beverage composed of rum, beer, and sugar, was a general favorite throughout New England.

44. The hero of Samuel Butler's mock-epic poem of the same name (1663–78); *Hudibras* provided one of the chief models for Trumbull's *M'Fingal.*

45. The Boston Tea Party, December 16, 1773.

46. On the morning after the Boston Tea Party, Massachusetts governor Thomas Hutchinson (1711–80) retired in alarm to his country estate at Milton. Tradition has it that when informed that a patriot mob was on the way to Milton, Hutchinson immediately took flight, bareheaded and half-shaved ("in the suds").

47. The allusion is to William Smith (1728–93), a noted New York lawyer, who after wavering in his allegiance finally became a Loyalist.

48. See note 38 above. William Tryon (1729–88) was the royal governor of New York at the outbreak of the Revolution. As commander of Loyalist troops, Tryon invaded Connecticut in 1777 and burnt the towns of Danbury, Fairfield, and Norwalk.

49. Joseph Galloway (1731–1803), a prominent Pennsylvania lawyer and influential political figure, represented Pennsylvania at the First Continental Congress, where his plan for colonial confederation based on American home rule was narrowly defeated. Shortly thereafter the conservative Galloway broke with his more radical colleagues, became a Loyalist, and actively took up arms with the British before sailing for London in 1778. Aboard ship Galloway is supposed to have received a trunk containing a halter.

50. James Rivington (1724–1802) was a well-known New York bookseller, printer, and newspaper editor of pro-British persuasion. In November, 1775, a party of patriots destroyed his press and carried off his types. Nonetheless, Rivington was soon back in business under the auspices of the British as editor of the *New York Loyal Gazette* (later shortened to the *Royal Gazette*) which emitted a steady stream of Tory propaganda throughout the war and hence became a

favorite object of attack for American writers.

13. HUGH HENRY BRACKENRIDGE

51. Though it is pointless to quarrel with the historical accuracy of Brackenridge's drama, the absence from the cast of characters of Colonel William Prescott (1726–95), who had command of the American troops on June 17, 1775, is somewhat surprising. At the time of the battle General Thomas Gage (1719–87) was commander-in-chief of the British army; Sir William Howe (1729–1814), John Burgoyne (1722–92), and Sir Henry Clinton (c. 1738–95) were all major generals but newly arrived in America; Robert Pigot (1720–96) held the rank of brigadier general. Captain George Sherwin (? –1775) was aide to General Howe. The career of Joseph Warren (1741–75) has been noted earlier. Israel Putnam (1718–90), "Old Put," a rugged veteran of the French and Indian War, hearing the news of Concord, dropped his plow and rushed from Connecticut to the American camp at Cambridge, just in time to take part in the Battle of Bunker Hill. Colonel Thomas Gardner (1723–75) of Massachusetts commanded one of the American regiments the day of the battle, and was mortally wounded.

52. Howe refers to events of the French and Indian War (1754–60) and its aftermath, the siege of Havana in 1762, when British soldiers and American colonials fought side by side.

53. Kings Henry VII, Henry VIII, and Edward VI, who ruled England between 1485 and 1553, periodically made war on France ("the Gallic shores"). John Churchill, the first duke of Marlborough (1650–1722), served as Queen Anne's commander-in-chief in her war against France, 1702–13. General James Wolfe (1727–59) was killed on the Plains of Abraham while attempting to storm the French citadel at Quebec. The allusion to John Hampden (1594–1643) is, in this context at least, obscure.

54. General Frederick Haldimand (1718–91), a veteran of the French and Indian War, was Gage's second in command.

55. John Stuart (1713–92), earl of Bute, the purported power behind the throne, and William Legge (1731–1801), earl of Dartmouth, the secretary of state for the colonies 1772–75.

56. Minden, a city in northwest Germany, was the site of an important English victory over the French in 1759.

57. The Boston Massacre of March 5, 1770.

58. See note 36 above. All three were opponents of political absolutism; Brutus, of course, was the slayer of Julius Caesar.

59. England won three celebrated victories over the French at Crécy (1346), Poitiers (1356), and Agincourt (1415).

60. Lieutenant Colonel James Abercromby, Major John Pitcairn, and Captain George Sherwin were all killed on June 17.

14. THOMAS PAINE

61. Paine is quoting the language of the Declaratory Act of 1766.

62. Actually the fifteenth century.

63. The allusion, apparently, is to William the Conqueror who became king of England in 1066; Voltaire (1694–1778), of course, was the great eighteenth-century poet, historian, and philosopher.

64. Philadelphia, where Paine had come to publish his first *Crisis* paper.

15. PHILIP FRENEAU

65. Saint James's Palace, the London residence of George III.

66. Captains and ships in the British navy, then employed on the American coast. –Freneau's note.

67. When the Virginia convention resolved to put the colony in "a posture of defense" in March, 1775, John Murray (1732–1809), the earl of Dunmore and

last royal governor of Virginia, seized the powder supply at Williamsburg and threatened to "lay the town in ashes."

68. John Montagu (1718–92), the earl of Sandwich, was the first lord of the admiralty.

69. In October of 1775 William Tryon (1729–88), New York's royal governor, was forced by the patriots to take refuge on a British warship anchored in New York harbor where he remained until the arrival of the British army.

70. Sir Henry Clinton (1738–95), who succeeded William Howe as commander-in-chief in 1778, made his headquarters in New York City. Freneau's poem satirizes the treatment accorded by Clinton to the Tories who sought his protection.

71. A poem in three cantos. Canto 1, "The Capture," recounts the capture of the American privateer *Aurora,* on which Freneau was a passenger, off Cape Henlopen, Delaware, by the British frigate *Isis,* May 26, 1780. In canto 3, "The Hospital Prison Ship," Freneau recalls his three weeks experience aboard the *Hunter,* lying in the East River, where he was conveyed, sick with fever, after twenty days aboard the *Scorpion.* Freneau was released on July 12, 1780.

72. David Sproat (or Sprout) was the commissary of naval prisoners at New York.

73. General Nathanael Greene (1742–86) engaged the British under Colonel Alexander Stewart at Eutaw Springs, South Carolina, on September 8, 1781. The initial advantage belonged to Greene, but a British counterattack forced the Americans to retreat, leaving the field and a nominal victory to the British. Because the British, weakened by their losses, were forced to fall back on Charleston, the end result of the battle was to insure American military ascendancy in the South.

74. Written by Freneau to celebrate the victory on April 26, 1782, of Captain Joshua Barney (1759–1818) and the crew of his Philadelphia privateer *Hyder Ali* over the British sloop *General Monk* which had long marauded the Delaware coast. The *General Monk* was commanded by Captain Josias Rogers (1755–95).

16. BENJAMIN FRANKLIN

75. Early in the morning of December 26, 1776, Washington crossed the Delaware River and fell upon the Hessian detachment at Trenton commanded by Colonel Johann Rall. The Americans had the advantage of surprise, and after a battle lasting less than two hours, Rall's troops, some 950 of the garrison's original total of 1,400, surrendered; 114 others were either killed or wounded. The Battle of Trenton, coming as it did at the end of the bleak campaign of 1776, which had seen Washington's army for the most part in retreat, did much to bolster sagging morale. Though Americans gave the name "Hessians" to all German mercenaries, only about half of the nearly 30,000 soldiers who served in America came from the German state of Hesse-Cassel.

17. WILLIAM LIVINGSTON

76. Sir Guy Carleton (1724–1808), then governor of Canada, had helped prepare Burgoyne's expedition.

77. The original British strategy for 1777 called for Burgoyne's army to rendezvous at Albany with Colonel Barry St. Leger, who was to move down the Mohawk Valley from Oswego on Lake Ontario, and with Sir William Howe, who was to move up the Hudson River from New York City. St. Leger was stopped at Fort Stanwix in August. Howe, unaccountably, turned south to take Philadelphia.

18. FRANCIS HOPKINSON

78. January 5, 1778.

79. The British, under the command of Sir William Howe, entered Philadelphia on September 26, 1777, and set up winter headquarters. During his occupation of the city Howe entered into an affair with Mrs. Loring, the wife of Joshua Loring, Howe's commissary of prisoners.

80. Sir William Erskine (1728–95), one of Howe's chief officers.

19. ETHAN ALLEN

81. Colonel Seth Warner (1743–84) was one of the leaders of the Green Mountain Boys; after Fort Ticonderoga was taken, a detachment under Warner moved up Lake Champlain and took Crown Point on May 11, 1775.

82. General Richard Prescott (1725–88), the commander of the British garrison at Montreal.

83. Guy Johnson (1740–88) was the British superintendent of Indian affairs; Daniel Claus was his brother-in-law and assistant. Both men became notorious Loyalists and took part in Joseph Brant's raids on the Mohawk Valley.

84. General Nathaniel Woodhull (1722–76) was supposedly hacked to death by the British officer to whom he surrendered in an incident following the Battle of Long Island (August, 1776). Captain Fellows is unidentified.

20. PATRIOT POEMS AND SONGS

85. The ballad, reproduced from the May, 1775, issue of the *Pennsylvania Magazine*, celebrates the British retreat from Concord and Lexington on April 19, 1775.

86. "Yankee Doodle," the most popular and widely known of all revolutionary songs, was apparently written by a British officer to make fun of the provincialism of the New England soldier. It was subsequently seized upon by the Americans, who reworked parts of it to suit their own purposes. Many variations are extant. The tune itself is of colonial origin.

87. First published in the *Pennsylvania Evening Post* March 30, 1776, and attributed to Benjamin Franklin. In order to ridicule the British Regulars, the author provides a catalog of their reverses in battle: at Prestonpans and Falkirk, near Edinburgh, Scotland, where they were defeated by Highlanders in 1746; at the Monongahela River near Fort Duquesne, where the French and Indians defeated General Braddock in July, 1755; at Fort George and Fort Oswego on Lake Ontario, taken by General Montcalm in August, 1757; at Fort Ticonderoga, at the head of Lake Champlain, where Montcalm threw back Abercromby's assault in July, 1758; and at Louisburg, the fortress on Cape Breton Island, which Lord Loudoun failed to take in June–July, 1757.

88. Nathan Hale (1755–76) was the young Connecticut schoolteacher who volunteered to enter British lines to obtain information on the disposition of enemy forces in and around New York. Captured in disguise and with incriminating documents in hand, he was ordered hanged without trial as a spy. His last words reportedly were: "I only regret that I have but one life to lose for my country." Hale quickly became a symbol to his countrymen of selfless patriotism

89. The ballad gives an accurate account of Burgoyne's career and of his campaign of 1777.

90. General Arthur St. Clair (1736–1818), in command of Ticonderoga, prudently surrendered the untenable fort to Burgoyne's superior army on July 5, 1777, and succeeded in escaping with most of his troops. Horatio Gates (1729–1806) was in command of the American army that accepted Burgoyne's surrender at Saratoga on October 17; Benedict Arnold, though without command, distinguished himself by personally leading an assault against Burgoyne on October 7.

91. Attributed to one Henry Archer, an Englishman, who emigrated to America in 1778.

92. "The Dance," to the tune of "Yankee Doodle," commemorates the 1781 campaign of General Charles Cornwallis (1738–1805), culminating in his surrender at Yorktown on October 19. Passing reference is made to four of Cornwallis's chief antagonists: General Nathanael Greene (1742–86), who engaged Cornwallis in a series of battles in the Carolinas during the winter and early spring of 1781, forcing him to fall back on Wilmington, N.C.; Marquis de Lafayette (1757–1834), the young French nobleman who fought Cornwallis in New Jersey in 1777 and opposed him again in Virginia (and at Yorktown) in 1781; and Comte de Grasse (1722–88) and Comte de Rochambeau (1725–1807), who at Yorktown commanded the French fleet and army respectively.

93. Sung to the tune of "Maggie Lauder," a favorite in both armies.

PART III

21. THE BATTLE OF BROOKLYN

94. Generals Israel Putnam (1718–90), John Sullivan (1740–95), and William Alexander (1726–83), the earl of Stirling, served as Washington's chief field officers during the Battle of Long Island, Stirling with particular distinction. Of the colonels, Joel Clark (? –1776) and John Lasher (1724– ?) commanded units of Connecticut and New York troops respectively; Abraham Remsen was a farmer of the Gowanus area. Why Lady Gates, wife of General Horatio Gates (1728–1806), should be included among the cast of characters is unclear; her husband did not see service on Long Island and, in fact, was then far to the north as second in command to General Schuyler.

95. The Battle of Brooklyn took place on and in front of a peninsula jutting into the East River across from New York City, bounded on the northeast by Wallabout Bay and on the southwest by Gowanus Bay.

96. Fort Greene (named after American general Nathanael Greene) was a star-shaped redoubt near the center of the American lines.

97. The allusion, clearly, is to Robert Harrison (1745–90), Washington's military secretary.

98. The gilt statue of George III in New York City's Bowling Green was pulled down by celebrating patriots on the evening of July 9, 1776.

99. Edmund Burke (1729–97), the English statesman, was noted for his oratorical ability. "Junius" was the pen name of an unknown writer who attacked George III and his ministers in the London *Public Advertiser* 1769–72.

100. Theodorus Polhemus, a representative to the New York Provincial Congress, whose ancestor was the first Dutch Reformed minister in King's County (N.Y.).

101. The allusion is unclear. Thomas Fitch (1700–74) served as governor of Connecticut between 1754 and 1766. A son, also named Thomas, was a colonel in the Fairfield County (Conn.) militia.

22. JONATHAN ODELL

102. Occasioned by the series of reversals suffered by Comte d'Estaing (1729–94) and the French fleet in 1778 and 1779. D'Estaing's inept maneuvers at New York and Newport were climaxed in October, 1779, by his failure to take Savannah. These setbacks led many Americans to question the advantages of the new Franco-American alliance, a disenchantment which Odell sought to exploit.

103. New York.

104. The Reverend George Duffield (1730–92), a Presbyterian chaplain to Congress. The allusion that follows suggests the length that Congress was willing to go to ingratiate itself with its new French allies.

105. Sir Hyde Parker (1739–1807), the British admiral.

106. D'Estaing's failure to pass Sandy Hook in July, 1778, cost him the opportunity of destroying or capturing Howe's fleet. Instead, he sailed off to Newport. Had d'Estaing been simply content to maintain a blockade, he might well have forced the British to evacuate New York.

107. Samuel Huntington (1731–96) of Connecticut, the president of Congress from 1779 to 1781.

108. La Motte Picquet, another French admiral.

109. The Oneida tribe of central New York was one of the Six Nations of Iroquois. Congress occasionally bestowed military rank and other awards on Indian chiefs in an effort to ensure their loyalty.

110. Henry Laurens (1724–92) of South Carolina succeeded Massachusetts's John Hancock (1737–93) as president of Congress in November, 1777. Hancock had been one of the leaders of Boston's Sons of Liberty.

111. General Charles Lee (1731–82), a former British officer and soldier of fortune, tendered his services to Congress in June, 1775; throughout the war he remained

a controversial figure.

112. William Livingston (1723–90), the governor of New Jersey.
113. John Jay (1745–1829), a wealthy New York lawyer, served as president of Congress (1778–79) before becoming minister to Spain.
114. Samuel Chase (1741–1811), a Maryland lawyer and member of Congress.
115. The Reverend Samuel Cooper (1724–83), pastor of the Brattle Street Church, Boston, was well known for his patriotic pamphlets and sermons. "Adams with Adams" refers, of course, to the two Boston cousins, Sam Adams (1722–1803), the master agitator and propagandist, and John Adams (1735–1826), a leading figure in Congress and the future president.
116. The allusion is to James Ewing (1736–1806) and Daniel Roberdeau (1727–95), both Pennsylvanians.

23. JOSEPH STANSBURY

117. Composed for a meeting of the Sons of St. George in New York. To the tune "Hearts of Oak."
118. Robert Cecil, Lord Burleigh (1563–1612), adviser to Elizabeth I.
119. The date of composition is unknown.
120. The Church-and-King Club was apparently a Loyalist association in Philadelphia.
121. Congress.
122. William and Richard Howe, the general and the admiral.
123. An allusion to the scheme for shipping lumber to the British which Stansbury devised and participated in while living in Philadelphia. Vessels were cleared from Philadelphia bound for Boston only to fall "by accident" into the hands of English warships like the *Savage* and *Triton.*

24. JOHN ANDRÉ

124. The blockhouse at Bull's Ferry, manned by a garrison of about seventy Loyalists, was used as a base for protecting woodcutting operations in the vicinity. Below the blockhouse, on Bergen's Neck, were a large number of cattle and horses, within too easy a reach of the British troops at Paulus Hook. Accordingly, on July 20, 1780, Washington dispatched Anthony Wayne (1745–96) with a force of something less than 2000 (including four cannon from Thomas Proctor's artillery and some dragoons under the command of Stephen Moylan) to destroy the blockhouse and bring off the cattle. After a spirited attack, heroic but somewhat foolhardy, Wayne withdrew, bringing with him his dead and wounded and a fair number of cattle.
125. Wayne, like his father before him, was a tanner by trade.
126. Cornmeal mush, more popularly known as hasty pudding.
127. An anachronism. Major Henry Lee (1756–1818)–"Light-horse Harry"–the most famous cavalry leader of the Revolution, was not with Wayne; the dragoons were commanded by Colonel Stephen Moylan (1737–1811). André may have deliberately made the substitution to capitalize on Lee's dashing reputation. Colonel Thomas Proctor (1739–1806) of Pennsylvania commanded the cannon.
128. A Liberty Pole located between Nyack, New York, and Orangetown, New Jersey.
129. George Washington.
130. Colonel William Irvine (1741–1804) was with Wayne at Bull's Ferry; he was a physician ("that gives a clyster"). The other "Irving," Brigadier General James Irvine (1735–1819) of the Pennsylvania militia, was a hatter.
131. James Irvine and his troops were repulsed by the British at Chestnut Hill, Pennsylvania, on December 5, 1777; Irvine himself was wounded and captured. William Irvine spent almost two years as a prisoner in Canada after being captured at Trois Rivières on June 8, 1776.
132. Washington, explaining the failure of Wayne's expedition in a letter to the president of Congress, noted that the cannon were "too light to penetrate the logs

of which it [the blockhouse] was constructed." But Washington also complained of the "intemperate valor" of Wayne's men, and then concluded: "I have been thus particular, lest the account of this affair should have reached Philadelphia much exaggerated, as is commonly the case upon such occasions." The letter was published in the *Pennsylvania Packet* on August 1, 1780, and André in writing his poem had obviously seen and made use of it.

133. An allusion to Washington's two military secretaries Alexander Hamilton (1757–1804) and Robert Harrison (1745–90).

134. These two lines parody a stanza from the ballad "Chevy Chase": "For Witherington needs must I wayle/ As one in doleful dumps;/ For when his legges were smitten off/ He fought upon his stumpes."

135. "Chevy Chase": "Against Sir Hugh Montgomery/ So right the shaft he sett,/ The grey goose-wing that was thereon/ In his hearts blood was wett."

136. William Cunningham (1717–91), the British provost marshal in charge of the New York prisons.

137. André himself supplied the following annotation: "Five refugees ('tis true) were found,/ Stiff on the block-house floor;/ But then 'tis thought the shot went round,/ And in at the back door."

138. The Reverend James Caldwell (1734–81) of New Jersey, an active patriot and a deputy quartermaster general.

139. An allusion to Lord Stirling's mismanaged attempt to surprise the British on Staten Island on the night of January 14–15, 1780. The temperature was below zero, and about five hundred of his men returned with frostbite.

140. The Marquis de Lafayette (1757–1834), the young French nobleman who attached himself to the American cause.

141. Susanna Livingston (1748– ?), the daughter of New Jersey Governor William Livingston, was suspected in some quarters of engaging in political authorship like her father.

25. LOYALIST POEMS AND SONGS

142. General Richard Montgomery (1738–75), who was killed during the Americans' unsuccessful assault on Quebec in December, 1775.

143. Catiline (108–62 B.C.), the Roman politician and conspirator; Oliver Cromwell (1599–1658), the Puritan general who executed Charles I; and Jack Cade (d. 1450), the leader of the mob that seized London in 1450—all three defied the civil authority of their time.

144. Sir Guy Carleton (1724–1808), governor of Canada.

145. These three famous English generals arrived together in Boston on May 25, 1775.

146. John Murray, earl of Dunmore (1732–1809), the royal governor of Virginia.

147. General Charles Lee (1731–82).

148. The song celebrates the failure of the combined forces of General John Sullivan and French Admiral Comte d'Estaing to take Newport in August, 1778. The English garrison at Rhode Island was commanded by General Robert Pigot (1720–96).

149. Conrad Gerard (1729–90) was the ambassador to America from the court of Louis XVI, king of France.

150. John Hancock (1737–93) of Boston commanded the Massachusetts militia in the operations around Newport.

151. Contemporary opinion placed the blame for the American defeat on d'Estaing's decision to depart with his fleet for Boston at a time when Sullivan counted on his active support.

152. This poem appeared in Rivington's *Royal Gazette* on January 2, 1779.

153. John Byron (1723–86), "Foul-weather Jack," the British admiral, had failed to intercept the French fleet under d'Estaing in the late spring of 1778 as planned (largely, historians think, through his own incompetence).

154. The ballad celebrates the failure of the Franco-American attempt to take

Savannah in October, 1779.

155. General Augustine Prevost (1723–86), commander of the British forces in the South.

156. Comte d'Estaing (1729–94), the French admiral.

157. General Benjamin Lincoln (1733–1810).

158. On September 16 d'Estaing demanded the city's surrender. Prevost, playing for time, asked for and got twenty-four hours to come to a decision, during which time Colonel John Maitland (d. 1779) reached Savannah ("push'd in") with reinforcements of eight hundred men. Prevost decided to fight, and the siege was on. Captain James Moncrieff (1744–93) planned and built the fortifications at Savannah.

159. The main attack of the allies came on the morning of October 9.

160. Casimir Pulaski (1748–79), a native of Poland, was mortally wounded when he recklessly led his cavalry against Savannah's defenses. Prior to coming to America Pulaski had been involved in an abortive attempt to seize the king of Poland and was forced to flee the country.

161. Allied losses actually totaled a little over eight hundred.

162. The Volunteers of Ireland, composed entirely of Irish Americans, was a Loyalist regiment raised (1778) and commanded by Lord Francis Rawdon (1754–1826).